A HISTORY OF BRITAIN THROUGH BOOKS

1900-1964

CHRISTOPHER TUGENDHAT

First published in 2019 by whitefox
This edition published in 2022

ISBN 978-1-915036-80-3

Also available as an ebook
ISBN 978-1-912892-35-8

Typeset by seagulls.net
Cover design by simonlevyassociates.co.uk
Cover images: Shutterstock, iStock
Project management by whitefox

Printed and bound by CPI Group (UK) Ltd,
Croydon, CR0 4YY

For my grandchildren, Lily, Eva,
Christopher, Rachel and Isobel

Contents

Cold War

Imperialist Complexities

Provincial Life

Early Feminism

Conclusion

Introduction

This book has two wellsprings. The first is my collection of books by British authors, written or published between 1900 and the early 1960s, that I believe shows what it was like to live in this country during those years. The second is Neil MacGregor's great work *A History of the World in 100 Objects* in which he examines previous civilizations through the prism of objects that have come down to us from the past. This has inspired me to use my collection as a prism through which to convey the British experience during the first two-thirds of the twentieth century.

It was a tumultuous period that began with the British empire at the plenitude of its power and ended with the empire's dissolution and the reversal of a population flow that had been in place for some two centuries. Instead of people going out from these islands to settle overseas, people from the former colonies began to come here. Because of the two world wars, the build-up to them and the Cold War the nation was, for much of the time, facing an existential threat. It witnessed a transformation in the lives of the great mass of the people from poverty to relative prosperity. And it saw some traditional prejudices begin to crumble while others endured.

The books I write about, fiction and non-fiction, have been chosen for the light they cast on the period or for the influence they exercised on the minds of men and women at the time. Some occupy a permanent place in the canon of English literature or as part of the nation's intellectual heritage. Others have fallen into obscurity. Together they provide a kaleidoscope of perspectives, unencumbered by hindsight, into the way people lived, the challenges they faced and the assumptions and ideas that lay behind their actions.

Like archaeological objects the books and their contents cannot be altered. But they can be mixed and matched and read in different combinations – an exercise that both deepens understanding of the past and throws up unexpected insights that in turn stimulate a reassessment of received opinions. To give three examples:

I had always assumed that it was the suffragettes and winning the right to vote that, more than anything else, made it possible for women to engage in active politics and to influence public policy. The autobiography of Margaret Bondfield, the first woman to enter the Cabinet, overturned that view. For many years before the vote was won, she had been actively engaged as a trade unionist in bringing about change in the workplace. More than fifteen years before women cast their first vote, and even before the suffragettes had broken away from the main body of the women's suffrage movement, she was giving evidence before a parliamentary committee and helping to mould legislation. Crucial as the right to vote was to the advancement of women's aspirations, the largely middle class-led campaign to acquire it has diverted attention away from the practical work done on behalf of working-class women by women in the trade union movement.

Another surprise was to discover that perhaps the first person to call time on the British empire in Africa was that arch-reactionary Evelyn Waugh in his 1931 travel book *Remote People*. One of its sections is on Kenya where, with the active encouragement of the British government, men and women from this country were between the wars building new lives in the confident expectation that British rule would last beyond their lifetimes. He wrote with approval of their efforts to reproduce the life of the English squirearchy in Africa and with sympathy of their colour bar and discrimination against the Africans. Yet he forecast that the European colonization of Africa might not last for more than another twenty-five years, which proved to be only a few years out.

My third example is about looking back rather than forward and is drawn from John Braine's 1957 novel *Room at the Top*. The narrator, Joe Lampton, explains that his lucky break during the war was to have been shot down while on an RAF bombing raid over Germany and to have been kept safe from danger in a prison camp. Under the auspices of the International Red Cross, he used his time there to pass the accountancy exams which, after the war, enabled him to jump from his working-class background into the middle class. It is hard to imagine a wartime reminiscence more at variance with the patriotic terms in which they are conventionally expressed both in biography and in literature.

I begin my book by considering two titles that set out to debunk the Victorian era and which contain within them the seeds of the iconoclasm that became the hallmark of the first part of the twentieth century: Samuel Butler's *The Way of All Flesh* and Lytton Strachey's *Eminent Victorians*. I end with three books by George Orwell and two by John Maynard Keynes: *Homage to Catalonia*, *Animal Farm* and *Nineteen Eighty-Four* by the former and *The Economic Consequences of the Peace* and *The General Theory of Employment, Interest and Money* by the latter. To the extent that anyone could be said to have had answers to the problems of the age it was these two men.

The chapters in between range widely: from the two world wars and issues arising out of them to the rise of feminism, from working-class life in the North of England to life in the great public schools, from racism and anti-Semitism to sexual relationships, from living in the empire to medical care before the NHS and from class distinctions to cookery. The result is not so much a panorama of the age as an eclectic collage – a big picture made up of many smaller ones with a good deal of overlap between them. In more than half the chapters I cite experiences and recollections of my own and my family.

One of the strongest themes to run through the period was fear of mass destruction and the end of civilization. In 1903 Erskine Childers, in his pioneering espionage novel *The Riddle of the Sands*, had fanned the already widespread fears that Britain might be invaded with his detailed fictional account of German plans to launch an assault across the North Sea. H. G. Wells then added an altogether more frightening dimension. In his 1908 novel, *The War in the Air*, he described a war in the near future in which the aerial bombing would be so intense and so widespread that civilization would be brought to an end. In 1914 he forecast in *The World Set Free* that there would be a nuclear war by the middle of the century, as indeed there was. The fear of universal mass destruction that he conjured up, and to which subsequent technological advances gave increasing credibility, would hang over society throughout the following decades.

Between the wars Stanley Baldwin, who was Prime Minister for much of the period, was among many who forecast that in a future war bombing from the air would destroy civilization. This fear, rather than a repetition of the trenches of the First World War, was the major driver of the pacifist movement that was so strong in this country at that time, as Storm Jameson's 1934 collection of essays, *Challenge to Death*, shows. The same fear drove the Campaign for Nuclear Disarmament during the Cold War and is reflected in Nevil Shute's 1957 novel, *On the Beach*, which describes how the world ends after a nuclear exchange.

The two wars left a legacy with which Britain is still living. Though very different from each other, they involved the whole population directly and indirectly as no previous wars had ever done. The diaries and letters I write about give some idea in a highly personal way of the extent to which the ultimate victory in both was the result of a national team effort. No other European nation can look back on its wartime experiences with such unalloyed satisfaction. For their part the British people have experienced nothing so dramatic, so unifying or so unequivocally successful since 1945. The result is a national obsession with those wars, especially the second, that continues to generate endless books, television programmes and films and to influence contemporary political attitudes towards our European neighbours and our place in the world.

At the beginning of the century the British were in the peculiar position of fearing an invasion at home while ruling a vast empire overseas. This created tensions in the national psyche that are reflected in the original 1908 edition of Robert Baden-Powell's basic text for the Scout Movement, *Scouting for Boys*. It is about much more than the organized camaraderie and outdoor pursuits now normally associated with scouting. It is a call to arms. He encourages scouts to be prepared for an invasion of Britain in which eventuality their tracking and signalling skills will be of great help to the defending forces. He also preaches the pure doctrine of white racial superiority over other ethnic groups and the importance of maintaining it in order to uphold the empire. As training in how to do this, he urges scouts to stage plays as a means of learning the techniques by which white men can impose their will on subject peoples of other races and provides allegedly real-life incidents on which to base them.

The corrosive effect of the belief in racial superiority on the characters of those who ran the empire is central to E. M. Forster's classic, *A Passage to India*, published in 1924. The extent to which it prevented the white settlers in Kenya from establishing a modus vivendi with the Africans that might have enabled them to remain there on a permanent basis is explained in the autobiography of the colonial-era

Kenya politician Michael Blundell, published in 1964. Those chapters in our history are now closed. The one concerning racism in this country is still being written.

Until after 1945 there were only minuscule numbers of people of black and minority ethnic origin in Britain itself. But when immigrants from the Caribbean and the Indian subcontinent began to arrive in significant numbers in the 1950s they found themselves facing a wall of racial prejudice. Among the early arrivals was the West Indian Sam Selvon, who, based on his own experiences, describes what this meant to them and how they reacted in his remarkable 1956 novel *The Lonely Londoners*. It provides a base position against which can be judged the efforts that have since been made to break down prejudice and to achieve racial equality.

Anti-Semitism is another prejudice that recurs in several of my commentaries. Somerset Maugham's 1936 short story, *The Alien Corn*, provides a vivid example of the form in which it was widely expressed in literature and socially until the revelations about the Holocaust after the war changed attitudes or at least made the expression of old ones unacceptable. Britain avoided the anti-Semitic excesses that on the Continent led to this catastrophe. It also benefited greatly, as I explain when writing about Ernst Gombrich and Nikolaus Pevsner, from providing a safe haven for some of those fleeing from persecution. But few in this country are aware that among the basic anti-Semitic texts from which the Nazis drew their inspiration was the work of a British author, Houston Stewart Chamberlain's *The Foundations of the Nineteenth Century*, which I discuss in conjunction with *The Alien Corn*.

Prejudice against gays and lesbians was deeply felt and loudly expressed throughout the period covered by this book. Sex between men was against the law and punishable by imprisonment in Britain, unlike other European countries, and remained so until 1967. Lesbianism, though not illegal, attracted a similar degree of opprobrium.

E. M. Forster's *Maurice*, written before the First World War, and Mary Renault's *The Charioteer*, set during the Second, convey something of what it was like to have been gay. Radclyffe Hall's *The Well of Loneliness*, published and almost immediately banned for being obscene in 1928, does the same for lesbians. The agonizing of the characters in these books over their orientation, how they come to terms with it and what it means for their lives will shock readers who have grown up in a world where sexual relations between people of the same sex have long since ceased to be taboo. The contrast between then and now is an encouraging example of how, over time, even the most deep-seated national attitudes can change for the better.

During the period itself the greatest improvement was in the lives of the working class. Robert Tressall's* influential and readable socialist novel, *The Ragged-Trousered Philanthropists*, is about a group of men and their wives on the south coast in the early years of the century. In *Love on the Dole* Walter Greenwood describes the hardships of a family in the North-West during the Great Depression in the early 1930s. Fear of debt and unemployment are dominant themes in both and life a constant struggle against adversity. By 1958, when Alan Sillitoe's *Saturday Night and Sunday Morning* became a bestseller, everything had changed. The crucial leap had been made to the dawn of the consumer society underpinned by the welfare state.

Throughout the period questions of class arise, sometimes in terms that almost take one's breath away, as in the case of an entry in *The Bickersteth Diaries* recording life in the trenches during the First World War. In the summer of 1917, after serving for three years at the front as an army officer, Burgon Bickersteth records in a letter home, 'the first time I had ever sat down to eat out here in uniform with soldiers.' On other occasions it is the frame of reference within which issues are

* This is how the name is spelled on the title page of the book's first edition, which I have used. In subsequent editions it is Tressell.

discussed that is striking. Virginia Woolf's *A Room of One's Own* and her lesser known *Three Guineas* provide a case in point. The former, published in 1929, is among the most important feminist texts of the twentieth century. The latter, which followed in 1938, argues the case for equal pay and equal opportunities for women in the professions. Although of ground-breaking significance, they only address matters of concern to middle- and upper-class women, those whom Woolf describes in *Three Guineas* as 'the daughters of educated men'. They have nothing to say of relevance to the majority of women then working in shops, factories and domestic service.

Graham Greene's collection of essays entitled *The Old School*, published in 1934, casts an interesting light on the class question. The contributors argue that the schools were machines for turning out 'gentlemen'. Whether the fathers of the boys who attended them were established members of the middle and upper classes or had only recently made money didn't matter. So long as they could pay the fees the schools would ensure that their sons (daughters did not yet enter the equation) would emerge with the right credentials and consequential advantages in terms of career opportunities. The schools were thus simultaneously vehicles for validating new money and integrating the sons of those who had made it into the 'gentleman' class while acting as barriers for those who had not been educated by them.

Each of the two wars broke down barriers and opened up previously undreamed-of opportunities for those with the right attributes and lucky enough to be in the right place at the right time, regardless of where they had been educated. C. P. Snow's *Strangers and Brothers* sequence of novels charts the rise of Lewis Eliot from provincial obscurity to influence in the heart of government, an ascent that closely paralleled that of his creator. A fictional character who turned down the chance to move up in the world was Lady Chatterley's lover, the gamekeeper Mellors. During the 1914–18 war he had risen from the ranks to become an officer and could, had he so wished, have been assimilated into the 'gentleman' class after it ended rather than return to his origins. Lady Chatterley remarks when they first meet on how like a gentleman he is and I doubt that she would have wanted to marry him if he had been an ordinary working man.

In real life a far more extreme renunciation than Mellors' was that of Erskine Childers, who had inherited an established position in society and built on it with the success of *The Riddle of the Sands*. After distinguished service in the Royal Navy, he became so disgusted by what he regarded as British hypocrisy in claiming to be fighting for the rights of small nations while denying those rights to Ireland that he threw in his lot with the most extreme wing of the Irish rebels fighting for independence from Britain.

The complexities and inconsistencies in the way people behaved in the past are often hard for later generations to fathom. In the words of the novelist L. P. Hartley, 'The past is a foreign country: they do things differently there.'[1] To explain what they did and the consequences is one thing; to capture the mentality that led to their actions is quite another. To examine a period through the prism of contemporaneous books is a means of at least partially achieving that. In the case of the years from 1900 to the early 1960s that is not only interesting in itself; it also casts light on the background to some of the issues that still perplex us today.

Debunking Victorianism

The Way of All Flesh by Samuel Butler, 1903.

Eminent Victorians by Lytton Strachey, 1918.

The Way of All Flesh

by Samuel Butler (1903)

The Way of All Flesh by Samuel Butler, published in 1903, is the first great twentieth-century literary blast against Victorian values and institutions. With a title inspired by the Book of Genesis,* its enormous popularity and the influence it exercised tell us a great deal about the intellectual climate of that time. The cultural historian Richard Hoggart has described it as 'one of the intellectual watersheds between the Victorian age and the twentieth century'.[1]

Butler in fact wrote it during the 1870s and 1880s, but never sought a publisher during his lifetime – whether because he felt he could not get it quite right, as some suggest, or, as others claim, because he did not want its similarities with their own family history to cause pain to his sisters. Whatever the reason, its attack on the whole edifice of what came to be called Victorianism is so excoriating that, had it been published during the high noon of the Victorian era, its reception would have been very different from the accolades it received when it finally appeared a year after Butler's death.

The timing was ideal. With Queen Victoria's death in 1901 the intellectual revolt against the bourgeois orthodoxies of her reign,

* And God looked upon the earth and behold, it was corrupt: for all flesh had corrupted his way upon the earth. Genesis 6.12.

already simmering beneath the surface of society while she was alive, broke into the open. *The Way of All Flesh* captured and articulated the mood of the moment. Leonard Woolf, Virginia's husband and the founder of the Hogarth Press, recalls in his memoirs, 'We read it when it came out and felt at once its significance for us.'[2] The playwright George Bernard Shaw wrote to his friend Henry Salt: 'Get it instantly, it is one of the great books of the world … I do not exaggerate: it is enormous.'[3] Other young writers were similarly enthused. It always remained one of Somerset Maugham's favourite novels while E. M. Forster, in a characteristic phrase, thought that, 'If Butler had not lived, many of us would now be a little deader than we are, a little less aware of the tricks and traps in life and of our own obtuseness.'[4]

These words go to the heart of what made the book popular. It helped those wanting to rebel to think for themselves and to find words to express those thoughts. In 1928 Virginia Woolf suggested[5] that Victorian family life had been disrupted by two great forces. *The Way of All Flesh* was one, the other was Constance Garnett's translations of the great Russian authors, which first brought them to the attention of English-speaking readers during the opening decades of the century.

It is never easy to assess how much influence one writer exercises over others. All writers are open to a variety of influences of various kinds. George Bernard Shaw, however, was in no doubt about his debt to Butler. In the preface to his play *Major Barbara*, first performed in 1906, he castigates those critics who claimed that he drew inspiration from Ibsen and Nietzsche and failed to see that 'Butler's extraordinary fresh, free and future piercing suggestions have an obvious share'. The reference to 'future piercing' suggests he had in mind Butler's earlier utopian satire *Erewhon*, as well as *The Way of All Flesh*. Other notable works in which traces of the latter are clearly detectable, or for which it at least paved the way, include Arnold Bennett's *Clayhanger*, published in 1910, D. H. Lawrence's *Sons and Lovers* (1913), Somerset

Maugham's *Of Human Bondage* (1915), and, in the view of some critics, James Joyce's *A Portrait of the Artist as a Young Man* (1919).

At over four hundred pages and covering five generations of the Pontifex family, *The Way of All Flesh* looks at first sight as if it belongs with John Galsworthy's *Forsyte Saga*. But there the similarity ends. It begins with the rise of the Pontifex family from the working class to the bourgeoisie. But instead of rejoicing in this upward mobility, as Galsworthy does, Butler presents it as a downward progression in moral terms. Old Mr Pontifex, a village carpenter, who we meet aged eighty in the opening pages, is portrayed as being both a happier and a better man than his son George, a successful businessman, and his grandson, Theobald, who completes the gentrification process by moving out of trade to become a clergyman.

The hero, if such he can be called as he is far from being heroic, is Theobald's son, the naïve and well-meaning Ernest, who reverses the family's social advancement. After obediently following his father into the priesthood, he becomes a curate at a fashionable London church where he is expected to confine his ministrations to its well-to-do parishioners. Instead he tries to proselytize among the poor, with disastrous results, when he becomes involved entirely innocently with a prostitute. He is accused of an offence he didn't commit, prosecuted, found guilty and sentenced to six months in prison. His father is appalled by the disgrace and banishes Ernest from the family circle. After his release Ernest tries his hand as a tailor and as a shopkeeper but fails again, marries and fathers two children by a woman he subsequently discovers is already married. These misfortunes persuade him that the values he was brought up with are false and that the paternal tyranny of his childhood has ruined his chances of achieving happiness and fulfilment.

At this point he seems destined for a life of penury from which he is saved by a legacy from a long-forgotten aunt. He uses this to become a writer, but his most significant decision is to keep his children with the family of a bargee on the Thames to whom he had entrusted them when their mother left him. Instead of restoring them to the bourgeois fold, he wants them to grow up without the pretensions and restrictions of gentility. When, in due course, they become adults he enables his son to buy a boat of his own while his daughter marries within the river community. Thus, the wheel turns full circle. The new generation is back in more or less the same social stratum as was old Mr Pontifex. In defiance of the conventional view of how social mobility should work, this is a matter for celebration rather than regret.

Several themes relating to middle-class life and values run through the book and interact with each other – paternal tyranny, hypocrisy, the corrosive effect of money on family relationships and the absence of any real emotional commitment both within the family and in the discharge of clerical duties. The family is presented as a unit that revolves round the paterfamilias whose principal concern is to exercise power over his wife and children.

The women too are ruthless in pursuit of their own ends. Among the book's most memorable passages, so vivid one feels it must have been drawn, or at least derived, from life, is the description of how the Reverend Mr Allaby's five daughters react when, as a young curate, Theobald arrives to assist their father in his parish duties. All 'are in want of a husband', as Jane Austen would have described them. They resolve the matter by 'playing at cards with Theobald for the stakes', behaviour beyond anything one can imagine Austen's characters engaging in.

The winner is Christina, the second unmarried daughter and, at twenty-seven, four years older than Theobald. Mrs Allaby immediately packs the other girls off to stay with friends to give her a clear run. She duly catches him, but, as they drive away from the church after their marriage, remorse sets in. Theobald experiences that feeling akin to death, 'what the Italians call la figlia della Morte', that a man suffers during 'the first half-hour that he is alone with a woman who he has married but never genuinely loved'. The language of love and of the marriage service is shown up to be a sham, but Theobald and Christina have each fulfilled a social requirement. She has escaped spinsterhood while he has acquired a housekeeper and both can form a family with children.

The relationships between fathers and sons – George with Theobald and Theobald with Ernest – are bleak and violent, but in that respect, we are assured, similar to those around them. George thrashes Theobald and his brother 'two or three times a week and some weeks a good deal oftener', which 'may have been a little sterner … than some of his neighbours, but not much'. Theobald does the same to Ernest. The purpose is always for their own good: to make them work harder at their lessons, to inculcate obedience and, as Theobald and Christina say to each other in the case of Ernest, 'so that from the first he might have been kept pure from every taint of evil'. As the sons grow older the fathers threaten to withhold allowances and to alter wills to ensure that they follow the careers laid down for them. When they comply with their fathers' desires they are rewarded financially. Again, all is couched in terms of being in their own best interests. This is the cycle from which Ernest wishes to escape though it requires a series of accidents rather than deliberate action on his part to do so.

The violence adds colour to Butler's argument, but is peripheral to his central point, which is the conflict between filial obedience and free will at a time when it was taken for granted that sons should do as their fathers wished and often follow them into the same profession. It was the questioning of this assumption that many found so liberating. George Orwell, who, as a young man, followed his father into a branch of the imperial administration, in his case the Burma Police, from which, after some years' service, he resigned to become a writer, reflected that feeling in a radio broadcast many years later. He called *The Way of All Flesh*, 'A great book because it gives an honest picture of the relationship between father and son.'[6]

At a time when Darwin's theory of evolution was beginning to eat away at the foundations of Christian belief, the Church of England was vulnerable to Butler's attack upon the clergy. It went much further than portraying Theobald as violent, selfish and narrow-minded. A clergyman, Butler claimed, could never make an 'unbiased examination' of facts or issues because, in preaching the gospel, he 'is as much a paid advocate as a barrister who is trying to persuade a jury to acquit a prisoner'. Moreover, he suggests, social ambition, rather than a vocation to serve God, was often the reason why men wanted to become clergymen. Among Ernest's fellow students at Cambridge were some imbued with the missionary spirit, but for many, 'the fact of becoming clergymen would be the entrée into a social position from which they were at present kept out by barriers they well knew to be impassable; ordination, therefore, opened fields for their ambition'. In a telling passage, Christina whispers to the book's narrator as the congregation 'bobs' before Theobald as they enter his church for Sunday service, 'The people hereabouts are truly respectful, they know their betters.'

In Butler's view, both the clergy and the Church as an institution are fundamentally no different from the society of which they were a part and deserving of no special respect. This analysis had the same impact on public opinion, when *The Way of All Flesh* was published, as that of the child in Hans Christian Anderson's fairy story who dares to proclaim that the Emperor has no clothes when everybody has been pretending to admire them. As such it made a significant contribution to the decline in respect for the clergy and in religious observance that were already under way and would gather momentum as the century progressed.

Butler's relationship with his own clergyman father to some extent mirrored that of Ernest and Theobald. He too was destined to follow his father into the Church. After leaving Cambridge he served as a lay reader at St James's, Piccadilly, in London, a fashionable church similar to the one at which Ernest served as a curate in the novel. He then rebelled and announced that he wanted to become an artist. His father regarded this as ridiculous but behaved more generously than Theobald. In a grand Victorian gesture, he gave his son a substantial sum of money and told him that if he could make his fortune in the colonies, he would be free to do as he wished. In 1859 Butler sailed to New Zealand where he achieved such success as a sheep farmer that in 1864 he was able to return to London as a man of independent means.

Thereafter he embarked on an astonishingly eclectic literary career. The most successful of his books in his own lifetime was *Erewhon*, an anagram of nowhere, published in 1872, which has been compared with *Gulliver's Travels* as a satirical utopia. Others followed on Darwin and Darwinism, his travels in Italy and his rediscovery of forgotten artists and craftsmen associated with pilgrimage sites in that country. Two that appeared towards the end of his life attracted particular attention. In one he argued that Homer's *Odyssey* and *Iliad* had been written by a woman and set in Sicily, an idea later pursued by Robert Graves in his novel *Homer's Daughter*. In the other, published in 1899, Butler suggested that Shakespeare's sonnets were about homosexual love; a less original theory, but a brave one for a man, widely supposed to be gay, to propound at a time when a wave of homophobia was sweeping the country following the trial of Oscar Wilde.

Eminent Victorians

by Lytton Strachey (1918)

In *Eminent Victorians*, published in 1918, Lytton Strachey's angle of attack on the Victorians was quite different from Samuel Butler's. Whereas Butler directed his fire at institutions – the Church of England and the family – Strachey's aim in his book of four short biographical essays was the character assassination of named individuals. The only one who is still famous is Florence Nightingale. Most people today would not be able to place Cardinal Manning, Dr Arnold or General Gordon, but in Strachey's day they were household names and Victorian icons. In an age of deference, they were people his readers had been brought up to revere. His purpose in attacking them was to indict an age, one whose values he believed had helped to bring about the First World War.

He achieved his objective. After Strachey's death in 1932, the great American critic Edmund Wilson wrote, 'neither the Americans nor the English have ever, since *Eminent Victorians* appeared, been able to feel quite the same about the legends that had dominated their pasts. Something had been punctured for good.'[7] In his influential book *Enemies of Promise*, the British author and critic Cyril Connolly made the same point in more hyperbolic terms. He described *Eminent Victorians* 'as the work of a great anarch, a revolutionary textbook on bourgeois society written in the language through which the bourgeois ear could be lulled and beguiled, the Mandarin style'.[8] These judgements remain valid. Although much has since been written about the Victorian era, *Eminent Victorians* has proved to be one of the most enduring templates against which subsequent generations have formulated their own assessments of that era.

It also had a significant literary impact. On the one hand Strachey's wit and irreverence helped to create the climate in which the iconoclasm and satire of such writers as Michael Arlen, Noël Coward and Evelyn Waugh, whom I write about in later chapters, could flourish in the 1920s and 1930s. On the other Strachey contributed to the evolution of biographical writing into the literary art form that it is today. His approach represented a dramatic break from the way in which biography had up till then been written – those great ponderous volumes, often two or even three, with which the lives of the great had traditionally been commemorated. In the preface to his own book, Strachey compares them to the 'the cortège of the undertaker'.

Whereas their objective was comprehensiveness, Strachey aimed for brevity and lightness of touch. While they tended towards hagiography, he sought to unravel and expose his subject's mentality and motives. In the words of his biographer Michael Holroyd, he believed 'that history yielded up more of her secrets to the heightened intuition of the artist than to the over-diffident, over-earnest, humdrum and humourless investigations conducted by scientific minds'.[9] His technique was similar to that of those producers of films about the past who tamper with their material, rearrange events and redraw characters, often unfairly, in order to achieve a desired dramatic effect. The result frequently misrepresents what actually happened while conveying such a powerful feeling for the period as to carry complete conviction.

The extent to which Strachey achieved this may be judged by the reaction of the publisher to whom he sent his manuscript, Frank

Swinnerton of Chatto & Windus. Swinnerton replied saying that he had read it during an air raid: 'The whirring of aeroplanes overhead, the rattle of machine gun fire, and finally the frightful thunder of a gun in the field at the bottom of our garden, would all have served to distract a mind less happily engaged; but as it was, with the curtain closely drawn to prevent the escape of light, I consorted that evening with Cardinal Manning, Thomas Arnold, Florence Nightingale and General Gordon. The nineteenth century had come alive again.'[10]

Eminent Victorians was published in May 1918 just as the fighting in France began tilting in favour of the Allies, but while the outcome of the war was still in the balance. Thousands of men were being killed or wounded every day. Even so, it received long and laudatory reviews and an accolade, as important as it was unexpected, from the former Prime Minister Herbert Asquith, who praised it in the course of a prestigious lecture at Oxford.[11] There were denunciations too, but these were often of the kind that attract readers. By July it was into its third, albeit small, edition, making three thousand copies in all. In November, the month the war finally ended, an American edition was published to be followed by Swedish, German, French, Italian and Spanish translations. The proceeds and the spin-offs made Strachey financially secure as well as famous for the rest of his life.

The book's timing turned out to be impeccable. Before the outbreak of the First World War in 1914, it would not have made the same impact. Many would have been shocked by the disrespect and often contempt that characterize Strachey's portraits. By 1918 attitudes had been transformed as a result of the dreadful loss of life in the trenches. Virtually everyone had lost family members or friends, very often both, and a deep shadow had been cast over the way they regarded the past. A book about the Victorian age that sought to undermine the moral foundations on which it was built turned out to meet a deep psychological need, regardless of the misrepresentation involved.

This is most extreme in the case of Cardinal Manning. The position Manning had held in public life is perhaps best illustrated by what happened when he died in 1892. The queues to file past his body as it lay in state at Archbishop's House in Victoria blocked traffic for four days. When his coffin was carried along a four-mile route from the Brompton Oratory to Kensal Green cemetery the streets were packed with mourners all the way.[12] That the head of the Catholic Church in England, then still a minority sect and an object of suspicion, if not anathema to many, should have evoked such an outpouring of public grief was extraordinary. It arose because of the practical concern Manning had shown over many years for the poor and disadvantaged and the way he had used his office and connections on their behalf in stark contrast to the hierarchy of the Church of England.

Strachey was not interested in any of that. His focus is on how Manning advanced his career in the Church of England before his conversion to Catholicism, on how he used his influence behind the scenes in Rome to work his way up in his new Church and how, in Strachey's view, he sought to do down that other great Catholic convert from Anglicanism, Cardinal Newman. That Manning was one of nature's executives, born to command and always in search of promotion, as well as an effective political operator, is not in doubt. But that is not at all the same as being a vindictive careerist forever justifying his manoeuvres to himself as being the fulfilment of God's will, which is how Strachey portrays him. Moreover, Strachey fails to answer the crucial question of why, if Manning was so driven by worldly ambition and so skilled at presenting his machinations to himself as being divinely led, he did not stay in the established Church whose bishops at that time lived in palaces and enjoyed large incomes. Had he done so, Manning would undoubtedly have secured one of the most prestigious dioceses with the wealth and status that went with it. His life would have been much easier and he would have avoided the painful break with old friends, including Gladstone, who regarded his conversion to Catholicism as an apostasy.

The portrait of Manning stands out for its unremitting hostility. In the others the denigration is tempered with humour. This is particularly so in the case of Dr Thomas Arnold, the famous headmaster of Rugby from 1828 to 1841. The reforms he introduced there were so widely copied by other schools that he is generally credited with creating the public school ethos that was for so long afterwards such a distinguishing feature of British life. Strachey treats him as a figure of fun: a pompous little man filled with a sense of his own importance and rushing around in pursuit of petty objectives.

Strachey's mockery of Arnold's belief that the classical languages and a devotion to the Anglican religion should provide the bedrock of an educational system and that discipline should be maintained by flogging set the tone for much of the future criticism of that ethos. But *Eminent Victorians* lacks any examination of the reasons why such a system, promulgated by a man as ludicrous as Arnold is made out to be, should have been so widely adopted by his contemporaries. Nor did Strachey's criticism have any practical effect as parents continued to send their sons to the public schools. In the 1930s, as I describe in a later chapter, it was thought they might become priced out of the market, but that proved to be a false alarm.

General Gordon is portrayed as a credulous and somewhat ridiculous Christian obsessed by the Bible. His death at the hands of the Sudanese at the siege of Khartoum in 1885 was the most memorable feature of one of the greatest British imperial defeats of the nineteenth century. Strachey set out to strip it of its aura of martyrdom and to present it as typical of the type of bungling that had cost so many lives during the First World War. He glories in describing buck-passing in government circles, the obtuseness of politicians, the self-interest of high officials and the muddles that combined to leave Gordon and his troops isolated and at the mercy of the Sudanese. His readers would have drawn an immediate connection with events during the war. They would also have appreciated his cynical comment on the British victory over the Sudanese some years later: 'At any rate, it all ended very happily – in a glorious slaughter of 20,000 Arabs, a vast addition to the British Empire, and a step in the peerage for Sir Evelyn Baring.'

The essay on Florence Nightingale left me with a surprising sense of déjà vu. It reads so like the things I used to read and hear about Margaret Thatcher in her prime – the same male sense of awe tempered by outrage that a woman should be able to move such mountains and dominate the men around her mingled with mockery at the exhibition she thereby makes of herself. Strachey cannot but approve of her nursing activities during the Crimean War and of her subsequent campaign back in London to overcome official resistance to reforming the archaic army medical services. But he has to present her as a harridan until, worn down by her efforts, she loses her mind and becomes a gentle old woman, as happened to Margaret Thatcher at the end of her life.

The idea that a strong woman in the public sphere is somehow an aberration and against nature is deeply embedded in his text and it was not only in this country that it endured into the 1980s and beyond. In 1980, when I was a European Commissioner, Thatcher had a particularly bruising encounter with the German Chancellor, Helmut Schmidt, after which a German minister came to see me to convey a message. 'You must tell your Prime Minister,' he said, 'that she has hurt my Chancellor in his male pride. If things are to be put right between our two countries, she must find a way of making it up to him.' I had to explain why I thought it would not be helpful to British-German relations to pass it on.

Strachey's work strikes another chord in my memory. His portrayal and mockery of his subjects and their motives, and his use of ridicule and misrepresentation to puncture their pretensions, are reminiscent of the 'satire boom' that, in the early 1960s, first brought to prominence such varied characters as the writer and dramatist Alan Bennett, the theatre and opera director and all-round polymath Jonathan Miller, the comedian Peter Cook and the television interviewer David Frost, among others. There is the same youthful exuberance, the same delight in being irreverent and pushing back the boundaries of taste. Both Strachey and the satirists reflected and helped to mould the spirit of their age; in the case of the satirists by undermining the anachronistic pretensions of the then Conservative government and the Establishment in general, in the case of Strachey by making Victorian icons appear ridiculous.

It is not only because of its own intrinsic merits and the social and literary influence it once exercised that *Eminent Victorians* has so successfully outlived the period of its own youthful exuberance. It has benefited from Strachey having been a colourful member of the Bloomsbury Group of advanced, free-thinking intellectuals that revolved round the writer Virginia Woolf and her sister, the artist Vanessa Bell. This remarkable coterie, named after the part of London in which Woolf and Bell originally set up house together, included the great economist John Maynard Keynes, the artist Duncan Grant, the artist and critic Roger Fry and the writer E. M. Forster, to name only the best-known. Their reputations have become mutually reinforcing as, among later generations, those who become interested in the books and paintings of one member frequently then wish to know more about the work of the others.

Besides that, the Bloomsbury Group has become a sort of composite cultural celebrity. The heady mix of their unconventional sex lives – gay, straight and promiscuous – their disregard for the social mores of their time and their high intellectual and creative achievements has made them the subject of countless books and television documentaries. These tend to concentrate on their sexual activities and their flouting of convention rather than on their contribution to the nation's cultural life.

That contribution was, however, considerable. In the twentieth century there was no other group of friends whose combined influence has been remotely as great. I shall have more to say on this when writing about other members of the group in subsequent chapters.

War 1 – Warnings and Reality

The Riddle of the Sands by Erskine Childers, 1903,
and *The Thirty-Nine Steps* by John Buchan, 1915.

The War in the Air by H. G. Wells, 1908,
The World Set Free by H. G. Wells, 1914,
and *The Great Illusion* by Norman Angell, 1910.

The Bickersteth Diaries, 1914–18, edited by John Bickersteth, and *Private Lord Crawford's Great War Diaries*, edited by Christopher Arnander.

The Riddle of the Sands

by Erskine Childers (1903)

The Thirty-Nine Steps

by John Buchan (1915)

As the twentieth century opened, the British empire stood at the plenitude of its power. The government in London held sway over some 24 per cent of the earth's surface and 23 per cent of its people. Yet fears about the country's vulnerability and of what the future might hold were germinating. In his famous poem 'Recessional', published for Queen Victoria's Diamond Jubilee in 1897, Rudyard Kipling had prayed to God that the British empire might not go the way of the biblical empires of Nineveh and Tyre.[1] The Boer War against the small and scattered population of Afrikaans-speaking farmers of Dutch and Huguenot origin in South Africa known as Boers, which began in 1899 and ended in 1902, had proved to be a salutary experience. At its outset the British Army had suffered defeats. In the end it emerged victorious, but victory had been hard-won. Britons had also been shocked to find how much support the underdog Boers had enjoyed in Europe and the United States. Beneath the surface of their imperial pomp and splendour they were beginning to feel isolated and insecure. So called 'invasion novels' envisaging an invasion of Britain had become a popular genre and in his maiden speech to the House of Commons in 1901 the young Winston Churchill made a passing reference to such a possibility.[2]

It was in this atmosphere that Erskine Childers, then working as a clerk in the House of Commons, captured the imagination of the nation with *The Riddle of the Sands*, published in 1903. It did so because of the detail it deployed in explaining how Germany could mount an invasion of the east coast. It was this rather than the naming of Germany as a likely invader that marked it out from other invasion novels. Germany had been named before, although at the time of *The Riddle of the Sands'* publication relations between Britain and Germany were good. The memory of how, only two years before, the Kaiser, Wilhelm II, as Queen Victoria's grandson had been present at her deathbed with his cousin, Edward VII, was still fresh in the public mind and there was, as yet, no ostensible quarrel between the two countries. By contrast, Britain was at odds with France in Africa and competing for influence with Russia in central Asia. With strategic acumen, Childers identified the North Sea as the point at which Britain would be at greatest risk in a future naval war with Germany and when war came it was indeed there that the decisive Battle of Jutland was fought.

The Riddle of the Sands tells the story of two friends, Charles Carruthers of the Foreign Office and Arthur Davies, a solicitor, on a yachting holiday cruising round the Frisian Islands off the coast of Germany. When Davies had sailed in those waters before he had become suspicious that something sinister and mysterious was afoot and, with Carruthers' help, he had set sail determined to find out what was happening. What they discover, after various adventures, is nothing less than well-advanced preparations to enable a German army to be secretly transported across the North Sea to England. At great risk to themselves, they then succeed in bringing the information back to London.

Childers' taut, straightforward prose and the professionalism of the accompanying maps, charts and technical data, drawn from his own experience as an enthusiastic yachtsman, all combine to give their account of their adventures an alarming verisimilitude; an impression enhanced by the book's subtitle, *A Record of Secret Service Recently Achieved*. The novel's patriotic tone and its tale of how a pair of British amateurs gets the better of highly professional opponents played precisely to how the British liked to think of themselves, which added to its popularity.

Eleven years were to pass before the war Davies prophesied 'was bound to come' actually broke out. During that time, while the naval arms race between Britain and Germany gathered momentum and Britain formed an alliance with France and Russia, *The Riddle of the Sands* exercised influence in two directions. In the literary sphere it became, in conjunction with John Buchan's famous book *The Thirty-Nine Steps*, published in 1915, one of the progenitors of the espionage spy thriller that has ever since been such a notable feature of British popular literature. In the government, it was credited with having been among the factors that led to the establishment of the naval bases at Scapa Flow, Invergordon and Rosyth to protect the east coast from the German fleet.

Whether, as is widely claimed, Churchill as First Lord of the Admiralty was directly influenced by *The Riddle of the Sands* I have been unable to verify. But it is certainly the case that within days of war having broken out the Director of Naval Intelligence at the Admiralty was instructed to find Childers and recruit him into the Royal Navy.[3]

Naval secrets are also at the heart of *The Thirty-Nine Steps*, but this time with the Germans trying to steal Britain's. After a thrilling chase, mostly set in the Highlands of Scotland, that, for perhaps the first time in literature, features an aeroplane, they are thwarted by the book's hero, Richard Hannay. As in *The Riddle of the Sands* the Germans are portrayed as highly professional and fiendishly clever, but somehow too clever by half, which results in them being outwitted by the brilliant improvisation of their British antagonist.

As Buchan, who already had a string of books to his credit, published *The Thirty-Nine Steps* after hostilities had begun, it has none of Childers' foresight nor did it in any way influence government policy. But it is notable for other reasons. In Hannay, Buchan created the prototype of the resourceful, intelligent and tenacious hero of so many subsequent thrillers. They include Bulldog Drummond, who remained popular from the 1920s to the 1950s, BBC Radio's Dick Barton 'special agent', to whose adventures boys of my generation, as well as adults, listened avidly in the 1940s, and above all James Bond, launched in the 1950s and still going strong, among a host of others.

Hannay has another significant characteristic. He had been brought up in Africa and felt himself to be an outsider in London among the native English. His element was the 'veldt', that great open landscape comprising mostly grass or scrub of southern Africa. There, fighting African tribesmen and hunting big game, he had learned the skills that enable him to outwit his German pursuers. In this he personified an idea, widespread in the early twentieth century, that a stronger, more resourceful breed of Briton was to be found in the wild new lands of the empire than in the urbanized mother country and that they would come to Britain's rescue if it ever found itself in danger.

Hannay fulfils that expectation. In the book's closing pages, after his adventure has been successfully concluded, war is declared between Britain and Germany. He immediately joins the army and, thanks to his African experience, is straightaway commissioned as a captain, thereby leapfrogging the junior ranks. His example, though not the leapfrogging, was followed in real life by many hundreds of thousands of other young men from the empire, as happened again in the Second World War. Paradoxically, however, far from strengthening the sense of Britishness in the countries from which they came, the experience of war fostered the evolution of distinctive Australian, Canadian and New Zealand identities.

In its admiration for Hannay's colonial background *The Thirty-Nine Steps* reflects one aspect of early twentieth-century attitudes. Another was suspicion and fear of Jews. At the outset of the novel Hannay is warned by the man whose murder precipitates him into his adventures to beware of Jews. 'The Jew is everywhere, but you have to go far down the backstairs to find him,' he is told. This is particularly so with Germany. In 'any big Teutonic business', if you get to the real boss, 'ten to one you are brought up against a little white-faced Jew in a bath-chair with an eye like a rattlesnake. Yes, sir, he is the man ruling the world just now.' Somewhat surprisingly after this warning, Jews play no further part in the story.

Childers and Buchan are remembered for their books, but their careers and the contrast between them cast an even more revealing light upon the age they lived in. That of Childers is the more astonishing. His father was English and his mother Irish and, after their deaths while he was still a child, he was brought up by her family in Co. Wicklow. His education in England at Haileybury and Cambridge provided him with an assured position in the English upper middle class and, after the success of *The Riddle of the Sands*, he had the world at his feet. His drama and his tragedy arose from the fact that his Irish identity proved to be stronger than his English, leading him to turn against Britain and to meet his death as an Irish martyr.

His first intervention in Irish affairs came in 1910 when he gave up the parliamentary seat in Plymouth where he was a Liberal candidate in protest at the Liberal government's decision to exempt the six counties of Ulster from the provisions of its bill to give Home Rule to Ireland in an attempt to buy off the Unionist opposition. This did not satisfy the Unionists and in the early months of 1914 a group of them imported guns into Ulster in preparation for taking up arms against the bill's implementation. Childers decided to respond in kind and, in an echo of his novel, used his yacht to bring guns into Howth, near Dublin, for the Nationalists supporting the bill.

The outbreak of war distracted Childers from Irish affairs. Having been invited to join the navy he served with such bravery and distinction that he was awarded a Distinguished Service Cross. But Ireland was never far from his mind. When Sinn Fein mounted the Easter Rising in 1916, he was shocked by the brutality of the government's response. In 1918, he was further outraged when conscription, which had been in operation in Britain since 1916, was extended to Ireland. A central plank of the government's wartime propaganda was that Britain was fighting for the rights of small nations and Childers believed that it was hypocritical to deny those rights to Ireland.

When the war ended and Ireland was in open revolt he joined the Sinn Fein rebels.* To those in Britain who remembered how, in his novel, a renegade British naval officer who had been working for the Germans preferred to commit suicide rather than allow Carruthers and Davies to bring him home to face justice, this was a shocking and incomprehensible betrayal. In 1922 he went a step further when a majority of the Sinn Fein leadership settled with the British government and set up the Irish Free State, owing allegiance to the King. A dissident faction led by Eamon de Valera determined to fight on until a completely independent republic could be established, and Childers joined them. During the bitter Irish civil war that followed, he fell into the hands of Free State troops and was sentenced to death by the government in Dublin.

The manner of his dying became the stuff of legend. On the night before the execution he told his sixteen-year-old son, also called Erskine, to shake the hand of each of the men who had played a role

* See the essay on *The Last September* by Elizabeth Bowen.

in sentencing him and never to use his name for political advantage. When the firing squad was drawn up, Childers shook hands with each of its members. When he was facing the guns, he called out, 'Take a step or two forwards lads. It will be easier that way.'[4] In 1973 the wheel turned full circle when the younger Erskine succeeded de Valera as the fourth President of the republic.

Buchan's career could not have been more different. The privileged position in British society that Childers threw up to join the Irish was what Buchan strove successfully to acquire. He was born in 1875 in Fife, where his father was a minister of the Free Church of Scotland. From the local board school he progressed via a grammar school to Glasgow University and thence, with a scholarship, to Oxford. While there he published his first novel. In 1901 he became Private Secretary to the British High Commissioner in South Africa, the influential Alfred Milner, which gave him his entrée into political circles. In 1907 he married a cousin of the Duke of Westminster. Poor health kept him away from the fighting during the war, which he spent working in various branches of government propaganda and as a *Times* correspondent, roles that enabled him to build up a huge network of useful friends and contacts.

Thereafter, he pursed a varied career as a successful writer, as a publisher, as an MP and as a pillar of the Church of Scotland. In 1935 he became Lord Tweedsmuir on his appointment as Governor-General of Canada, an office he filled with great distinction. When he died in 1940 he was accorded a state funeral in Canada and the British government sent a Royal Navy destroyer to bring back his ashes for burial at the estate he had acquired in Oxfordshire.

The contrasting trajectories of these two authors' lives show how much more complex issues of loyalty, identity and class sometimes were in the first part of the twentieth century than they appear in hindsight.

The War in the Air

by H. G. Wells (1908)

The World Set Free

by H. G. Wells (1914)

The Great Illusion

by Norman Angell (1910)

If these three books, all of which were bestsellers before the outbreak of the First World War in 1914, had been taken to heart by the governments of the major European powers, how different the twentieth century might have been – how much suffering and destruction might have been avoided. Someone who read them when they first appeared and then read them again in the late 1940s must surely have thought, 'we were warned'. They would have lived through and either witnessed or experienced much of what had been the stuff of fantasies and nightmares when they were young.

In *The War in the Air*, published in 1908, H. G. Wells foresaw how air power would transform the nature of war, putting the civilian populations of large cities as much at risk as front-line troops and trumping the sea power on which Britain relied. In *The World Set Free*, published in 1914, he foresaw the atomic bomb. In *The Great Illusion*, published in 1910,* Norman Angell analysed in meticulous detail how, as a result of the growth of international credit markets and of international trade based upon them, national economies had become so dependent on each other that a war between major powers would be ruinous to victor and vanquished alike. It was not until the Second World War that most of Wells' prophecies were fulfilled and then in different circumstances from those he had envisaged. Angell's warnings were vindicated almost immediately by the irreparable damage wrought by the First World War on Britain and France as well as on Germany and its allies.

Wells sets *The War in the Air* a couple of decades or so after 1908. The world has been living at peace throughout that time while Germany and the United States have become the world's leading powers with New York overtaking London as the leading financial centre. Instead of going to war with Britain and France, as happened in 1914, the German government decides to establish a colonial empire in South America. It denounces the Monroe Doctrine, on the basis of which the United States had, since 1823, proclaimed that European powers should keep out of the American continent, and launches a huge fleet of airships† to invade New York. Following a series of improbable accidents and misunderstandings, the novel's hero, Bert Smallways, a young man from south London, is a captive on the flagship. It is partly

* The book grew out of a pamphlet published the year before under the title *Europe's Optical Illusion*.

† An airship is a balloon with a rigid frame that can navigate through the air under its own power. It derives its lift from large bags filled with gas. A gondola suspended beneath houses the crew, passengers and engine. The most famous was the German Zeppelin, named after its designer, Count Ferdinand von Zeppelin, and Zeppelin became a generic term. During the 1914–18 war airships were used to bomb Britain and France. Both before and after the war they were used for commercial flights and during the 1930s for a regular transatlantic service between Germany and North and South America.

through his eyes and partly in the form of a history written after the event that the story unfolds.

Wells was writing when the naval arms race between Britain and Germany was in full swing and just as the United States too had become a great naval power. The prestige weapon on which all three, and other powers as well, were spending millions of pounds was the big battleship, or dreadnought. In *The War in the Air* he showed that the development of air power would soon render these behemoths obsolete, though he was wrong in believing that the future of air power lay with the airship rather than the aeroplane. On their way to New York the German airships destroy the United States' Atlantic Fleet with ease. They then blitz New York, much as London would be blitzed in 1940. Unlike London, New York surrenders, but, as would be demonstrated many times subsequently, the Germans find that an attacker can't take possession of enemy territory without having troops on the ground. The United States fights on and, as winter sets in, the German airships are stranded over the Atlantic seaboard at the mercy of powerful winds.

At this point the German plan falls apart as other countries enter the war. In Europe Britain, France and Italy turn on Germany, violating Swiss neutrality in the process, just as the Germans would violate Belgian neutrality in 1914. The two sides mount bombing campaigns against each other's cities as would later happen during the Second World War. But the biggest sufferer is the United States. Japan and China form an alliance and dispatch a massive air fleet across the Pacific to attack Americans and Germans alike with airships that prove superior to both. As the war rages in the air the great American cities are blown to smithereens.

To suggest, as Wells did, that Asian countries could technologically outstrip Europeans and Americans required a huge leap of the imagination in the early twentieth century. At the same time, it tapped into deep-seated fears about what might happen should the Asian giants ever find the means to hit back at the white races then riding roughshod over their continent. Some thirty-four years later, in 1942, his scenario looked very prescient after the Japanese attack on the American fleet at Pearl Harbor and their victories over the British land and sea forces in South East Asia. It does so again today as China asserts itself militarily as well as industrially on the world stage and a host of other Asian economies outperform those of the West.

The War in the Air ends with the collapse of civilization. 'As the exhaustion of the mechanical resources of civilization clears the heavens of airships at last altogether, Anarchy, Famine and Pestilence are discovered triumphant below. The great nations have become but names in the mouths of men. Everywhere there are ruins and unburied dead, and shrunken, yellow faced survivors in a mortal apathy.' In the final scene, set thirty years after the end of the war, an old man and a boy, Smallways' brother and son, wander through the ruins of south London as the old man describes what it had once been like before the war and the plague, famine and other horrors that followed it. This was the future that those who campaigned for peace between the wars feared would follow a war in the air while later, during the Cold War, it was feared that a nuclear exchange would go a step further and destroy the world itself.*

In *The World Set Free*, Wells describes a nuclear war, which he envisages taking place in the 1950s, the decade after the Americans actually dropped atomic bombs on Hiroshima and Nagasaki. The book's most remarkable feature is that in 1914, on the basis of the scientific knowledge then available, he was able to foresee the potential of nuclear power both as a limitless source of energy to the great benefit of the human race and as the ultimate weapon of mass destruction. Initially he sees it being developed for peaceful purposes with two Indian inventors producing some of the most spectacular results, an idea that would have seemed outlandish to British readers, accustomed to regarding Indians

---

* See the essays on *Challenge to Death* and *Guilty Men*, and on *Lord of the Flies* and *On the Beach*.

as a subject race. Then in 1956 comes a financial crash, even more calamitous than the one that in fact occurred in 1929, and war follows.

The war pits Britain and France against a central European alliance led by Germany. After an attack by the Germans has destroyed the Franco-British headquarters in Paris, the commander of the French special scientific corps and his lieutenant take it upon themselves to drop three atomic bombs on Berlin. These are small devices that can be dropped by hand over the side of an aeroplane, but their effects are devastating. When the pilot looks down after releasing the first, 'it was like looking down upon the crater of a small volcano'. Thereafter the war spreads. There are battles on the ground and in the air in Europe, China and Japan attack Russia and the United States attacks Japan. Atomic bombs that continue to pour out radioactive substances with diminishing force for several weeks on a seventeen-day cycle are freely used.

'By the spring of 1959 from nearly two hundred centres, and every week added to their number, roared the unquenchable crimson conflagrations of the atomic bombs, the flimsy fabric of the world's credit had vanished, industry was completely disorganized and every city, every thickly populated area was starving or trembled on the verge of starvation.' In the real world, fears of a nuclear holocaust ran particularly high in the late 1950s and early 1960s. In Britain each Easter was marked by a march of tens of thousands of people from the Atomic Weapons Research Establishment at Aldermaston to Trafalgar Square in London. Wells' scenario exemplified the fears blazoned on their banners and expressed in their chants and the speeches at their final rally.

In *The War in the Air* the world never recovers from the effects of the fighting. In *The World Set Free* the nuclear exchange ushers in an improbable utopia that reflects to an extreme degree the hopes that were to be reposed in the League of Nations after the First World War. Faced with the prospect of the collapse of civilization, the world's leaders come together at a conference at Lake Como in Italy and agree to set up a World

Republic to be based there. Monarchs give up their crowns, governments pool their sovereignty and war is outlawed. There are difficulties at the outset in bringing a recalcitrant Balkan ruler into line. A prominent role in outwitting him is played by Egbert, the idealistic former British King. The great cities remain as radioactive no-go areas while a new society, stripped of the national rivalries that lead to wars, is created around them. Towards the end of the book the situation in London has improved to the point where work can begin on repairing the ruins.

The Great Illusion has none of the leaps of the imagination that characterize Wells' books. While writing it, Norman Angell was the managing editor of the continental edition of the *Daily Mail* in Paris,* a more serious publication than today's tabloid *Daily Mail*, and it reads somewhat like an extended think piece in a good newspaper. Its central thesis is that a new form of international economy had evolved over the preceding decades with the result that military and commercial security were no longer linked as they had been in the past. British prosperity, he argued, no longer resulted from its command of the oceans and acquiring a large navy or conquering more territory would not make the German people more prosperous.

Angell argues that in the world of 1910 a country's prosperity stemmed not from military or naval might, but from the competitivity of its products on world markets and the creditworthiness of its governments on financial markets. From this it follows that the citizens of small countries, such as Holland and Belgium, could be richer than those of a large one with a large army, like Germany, let alone Russia. Likewise, their governments could raise money on better terms. Nor, he points out, does imperial power promote commercial success in a free

---

* His full name was Ralph Norman Angell Lane. He wrote the book under his two middle names to conceal his identity from the paper's proprietor, Lord Northcliffe. After leaving the *Daily Mail* and becoming a celebrity, he adopted the name of Norman Angell and that is how he has been known ever since.

trade environment. 'Although England "owns" Canada, the English merchant is driven out of the Canadian markets by the merchant of Switzerland, who does not "own" Canada.'

Because of the changes that had taken place since the Franco-Prussian war of 1870–71 a decisive victory, like Prussia's in that conflict, was, he believed, no longer possible. The cost of a war would be catastrophic, whichever side won. With considerable foresight he added that for the victor to force the loser to pay reparations, as Prussia had forced France to do in 1871, would, in the new circumstances, be self-defeating as it would hold back the recovery of world trade and so damage the victorious power as well as the defeated. His explanations and arguments on both these points were later borne out by what happened during the First World War and afterwards with the Treaty of Versailles. In many respects they are similar to those put forward after the event in 1919 by Keynes in his great polemic, *The Economic Consequences of the Peace*.*

Another of the book's features is its attack both on the glorification of martial valour and on the view that expansionist foreign and colonial policies reflected a praiseworthy national spirit. Such notions were by no means confined to imperial Germany. They enjoyed widespread support in Britain and France. Among their most eloquent advocates was the former President of the United States, Theodore Roosevelt, whom Angell quotes as saying: 'We must play a great part in the world, and especially … perform those deeds of blood, of valour, which above everything else bring national renown.'

For his part Angell argued that just as duelling had fallen out of fashion in Britain as a means of settling disputes between individuals, so should war as a means of settling disputes between nations. He saw that for as long as it was widely believed 'warlike qualities alone can give the virile energy necessary for nations to win the struggle for life' and for as

* See essay on *The Economic Consequences of the Peace* and *The General Theory of Employment, Interest and Money*.

long as governments poured money into building more battleships and other armaments wars might easily break out. He sought to persuade his readers that 'human nature is not unchanging … that the struggle between nations is no part of the evolutionary law of man's advance', and that the concept of victory had become a great illusion.

The book turned Angell into a celebrity pundit, which proved to be his undoing. He had not in its pages ruled out the possibility of war nor had he argued that war was no longer possible. It is, however, easy to draw that conclusion from a casual reading of his text and some of his own subsequent statements, after he had become a publicist for peace, encouraged that interpretation. As a result, when war broke out he found himself being pilloried for having been wrong. For the rest of his life – he lived until 1967 – he argued with only limited success to put the record straight. At the same time, he continued to campaign and in 1934 was awarded a Nobel Peace Prize.

Besides being a prolific, popular and imaginative author with a huge body of work to his credit, H. G. Wells was one of the most outspoken public intellectuals of his day and a prominent figure in left-wing political circles. There were few subjects on which he did not speak and write, from art and design to women's rights, the organization of society and world government. He was a polymath, who would like to have been remembered as a serious novelist and political thinker. Had he known that subsequent generations would think of him mainly as a founder of science fiction he would probably have been disappointed. His most famous book, and one of the most celebrated of all science fiction books, is *The War of the Worlds*. In its original form, when published in 1898, it is about a Martian invasion of England. In 1938 Orson Welles adapted it for radio in the United States and transferred the setting to that country. The result was so realistic that it was taken by many to be a genuine news broadcast and provoked a mass panic.

The Bickersteth Diaries, 1914–1918

edited by John Bickersteth and published in 1995

Private Lord Crawford's Great War Diaries

edited by Christopher Arnander and published in 2013

The First World War, or The Great War as it was always called until the Second one came along, is the greatest calamity to have befallen the British people in the twentieth century. The war memorials in every city, town and village the length and breadth of the country and the commemorative plaques in so many churches and institutional buildings show the extent to which it affected every community, urban and rural, rich and poor, alike. The names of the fallen in the First War always substantially outnumber those who gave their lives in the Second. Precise overall figures differ from one source to another, as some include men from what were then the colonies and others not. For the British Isles alone the total is something over 700,000, which is more than double the figure for the Second, even when civilian deaths from the bombing of British cities are included. In terms of deaths as a percentage of their population France, Germany and Italy lost even more men in the First War than this country. Australia, Canada, New Zealand, India and other Commonwealth countries that fought alongside Britain also suffered grievously.

It is impossible to encompass the scale of the grief that overwhelmed the nation during the four years of war from August 1914 to November 1918 – the women who lost their husbands, parents their sons and children their fathers. In many cases two or even more sons from the same family were killed and instances were recorded of as many as five. It is through what happened to named individuals that the full extent of the horror can sometimes be most graphically illustrated. The society beauty Lady Diana Cooper told her son many years later that by the end of 1916 when she was twenty-four years old, 'with the single exception of my father, every man she had ever danced with was dead'.[5] By the end of the war, Vera Brittain, famous for her autobiography, *Testament of Youth*, had lost her fiancé, her brother and her two closest men friends.

That was not all. Many hundreds and thousands of the men who returned were physically maimed and often hideously disfigured and/or mentally and psychologically damaged as well. Their lives and those of their families never recovered.

Throughout Europe, on both sides, the war inspired an outpouring of writing – poems, novels, memoirs, histories, diaries and letters – commensurate with its scale. The flood began within months of the first guns being fired and continues to this day with new books being published and old records brought to light. No other conflict involving Britain has inspired so many words. Most have not endured, but wherever English is read the most famous poems written during the war by Rupert Brooke, Wilfred Owen, Edmund Blunden and others still resonate. The prose works published in the 1920s and 1930s by Robert Graves, Siegfried Sassoon, Ford Madox Ford and others who served are also still widely read.

The Bickersteth Diaries and *Private Lord Crawford's Great War Diaries* are among those that have only relatively recently become publicly available. They were private documents not intended for publication and written as and when the opportunity arose. They are snapshots that capture the thoughts and feelings of the writers at the moment they were committed to paper. As such they provide an intimate account of how the war was seen through the eyes of the writers.

Canon Sam Bickersteth was a well-connected Anglican clergyman. He and his wife, Ella, had six sons. By the spring of 1915 four were on active service while one was in the War Office and another a rector in the Midlands. The sons wrote home regularly and Ella transcribed and circulated the letters within the family. As published the *Diaries* consist mainly of letters written by Julian, a chaplain, and Burgon, an officer in a cavalry regiment. Occasionally, the editor, a nephew of the writers, includes a contribution from one of the others or a comment by Ella herself.

The Earl of Crawford and Balcarres, to give him his full title, was a great aristocrat, Scotland's premier earl with a title dating from 1398, and a man of many parts. When the war began he was forty-three and a former Conservative Chief Whip in the House of Commons. He had written a book about the Italian Renaissance sculptor Donatello, helped to found what is now the Art Fund and was chairing a coal and iron company. In 1915, when it became apparent that the war might last a long time, and having turned down an offer to enter the government, he felt he should do something practical to help. Instead of seeking a role in keeping with his status, he joined the Royal Army Medical Corps as a hospital orderly with the rank of private, the lowest in the British Army, a crossing of the rigid class divides of the period that must have been greeted with incredulity by all who knew him.

His diary provides a unique worm's-eye view of how the war and the army appeared to a man with experience at the top of the social, political and business worlds. He served for some fourteen months, in the course of which he refused another ministerial offer, before being persuaded to return to London during a political crisis to become Minister of Agriculture. He was the only member of the government throughout the war to have served in the ranks with the ordinary soldiers, as distinct from being an officer.

When the war began it was greeted with enthusiasm all over Europe and men flocked to the colours – over one million two hundred thousand in Britain by the end of 1914 and double that number by the end of 1915. That they should have continued to do so in 1915 when the horrors had become apparent says a great deal about both the attitudes and condition of the British people at that time. Julian Bickersteth felt he owed it to the country to return from Australia, where he was working, to join up. Ford Madox Ford, who volunteered at the age of forty-one, expressed a widespread feeling when he wrote to his mother: 'If one has enjoyed the privileges of the ruling class of a country all one's life, there seems no alternative to fighting for that country if necessary.'[6]

Others who had not enjoyed such privileges felt similarly impelled. In October 1915 a private suffering from rheumatism was admitted to Crawford's Casualty Clearing Station. He turned out to be sixty-one and had misled the recruitment office about his age. As he had three sons at the front he 'thought it my duty to come out and help them'. Not many elderly men would have lied about their age to join the army, but it is estimated that some quarter of a million underage boys claimed to be nineteen in order to get accepted.

Many volunteers were swept up by the fervour and effectiveness of the recruitment campaigns, epitomized by the famous poster of the mustachioed Lord Kitchener pointing a finger above the caption

'Your Country Needs You'. Some were influenced by the intense social pressure that was put on young men to join up. Others were escaping from boring jobs and marriages. In many cases need was the motivation. Men were better clothed and better fed in the army than leading the kind of lives described in the chapter on *Anna of the Five Towns*, *The Condition of England* and *The Ragged-Trousered Philanthropists*. 'In my four months' training with the regiment I put on nearly a stone [fourteen pounds] in weight and got a bit taller,' remembered one survivor from a Suffolk village.[7]

Both Burgon Bickersteth and Crawford inveigh against those who don't volunteer. 'You have no conception of the contempt which men out here have for the non-combatant corps,' writes Burgon in 1915. He is strongly in favour of universal conscription while Crawford criticizes the government for its reluctance to introduce it, which it eventually did in 1916. Theirs was the majority view, but there were exceptions. One was the future Labour Prime Minister Clement Attlee, who joined up immediately while his brother Tom became a conscientious objector. Yet they remained on the closest terms of affection and mutual respect both then and for the rest of their lives.[8]

The letters Julian and Burgon sent home provide a vivid impression of the extent to which they were living in the midst of death and must have been agonizing for the parents to receive. Three are typical. In one Julian tells of how 'At least six men died in my arms at the Corps Main Dressing Station during the twenty-four hours following the opening of the battle and many more were hurried away to the Casualty Clearing Stations, only to die there.' Burgon writes in January 1916 about how his unit is to be moved 'to a pretty hot part of the line – an average of thirty yards between us and the Hun'. In another letter he describes breezily how a shell that landed twelve feet away from him turned out to be a dud and only covered him with earth instead of killing him. A letter that Julian found particularly harrowing to write describes an all-night vigil with a man who had been condemned to death for desertion and was to face a firing squad in the morning.*

In Crawford's diary the most striking passages, and those that reveal most about what it was like to be in the army at that time, are about how differently the other ranks, or ordinary soldiers, were treated by comparison with the officers. No social radical or left-wing firebrand could have been more indignant than he, who until then had enjoyed all the privileges of the aristocracy. He makes no complaint about the menial tasks he has to perform in the operating theatre, tending patients or doing manual work around the camp. It is what he signed up for. What shocks him is 'the disparity between the treatment of officers and men based on the old theory that one officer is worth twenty men'. He experiences this most vividly on landing in France with his unit to board the train to take them to the town where they are to be stationed. While the officers travel in a carriage he and thirty-one other men are crammed into a cattle truck of the sort that in the Second World War would be used for deporting Jews to the concentration camps.

One of his biggest complaints is about how much more often officers go on leave than their men, a source of bitterness, he writes, among the rank and file. He himself had to wait eight months for his first leave, during which time his Colonel had four. Whereas officers got leave every three months 'with mathematical regularity' that of the men was allocated in a very hit-and-miss manner. In his own unit it was settled by ballot, which he favoured.

---

* Execution by firing squad was the standard punishment for desertion, cowardice and mutiny in all the armies involved in the war. The Italian Chief of the General Staff when Italy entered the war, General Luigi Cadorna, took this a stage further when he revived the ancient Roman practice of decimation, that is executing one in ten men in units that mutinied, disobeyed orders or simply failed in some other way, although he did not insist on the exact ratio.

Another of his gripes was the way officers disregarded the rule that their baggage should be limited to thirty-five pounds. One of his tasks when wounded officers arrived at his Casualty Clearing Station was to unpack and disinfect their kit. Some would have several times as much as they were allowed with cases full of extra boots, overcoats and other comforts, such as primus stoves. Whatever their rank, officers and men faced the prospect of death together, but, for as long as they survived, these comforts made life somewhat less unpleasant for the officers.

The extent to which officers and men, while serving together in the mud and rat-infested squalor of the trenches and risking death and disablement together on a daily basis, remained members of different castes receives further confirmation in a letter written by Burgon in the summer of 1917. He mentions having a meal with some private soldiers and notes that it was 'the first time I had ever sat down to eat out here in uniform with soldiers'. As a chaplain with the rank of an officer and ministering to officers and men alike, his brother Julian sees the war as an opportunity to bridge this divide. In a passage that shows how far removed middle-class Anglican clergymen were from their working-class parishioners, he writes that the war 'has given parsons the opportunity which nothing else in their lifetime would have given them' to be 'in close touch with the ordinary men and opened one's eyes to their point of view'.

Much of Julian's correspondence deals with the religious services he has arranged, including – a chilling detail – the constant need to find new recruits to assist at them to replace those who have been killed or wounded. He writes about his efforts to spread the Faith through confirmation classes and describes the practical ways in which he consoles the dying, comforts the wounded and acts as an unofficial link between them and their families at home. 'Between us, my chaplains and I wrote and dispatched 3,000 to 4,000 postcards and letters to relatives,' he writes after a particularly bloody engagement in 1917. These added comfort, reassurance and further information to the official notification provided to relatives by the War Office.

Some two years earlier, in 1915, my maternal grandmother had received just such a letter from a chaplain after my grandfather, serving with the Royal Artillery, was killed at the Battle of Neuve Chapelle. The details it gave were so precise that in 1980 it enabled my brother and I to locate the field in which he most likely fell.

The Bickersteths, with four brothers at the front, were phenomenally lucky that only one was killed: Morris at the Battle of the Somme on 1 July 1916, the worst day for casualties in the history of the British Army. The depth of the family's grief is palpable and the language in which they communicate with each other about his death is deeply emotional. There is nothing of the stilted stiff upper lip that is supposed to have characterized that generation. As devout Christians, they believe he has gone straight to heaven. 'We may indeed be proud of him, and we know, don't we, darling ones that he is happy now,' Julian writes to his parents. The 'magnificence' of his death for his country is a recurring theme in the family's correspondence.

It recurs constantly on the memorials and commemorative plaques in churches and elsewhere that were erected after the war. It is part of the language by means of which society and individuals coped with the human cost of war. To this day the solemnity and the sonorous tone of the words on these plaques and memorials retain their power to evoke the grief of those whose sons, brothers and husbands are named on them.

The Bickersteths were a deeply religious family. These words had real meaning for them. But as Julian recognized, their faith was not shared by the vast majority. To most, he writes in one letter, 'religion is simply a name and has never touched heart or mind'. This applies not just to the men, but to the officers too. Despite the prominence of religious education in the curriculum of the public schools, those schools had in Julian's view 'not produced a type of man who feels any need for religion'.

Burgon confirms this analysis. On Good Friday, 1917, he writes, 'not one per cent of the Brigade are aware of the fact, certainly not the significance of the day'. A chaplain, he explains, is not valued for what he represents. He is only 'appreciated by the men in so far as he busies himself with their recreational and physical comfort and respected if he visits the front line and shares their dangers'. Far from being brought, even temporarily, to take religion seriously by their constant exposure to death and disablement, Burgon reports, 'The average British soldier is very fatalistic: "Well, Sir, yer'll be 'it when yer'll be 'it and not afore", sums up his approach.'

As the war dragged on attitudes towards it among those at the front evolved. This is reflected in the brothers' letters. When it began they, like the country at large, were confident of victory and full of animosity towards the Germans. 'As to the Germans!' writes Julian during the early months, 'May God help them! We shall win this war because God cannot allow such scum to exist.' Burgon talks of 'the hated Hun'. By 1917 Julian wonders how the war will ever end and wishes for 'a round table conference'. In 1918 he writes, 'men don't and won't hate the Germans – they only hate the war'. Burgon utters a *cri de cœur*: 'When will this grim butchery of unfledged boys, German and English end?' The trajectory of their feelings reflected that of many at the front, but by no means all, as an argument Burgon had with his Colonel shows. The Colonel intends 'to teach my children to hate the Germans, and to teach their children to hate the Germans'. Burgon replies: 'If you do that, what is to be the future of Europe?'

While those at the front were becoming disillusioned, the civilian population at home, egged on by government propaganda and the press, remained bellicose. When in 1917 the Conservative Lord Lansdowne suggested that the possibility of a negotiated peace should be explored he was howled down at home while, as Julian reports, widely supported at the front. As might be expected Crawford saw through the propaganda at an early stage, as an October 1915 diary entry about the Battle of Neuve Chapelle shows: 'a great victory as announced to the world, but in reality a costly and dangerous fiasco. Our casualties gigantic, our net gains negligible.'

Towards the end of 1916 Julian writes of how 'The country is hoodwinked. Facts are distorted or totally misrepresented by the press.' This follows a letter from Burgon about a lunch with the *Daily Mail* correspondent Philip Gibbs that casts a fascinating light on the contrast between what the troops were experiencing and how it was reported at home. 'I am not allowed to tell the truth or what is worse, I am made to tell lies,' Gibbs complained. He had received a letter from the celebrated author G. K. Chesterton, complimenting him on his articles and 'praising the great spirit of the Briton' to which he had responded with one explaining the true horrors of the war. 'Chesterton, sitting safely in England, wrote back totally unconvinced and spoke of the necessity for sacrifice.'

War 2 – Warnings and Reality

Challenge to Death edited by Storm Jameson, 1934, and *Guilty Men* by 'Cato', 1940.

My Early Life by Winston S. Churchill, 1930.

Flare Path by Terence Rattigan, 1942, *Few Eggs and No Oranges: The Diaries of Vere Hodgson, 1940–45*, and *Darling Monster: The Letters of Lady Diana Cooper to Her Son John Julius Norwich, 1939–52*.

Challenge to Death

edited by Storm Jameson (1934)

Guilty Men

by 'Cato' (1940)

So dreadful was the loss of life and suffering caused to all the combatant countries by the 1914–18 war that it was widely hoped, in a phrase originally coined by H. G. Wells, that it would prove to be, 'The war to end war'.* Only that, it was thought, could possibly, in any way, justify the sacrifice that had taken place. The yearning to ensure that there could be no repetition of what had happened was felt in all countries. Its tangible result was the formation of the League of Nations, under the terms of which the member states committed themselves to the peaceful resolution of disputes in the hope that war could be banished for ever.

This aspiration held sway in Britain to a greater extent than in the other major European countries because the nation was untroubled

* In the months following the outbreak of war Wells published a number of articles that were brought together in a book entitled *The War That Will End War*. This gave rise to the pithier 'The war to end war', which soon became a catchphrase.

by historic nightmares or grudges against its neighbours. France was haunted by the spectre of its defeat by Prussia in 1871, after which the new German empire had been proclaimed in Louis XIV's Palace of Versailles; a humiliating memory. It had also suffered more than any other country from the recent war as nearly all the fighting and destruction had taken place on its territory. Germany had not only been defeated; it also believed itself to be the victim of an unjust peace settlement in the Treaty of Versailles. Italy was one of the victorious powers, but believed it had been cheated of the fruits of victory by its allies. All three countries, like Britain, had peace movements and the League of Nations was active in promoting cooperation between them by means of conferences and other gatherings. But in each there was a significant body of opinion that believed in the need to prepare for another round of fighting and opinion was more divided than in Britain.

Challenge to Death was published in 1934 just as those preparations for another round were beginning to gather momentum on the Continent. It expressed the dreams and wishful thinking of the British peace movement based on the belief, in the words of its editor, the popular novelist (Margaret) Storm Jameson, that, 'Ours is the largest and most important political unit in the world.' She believed that, 'More than any other state, more even than those which exceed us in actual or potential wealth, we can influence world thought.' In this view she reflected the beliefs of many in this country at that time.

Guilty Men is a scream of rage and recrimination published in 1940, when all such illusions had been swept away, as the country fought for its life against the might of Nazi Germany after the evacuation of its army from Dunkirk and the defeat of its French ally. Its authors, writing under the pseudonym of Cato, the Roman statesman famous for his probity and tenacity in opposing Julius Caesar, were three left-wing journalists, one of whom, Michael Foot,* went on to become leader of the Labour Party in the 1980s.

The peace movement in Britain had reached its peak in 1931 when membership of its principal vehicle, the League of Nations Union, a sort of supporters' club for the League, rose above the million mark. Thereafter it had declined under the pressure of events. In 1932 the League failed to prevent Japan's invasion of Manchuria and in February 1933 Japan walked out of the League. In May 1933 Hitler came to power in Berlin. Germany then walked out too and embarked on a rearmament programme. In 1938, Hitler took over Austria and in March 1939 Czechoslovakia before finally triggering the Second World War with the invasion of Poland in September 1939. Italy invaded Abyssinia in 1935 and the Spanish Civil War raged from 1936 to 1939.

Despite the movement's declining membership and all that was happening abroad, anti-war feeling remained strong in Britain. In February 1933 the Oxford Union passed a resolution 'that in no circumstances will this House fight for King and Country'. It was widely reported across Europe and taken in some circles to mean that the elite of British youth had become irredeemably pacifist. In Britain too, it caused a considerable stir and led to similar votes in some other universities. In October of the same year a by-election was held in Fulham at which a Conservative pro-rearmament candidate defending a large majority was defeated by a Labour pacifist. In the winter of 1934–5 the League of Nations Union with the support of thirty-four other groups organized a ballot on the lines of a general election. A total of over eleven and a half million votes were cast of which 96 per cent were in favour of continued British membership of the League. In

---

* The other two were Frank Owen and Peter Howard. In a private letter in my possession to Donald McCormick dated 30 June 1969, Michael Foot wrote: 'We concealed our identities under the name of Cato partly for publicity purposes, and partly to hide the matter from our common employer at that time, Beaverbrook. But we did not have much success for long with the second aim.'

1936 the charismatic Canon of St Paul's Cathedral, the Reverend Dick Sheppard, founded the Peace Pledge Union that enrolled a hundred and thirty-five thousand men in favour of absolute pacifism in order to demonstrate that men were just as much against war as women.

These and other expressions of anti-war feeling led the government to play down the need for rearmament during the 1935 general election campaign and not to press ahead with it afterwards as vigorously as those, like Churchill, who were warning of impending danger, wanted.

Challenge to Death was conceived in the months after Hitler took power as a way of bringing together the various strands of the peace movement in a single propaganda exercise. It emerged from a dinner held in February 1934 at London's Wellington Club, an ironic choice of venue for an anti-war meeting, presided over by Viscount Cecil of Chelwood. As a Conservative minister in the wartime coalition, he had played a significant role in formulating the ideas on which the League of Nations covenant was based. Besides Storm Jameson, the list of contributors to the book included a number of then prominent public intellectuals, of whom only the writers J. B. Priestley, Rebecca West and Vera Brittain, the poet Edmund Blunden and the scientist Julian Huxley have any resonance today.*

When the book emerged later that year, it received widespread attention and not only in this country. The *New York Herald Tribune* hailed it as speaking for the post-war 'lost generation'.[1] Its assumptions and recommendations reveal much about the hopes and fears of the period. The authors correctly identified the link between dictatorship and nationalism on the one hand with a propensity to aggression on the other that made Germany and Italy such obvious sources of danger. They assumed, like everyone else in this country, that Britain would always be on the side of peace, although Lord Cecil made a telling point

* It is worthy of note that within only sixteen years of women gaining the vote in 1918, five of the sixteen contributors were women.

when he drew attention to the words of 'Land of Hope and Glory'. As he pointed out, a nation with a large colonial empire that sang, 'Wider still and wider may her bounds be set/God who made her mighty make her mightier yet' could hardly 'throw stones across the channel'.

Besides overestimating British power and influence, the authors' most serious geopolitical error was to take insufficient account of the United States and the Soviet Union. That it would be those two powers who, when war came, would determine its outcome simply did not occur to them. This was in part because their actual military strength, as distinct from its potential, looked modest in the 1930s. Extraordinary as it now seems, the United States' army was smaller than Portugal's. Another reason was the overwhelmingly Eurocentric focus of the authors. Unlike H. G. Wells in his novels *The War in the Air* and *The World Set Free*, they could not imagine the destiny of the world being shaped by anyone other than Western Europeans. In this they were typical of their time.

However, they shared Wells' fear that the outcome of the next war would be determined in the air rather than on the ground. It was not the prospect of a resumption of trench warfare that haunted them, it was the fear of being bombarded from the air. The essence of this fear was distilled in two oft-repeated phrases by the Conservative leader Stanley Baldwin, who was three times Prime Minister between 1923 and 1937. In 1927 he had asked, 'and who in Europe does not know that one more war in the West, and the civilization of the ages will fall with as great a crash as that of Rome?'[2] In 1932, during a House of Commons debate in which he was arguing in favour of rearmament, he warned that 'the bomber will always get through'[3] and that therefore the only defence was offence.

These fears, but not Baldwin's conclusion, lie at the heart of *Challenge to Death*. Gerald Heard, a broadcaster and writer, foresaw a situation in which, 'outside Whitehall, as soon as the attack begins,

London has ceased to function as a capital or even as a city'. He forecast that a dictatorship would follow. Philip Noel-Baker, a former Labour MP who later became a Cabinet minister in the 1945 Labour government, quoted various scenarios put forward by military experts. One suggested that within forty-eight hours of an attack 40 per cent of London's population would leave the city and within a week 80 per cent. Other forecasts were equally alarming. Noel-Baker suggested that, though these fears might turn out to be exaggerated, the question remained, 'How long will it be after war begins before London and Paris and Berlin will each be a shattered, flaming hell?' His conclusion was 'that the next war, if it should happen, will obliterate the civilization in which we live', as Wells had warned in his novels would be the case. In the event, that proved to be wrong. Civilization survived, but the fears were none the less real for that.

As Harold Macmillan recalled in 1962 when he was Prime Minister, 'We thought of warfare in 1938 rather as people think of nuclear warfare today',* a point not generally given sufficient weight when the government's efforts during the 1930s to avoid war are condemned as appeasement. Nor have subsequent generations been sufficiently understanding of how my parents' generation, which had lost husbands, fathers, sons and brothers in the previous war, dreaded the prospect of going through the same agony again. In their position I should have felt the same and, like them, wished the government to do everything it reasonably could to avoid a repetition. I only hope I would have realized in time when that policy became self-defeating.

The attempt by the British government to avoid another war by reaching an enduring settlement with Hitler failed, not least because it was based on a fundamental misjudgement of his character and capacity

* Macmillan was speaking during the Cuban Missile Crisis of that year when the United States and the Soviet Union probably came closer to a nuclear exchange than at any other time during the Cold War.

for evil, but, in the circumstances of the time, it is understandable that it should have enjoyed widespread support. Likewise, though the proposals put forward in *Challenge to Death* were misconceived and impractical, even at the moment they were launched they reflected real fears and should be seen as a constructive attempt by a group of concerned individuals to tackle the underlying problems of their age.

The contributors came up with a variety of ideas for creating an environment that would diminish the chances of war. Among the problems they identified was the relationship in all countries between arms manufacturers promoting their products and the armed forces wanting always to have the most up-to-date equipment. The novelist and journalist Winifred Holtby argued that the only way to break this link was for the arms manufacturing companies to be nationalized and subjected to international control.

The most ambitious scheme was for 'the transference of control over aviation to the League, and [the creation of] an international air force'. In a chapter headed 'The International Air Police Force', Noel-Baker developed this idea. He advocated the total abolition of all national air forces of every kind and the supervision and control of this disarmament by a permanent commission with the right 'to inspect at will all aerodromes and airports, aviation establishments of every kind and aircraft factories'.

The result would be that, 'Once it is established, the International Police will be the only armed air force in the world.' He discussed whether it should be composed of national contingents or be a homogeneous international corps and came down in favour of the latter. The commander, he suggested, should come from a small country, such as Sweden or the Netherlands, and that its working languages should be French and English. His description of how it would function and the facilities it would need went into considerable detail, but was weak on how and according to what rules and safeguards international civilian control would be exercised. Nor did he face up to the question of what to do if a non-member of the League, such as the United States, Germany or Japan, refused to sign up and created a powerful air force of its own.

The difficulties of gaining agreement to set up the force are glossed over. Noel-Baker was convinced that, if Britain would support the scheme, 'our acceptance would be decisive'. Jameson wrote, 'Of the politicians who throng that Hall of Hopes, the Assembly at Geneva [the League's headquarters], it is the English on whom all wait. It is therefore our duty, and should be our pleasure, to assume responsibility and show the bogged and strayed nations of Europe a road to follow.' This illusion that where Britain led others would follow did not end with the 1930s. Between the 1950s and 1970s the Campaign for Nuclear Disarmament, generally known as CND, argued that if Britain would unilaterally renounce its nuclear weapons, it would set an example that would influence others.

None of the contributors to *Challenge to Death* was among the twelve men the authors of *Guilty Men* held responsible for Britain's desperate plight in 1940. Their purpose was to praise the army evacuated from Dunkirk for its courage and to show how, by ignoring Churchill's warnings of German rearmament and their own ineptitude, those in power during the 1930s had been responsible for the mess the country was in. Apart from Ramsay MacDonald, who in 1931 had resigned the leadership of the Labour Party to lead the coalition National government, all those in the dock were Conservatives. The pacifist George Lansbury, who had briefly led the Labour Party, was excoriated, but not charged. Because Conservatives had dominated the National government, whose efforts to reach an accommodation with Hitler through the policy of appeasement had failed, the authors' accusations both reflected and confirmed the public mood. They also helped to form the subsequent judgement of history on the period.

Written in a matter of weeks, *Guilty Men* is a powerful and convincing narrative. The authors showed how at each step of the way, from Hitler's assumption of power in the spring of 1933 to Prime Minister Neville Chamberlain's agreement with him at Munich in the autumn of 1938, the government had misjudged both his intentions and the speed of his rearmament. Against that background, they were scornful of the government for allowing itself to be influenced by the 'Peace Vote' in the general election of 1935. Reading their denunciations alongside *Challenge to Death* is like being in two parallel universes at the same time. In one the politicians are blamed for endangering the country by not rearming enough, in the other they are condemned for not leading the way to international disarmament. In one they are condemned for not building up the strength of the Royal Air Force more quickly, in the other for not promoting an International Air Force Police. That was the political story of the 1930s.

The desire for peace was still deeply felt in 1938 when Chamberlain and the French Prime Minister signed their now notorious pact with Hitler in Munich. Chamberlain hailed it as 'peace in our time'. He returned home a hero to appear with the King and Queen on the balcony at Buckingham Palace to receive the plaudits of the crowds cheering in the Mall; an unprecedented demonstration of royal support for a government of the day, and a reflection of the widespread public support for the agreement at that time. Fortunately, the government was by then sufficiently seized of the impending danger that it pushed ahead with rearmament and, by the skin of its teeth, was able to provide the Royal Air Force with the men and machines that, in 1940, enabled it to defeat the Luftwaffe in the Battle of Britain, which followed the retreat from Dunkirk.

The Battle of Britain and Dunkirk were heroic exploits. They have become engraved on the national memory as emblematic of the British spirit. It is right that they should be remembered and commemorated.

But, as well as providing an inspiration to subsequent generations, they have given rise to a serious misreading of the national interest. Instead of being seen as an awful warning of the existential dangers of isolation, they have led some to believe that distancing ourselves from our continental neighbours, rather than joining with them in common enterprises, is inherent in our national character and destiny.

My Early Life

by Winston S. Churchill* (1930)

The one man, above all others, to whom Britain owes its salvation in 1940 is Winston Churchill, who became Prime Minister in May, the month before Dunkirk. Thanks to his leadership, this country, supported by its empire and Commonwealth, was able to hold out alone until June 1941 when Hitler invaded Russia and then in December declared war on the United States following the Japanese attack on Pearl Harbor. His role in 1940 and 1941 constitutes the hinge on which the history of this country, of Europe and, in many ways, the world turned during the twentieth century. He remained in office until victory was achieved in 1945 and was again Prime Minister from 1951 until 1955. But, to paraphrase the title of one of his own books, the period when Britain stood alone was his finest hour.

For many of the forty-three books in seventy-two volumes that he published during his lifetime he relied on teams of researchers and ghost writers whose drafts he then transformed, 'by adding insights, comparisons, metaphors and flights of fancy'.[4] *My Early Life* is all his own work, or at least very largely so. It is highly personal and

* His earliest books were signed Winston Churchill until in 1899 he became aware of a successful American novelist of that name and decided to add the initial S for Spencer.

self-revealing and covers the years and the experiences that moulded him between his birth in 1874 and his early years in the House of Commons after the 1900 general election. In his own words it goes a long way to explaining why he was so distrusted by the British public until the moment in 1940 when it became apparent that only under his leadership could Britain defy Hitler.

He was feeling rather out of sorts when he wrote it. He had recently lost office as a result of the 1929 general election. He had also lost a good deal of money in the financial crash of that year. At the same time the country's prospects were overshadowed by the onset of the Great Depression. His sombre mood is reflected in the preface where he compares 'these anxious and dubious times' to 'a vanished age' in the late nineteenth century, when he was young and 'the dominant forces in Great Britain were very sure of themselves and their doctrines'. His nostalgic recollections, which would have been shared by many of his fellow citizens, and not just of his class and background, cast a revealing, and, sometimes, surprising light on that vanished age.

Like almost all members of the more prosperous classes until well into the twentieth century, the most important influence on Churchill's childhood was his nurse, or nanny, a woman called Mrs Everest. His father was the charismatic politician Lord Randolph Churchill, whose rise to high office was followed by a precipitate fall and early death; his mother, Jennie, was a beautiful and promiscuous American heiress. They were distant and glamorous figures, rarely seen and to be adored from afar. It was to Mrs Everest, 'your loving old woom', as she signed her letters to him when he was away at school, that he felt closest. Although accustomed to the grandest of grand houses, including Blenheim Palace where he was born, he 'loved Ventnor' on the Isle of Wight, where Mrs Everest would take him to stay with her sister, whose husband was a retired prison warder. The bond between them remained very close. Recalling her death in *My Early Life*, he writes,

'She had been my dearest and most intimate friend during the whole of the twenty years that I had lived.'

His feelings towards her were later to influence his approach to public policy. In *My Early Life*, he writes that his awareness of how many such women, after leaving their employer, ended their lives in penury made him glad, as a minister in Asquith's Liberal government, to play a part in the introduction of old age pensions and national insurance in 1911. This measure, part of a package of far-reaching reforms initiated by the Chancellor of the Exchequer, David Lloyd George, was regarded as very radical by British public opinion, although Bismarck had pioneered it in Germany many years before. It marks the first step on the long road to the establishment of the welfare state after 1945. The credit for that great innovation lies with the Labour government of 1945–51, but its genesis was a famous report by Lord Beveridge in 1942 that was commissioned and published by the wartime coalition led by Churchill.

After a famously unsuccessful school career at Harrow, Churchill found his self-confidence and acquired the characteristics and attitudes that were to become his hallmark serving as a young officer in a British Army cavalry regiment, the 4th Hussars, in India. One was the love of reading and the omniscient knowledge of history that together enabled him to become such a successful writer and orator as well as forming his approach to politics. It was, he writes, 'when I had almost completed my twenty-second year that the desire for learning came upon me'. Thereafter, while in barracks, where his duties were very light, he read voraciously for four or five hours a day.

Beginning with Gibbon's *Decline and Fall of the Roman Empire** he moved on to Macaulay, Malthus and Darwin and touched on others, including Plato, Aristotle and Schopenhauer. This was a solitary exercise. He had no university tutor or supervisor to guide him and he formed

* He was delighted to find that Gibbon in his autobiography expressed gratitude to his old nurse.

his own conclusions as he went along; an extraordinary exercise in self-education. No such books would have been in the library of the officers' mess and he relied on his mother to dispatch them in enormous parcels from England; on one occasion eight volumes of Gibbon, on another twelve of Macaulay.

The other characteristic he acquired at that time, and which comes through strongly in *My Early Life*, was his delight in war. In those days there was almost always a small colonial war going on somewhere in the empire. Churchill invariably volunteered to go wherever the fighting was thickest, first in India and later in Africa where, in 1898, he participated in the British Army's last victorious cavalry charge at the Battle of Omdurman.* The frankness with which he records the thrill of combat and the rather casual way he writes about casualties jar with those of a less martial disposition. Books and articles about his adventures poured from his pen and turned him into a minor celebrity until he was captured during the Boer War. After a dramatic escape from the camp in which he was being held prisoner, and a hair-raising flight across hundreds of miles of enemy-controlled territory, he returned home a hero and a household name. On the back of this he was catapulted into the House of Commons in the 1900 general election and able to earn large sums of money lecturing both in Britain and the United States where his mother opened many plutocratic doors for him.

The pattern of his life was set. Politics replaced fighting. Otherwise the rhythm of action interspersed by writing and public speaking continued until the end of his life. His range was enormous, from his multi-volume account of the First World War, entitled *The World Crisis*, and his biography in four volumes of his great ancestor, the Duke of Marlborough, at one end of the spectrum to lightweight articles in the popular press at the other. All were highly paid, which helped to fund

* It is salutary to think that as a young man he took part in this cavalry charge and as an old man authorized the British hydrogen bomb programme.

his lavish lifestyle. *The World Crisis*, published in the United States as well as in Britain and serialized in *The Times*, is estimated to have earned him £25,000, or about £1,500,000 in today's money. A series of articles in the early 1930s for the *News of World* on 'Great Stories of the World Retold', from *Ben-Hur* to *Uncle Tom's Cabin*, was paid for at the rate of £330 each, or about £22,600 in today's money. Inevitably, however, his writing exposed his restless spirit, belligerent character and enormous ego. Arthur Balfour, a former Prime Minister and Cabinet colleague, mocked *The World Crisis* as 'Churchill's autobiography disguised as a history of the world'.[5]

His record in office reinforced his literary image. As Home Secretary in 1910 he earned the undying enmity of the Welsh miners by his handling of the so-called Tonypandy Riots. As First Lord of the Admiralty he initiated and was blamed for what turned out to be the disastrous Gallipoli campaign of 1915. Many were also disgusted by his frank enjoyment of the war, about which he spoke openly, as during the height of that campaign to Violet Asquith, the Prime Minister's daughter. 'I know a curse should rest upon me – because I love this war,' he told her over a dinner at the Admiralty. 'I know it's smashing and shattering the lives of thousands every moment – and yet – I can't help it – I enjoy every second of it.' During the previous month he had told her stepmother, Margot, 'I would not be out of this glorious, delicious war for anything the world could give me.' The bestselling author Arnold Bennett's lightly fictionalized portrait of him in *Lord Raingo*, a popular novel about the wartime government, brought this characteristic to the attention of the general public. His aggressive stance and divisive behaviour during the General Strike of 1925 further antagonized many people. His crossing the floor from the Conservatives to the Liberals when the latter were doing well in the early years of the century and his return to the Conservative Party in the 1920s, after the Liberal Party had collapsed, added to the aura of distrust that surrounded him.

In the 1930s India was injected into this volatile mix with calamitous consequences both for him and the country. In *My Early Life* Churchill had written in rapturous terms about his time there: the numerous servants – butler, syce, head groom and dressing boy – who 'formed the foundation of a cavalry subaltern's household', the polo matches between rival regiments and teams supported by Indian princes, the pleasures of regimental life and the thrill of skirmishing on the North-West Frontier. Shortly after the book's publication, and while it was being widely read throughout the country, the government brought forward plans to move India along the road to self-government and eventual independence.

Such plans were anathema to him. He seemed unable to grasp the extent to which India and the foundations of British power there had changed since the 1890s and opposed them root and branch. Coupled with the imperial nostalgia that suffused *My Early Life*, this created the impression of an anachronistic romantic out of touch with the temper of the times. The extreme tone of some of his rhetoric, notably when he mocked Mahatma Gandhi, the widely respected Indian advocate of non-violent resistance to British rule, as 'the half-naked fakir', damaged him badly. These errors of judgement were then reinforced by his emotional and ill-judged support for Edward VIII during the 1936 Abdication crisis. Against this background Churchill looked like a man whose time had passed; a man whose obituary would have read, had he died at that time, that he had been brilliant, but, like his father, fundamentally unstable and not to be trusted.

So, neither fellow politicians nor the public at large were disposed to listen when he insistently warned in speeches and articles about the threat posed by the rising power of Nazi Germany and the need for Britain to intensify its rearmament programme. He and his small band of followers were disregarded both in Parliament and outside. After he opposed the now infamous Munich agreement between the Prime

Minister, Neville Chamberlain, and Hitler in the autumn of 1938 hostility towards him within the Conservative Party became so great that he had to fight off a move in his constituency of Epping in Essex to de-select him as their parliamentary candidate.

The breakdown of the Munich agreement followed by the outbreak of war in September 1939 transformed the public's view of Churchill. He was proved to have been right about Germany all along and a far more acute and up-to-date observer of current European trends than his critics. His well-known love of battle was likewise transformed from being a disadvantage into exactly the characteristic the country needed. He was invited to rejoin the government as First Lord of the Admiralty, the post he had held in 1914. When, in 1940, it became obvious that Chamberlain was unable to prosecute the war effectively, Churchill, at the age of sixty-five, finally achieved his life's ambition to become Prime Minister.

There was nothing inevitable about this. Quite the contrary. Germany's military successes had badly shaken the British political establishment. When he entered No. 10 Downing Street at the head of a new National coalition government there were many more in British public life than is now generally recognized who would have preferred to look for a way out of the struggle than to fight on.

King George VI was not one of them. When France made peace with Germany he wrote to his mother, Queen Mary: 'Personally I feel happier now we have no allies to be polite to and pamper.'[6] Churchill himself was more realistic. He knew Britain had to find new allies and did all that he could to bring the United States into the war. When Soviet Russia resisted Hitler's attack in June 1941, he rushed to embrace it, although he had always opposed Communism and knew very well that its regime was as morally reprehensible as the Nazis'. Then, six months later, came the real turning point when Hitler, in a monumental act of folly, declared war on the United States a few days after the Japanese attack on Pearl Harbor. Together Britain, the Soviet Union and the United States eventually won the war against Germany and Japan, but they could never have done so if Britain had made peace or been defeated in 1940.

When it was all over Churchill, with a team of assistants, wrote a history of the conflict in six volumes entitled *The Second World War*. This time nobody could object, as Balfour had earlier done, when he put himself at the centre of the story.

Flare Path

by Terence Rattigan (1942)

Few Eggs and No Oranges: The Diaries of Vere Hodgson 1940–45,

published in 1971

Darling Monster: The Letters of Lady Diana Cooper to Her Son John Julius Norwich 1939–1952

edited by John Julius Norwich and published in 2013

The Second World War brought the British people face to face with the reality of war for the first time since the Civil War involving Charles I and Cromwell in the seventeenth century. Instead of being a safe haven from which men went out to fight on the high seas or in other countries, Britain itself became a battleground. There had been a foretaste of this during the 1914–18 war when both sides had launched aerial bombardments against each other's cities, but those had been on a small scale. The German bombing raids, the worst of which from September 1940 to May 1941 became known as the blitz, put the civilian population of major cities* as much at risk as front-line troops had ever been. The men of the Royal Air Force who fought back against the attackers and mounted counter-strikes against German cities spent their off-duty hours at airfields in the countryside in close contact with civilians. The war was part of people's daily lives, not something they read about in newspapers or letters home from the troops. These three books capture the feel of what that meant in the most personal terms.

Flare Path is a play set in 1941 in a hotel near an RAF base in Lincolnshire involving a group of airmen, their wives and the hotel staff. Terence Rattigan wrote it while himself on active service with the RAF as a flight lieutenant and it is derived from his own experience. Vere Hodgson, the author of *Few Eggs and No Oranges*, described herself as 'an ordinary commonplace Londoner'. She lived in the Notting Hill district of London, then a modest rather than a fashionable area, where she worked for a community doing religious and philanthropic work among the homeless and the poor. She wanted to keep her cousin in Northern Rhodesia (now Zambia) informed of what was happening in London, so kept a daily record of what she saw and heard, which she then dispatched by post. Lady Diana Cooper was the wife of Duff Cooper, the Minister of Information in Churchill's government during the blitz. Like many other well-to-do couples,† they had sent their son, John Julius, then aged ten, to North America to escape the bombing. She wrote her letters to provide him with a running commentary on

---

* Among the worst hit were London, Swansea, Cardiff, Bristol, Southampton, Plymouth, Birmingham, Coventry and Liverpool with many others also suffering severe damage.

† Although the practice was widespread, the Coopers were strongly criticized for sending their son to safety. For a government minister to do so was regarded as defeatist and, as Duff Cooper's ministry was in charge of propaganda and raising public morale, his action ran directly counter to his responsibilities.

what she and his father were doing. As an elderly man, when he had achieved fame as the author John Julius Norwich, he edited them before their publication in 2013. Vere Hodgson edited her diary herself before it was published in 1971.

Running through all three books is a theme captured by Maudie, the wife of one of the airmen in *Flare Path*. Her home in London had been bombed out and she was having to live and work in St Albans. When asked how she is managing the change, she replies: 'What I say is, there's a war on and things have got to be a bit different and we've just got to get used to it – that's all.' With everyone's life disrupted to some extent, and everyone knowing someone worse off than themselves, this response captures the mood of the time. What would have been unimaginable, not to say intolerable, in peacetime became a new normal.

This was as true of the Coopers as of others, albeit at a more privileged level than that of humbler folk. While the raids were in progress, most Londoners, men, women and children, were crammed hugger-mugger into basements, air raid shelters and Tube stations where they would often spend several nights at a stretch. The Coopers had closed their house and taken rooms at the Dorchester Hotel, then recently built and thought more likely to withstand bombs than the Ritz, Claridge's or the Savoy. The hotel's management set up dormitories below ground for its guests in the Turkish baths and the gym.

Lady Diana describes life in the latter where they are one of four couples, including the Foreign Secretary, Lord Halifax, and his wife. 'Conversations are conducted in whispers that take me straight back to childhood,' she writes. Snoring is a problem. 'If Papa makes a sound I am up in a flash and rearrange his position. Perhaps Lady Halifax is doing the same to his lordship.' Despite the difficulties they continue to give dinner parties, guests sometimes arriving 'pyjamas in hand' lest an inopportune air raid prevents them from getting home and they have to find somewhere to doss down. Later, she reports gleefully,

'The Dorchester stands up well so far. The water flows well, whereas at Claridge's no one has had a bath for a week.'

Not even the Dorchester's walls could protect its residents from the noise of the raids with the anti-aircraft guns in Hyde Park doing more to disturb Lady Diana's sleep than the bombs, unless they fell very close. Vere Hodgson makes the same complaint. At the start of the blitz both women constantly write about broken nights and how tired they are, but as it goes on they find they can sometimes sleep through the noise.

Understandably Lady Diana spares her son harrowing details of the damage and the deaths, although she does sometimes tell him when the houses of friends he knows have been destroyed and of the trouble she takes to move his father's extensive library to safety in the country. I asked John Julius in his later years whether receiving his mother's letters at his school in Toronto made him worry about whether his parents would be killed. He replied that they never did, adding, 'I must have been a very unimaginative child.'

Vere Hodgson, by contrast, is meticulous in recording the death and destruction. Her deadpan style and absence of adjectives enhances the horror. When two bombs go right through Whiteleys department store in Queensway a water main bursts and those in the shelter below who survived the blast are drowned, forty-seven in all. A direct hit on the Café de Paris at Leicester Square kills some thirty-four people dining and dancing there. Another on the Notting Hill police station kills twenty policemen. And so on, night after night. Vere Hodgson herself was never bombed out. When she writes about those who were her tone is as matter-of-fact, as if she was referring to some routine domestic drama: 'Ivy rang up and we arranged to lunch together. Said she had been bombed out again. Found it hard to believe! This is the third time.'

She lists the names of the historic churches that have been destroyed and goes for walks round different parts of London to make an inventory of the damage. A typical report reads: 'Down Whitehall, past Horse Guards, which had had a tremendous Biff and looks awful. Reached Westminster ... two definite holes in the roof of the Hall. Damage to the Abbey is not apparent from the outside. Up Victoria St., Christ Church there is finished. Great crater in front of the Army and Navy Stores – fit to hold a bus. Various biffs and wonks. Station looks battered, but eventually groped our way in to a cup of tea.'

But, as is always the case, in even the most extreme situations daily life goes on. Vere Hodgson writes about how scarce oranges have become and how, when she manages to find two, she feels obliged to give one away and to share the other. Eggs, by contrast, are still available. She records how the laburnum is coming out and how a hedgehog has disappeared from her garden. On a warm day in February 1941 she buys lingerie material at Barkers in Kensington High Street and watches gulls and ducks sunning themselves by the Round Pond in Kensington Gardens. Lady Diana records buying a dress from Molyneux, one of the most fashionable couturiers, of occasional excursions to the theatre and of her delight at spending weekends in grand country houses.

The absence of oranges (and bananas), that children like me born shortly before the war had never seen, became a sort of symbol of wartime shortages. The son of Field Marshal Montgomery, who in November 1942 became a national hero after defeating the Germans at the Battle of El Alamein in North Africa, once told me that as a schoolboy he only became fully aware of just how important his father was, when, on one of his returns to this country, his father presented a crate of oranges to his school.

Vere Hodgson makes no reference in her published record to her welfare work, although, according to Jenny Hartley of the University of Surrey, Roehampton, writing in the preface, it was sufficiently important to exempt her from conscription. Lady Diana's took the form of serving in a mobile canteen on RAF bases. She writes in one letter of how 'It's lovely because RAF men rush the van and are jokey and grateful for hot teas and doughnuts, Mars bars and fruit gums.' In another she records arriving at an airfield soon after 'it has had a "dusting" from the enemy. Not one hangar has missed that duster, and when a hangar gets an explosion of course it looks far worse than a house.' In a third, she tells how, 'after my canteen [I] buzzed down to Chequers to have lunch with Clemmie Churchill', the Prime Minister's wife, a juxtaposition of activities that speaks volumes about how topsy-turvy the world had become.

Strangely, neither woman seems surprised by the remarkable way the essential services kept going. Public transport continued to run, the post was collected and delivered, the telephone still rang. They grumble about delays, such as those when Vere Hodgson goes by train to visit her family in Birmingham, but there is no mention of the astonishing work of the fire brigades nor of how quickly services were adapted and restored to work round the bomb damage. It's as if they take it for granted that, one way or another, people will cope, as indeed they did.

It seems to have been much the same in Germany. While the Luftwaffe was raining bombs on British cities the RAF was doing the same, though initially to a lesser extent, to German cities. The effects of this in Berlin were recorded in her daily diary by a young aristocratic Russian émigré called Marie Vassiltchikov.[7] Her reactions and those of people she writes about to the bombing, her inventories of the damage and her descriptions of a city adapting to the disruption caused by bombing are remarkably similar to those of her British counterparts. So is her cheerfulness. Not until 1943 and 1944, when the Allied raids reached massive proportions, creating firestorms that killed thousands of people at a time, does the tone darken. By then too her social circle, from which came those involved in the plot to kill Hitler, was in grave danger with the Gestapo arresting many of her friends.

The raids over Germany were carried out by RAF Bomber Command from airfields on the eastern side of Britain, of which the one described in *Flare Path* was typical. These raids were so dangerous that at 41 per cent Bomber Command had a higher death rate than any other branch of the British armed services. *Flare Path*, named for the lights that guided the bombers as they took off into the night, deals fundamentally with what it means for a man to have to live in a state of perpetual fear and the particular form of courage required to keep on going. To drive the point home, the man in question is a highly decorated young officer, Flight Lieutenant Teddy Graham, who, besides being widely admired for his bravery, is worshipped by his crew for his special ability to bring them home safely regardless of the damage sustained by his aircraft.

The play opens in the hotel near the airfield where some airmen, their wives and the staff are expecting a quiet weekend. To their astonishment a famous Hollywood film star called Peter Kyle arrives in search of a room. He has come, we soon learn, to reclaim Patricia, Teddy's actress wife, with whom he had formerly lived in California. His career is on the wane and he wants her back to help him adjust to his decline. She had married Teddy on the rebound and Peter has no difficulty in persuading her that she should return to him.

However, before she can confront Teddy with her decision the squadron is unexpectedly ordered to go on a raid. Their talk has to be postponed for a few hours until he gets back and he sets off to risk his life completely unaware that his wife is planning to leave him. While he is away the Squadron Leader, who has remained behind, tells her how amused he and his fellow officers are by the way Teddy speaks with so much pride about her and being married to her. She begins to realize the extent of his dependence on her and her resolve is shaken.

The following morning, she finds out for herself how much she means to him. He has had a terrifying experience. His plane was badly damaged by enemy fire and he has had the greatest difficulty bringing it home. His crew are filled with admiration at his skill and gratitude to him for their safe return. He is the hero of the moment, but obviously not well, and he won't let her call a doctor. When she tries to insist, he confesses: 'Do you know what's the matter with me? Funk. Just ordinary, common or garden, plain bloody funk.'

He knows the doctor will recognize the condition and classify him as unfit for further service. He will be reassigned as an instructor and his pupils will guess that he had buckled under the strain of combat. The shame, he tells her, would be unbearable. Yet he can hardly bear the pressure of being responsible for the lives of others while living in perpetual fear. He has reached breaking point and it is only his marriage to her that enables him to keep on going. 'It was you who got us home tonight. Not me,' he tells her. She realizes that his need for her is of a wholly different order from Peter's and that she must stay with him.

When Churchill was taken to see *Flare Path*,* he declared himself 'very moved'.[8] He also commented approvingly on the understated dialogue. This takes different forms. One is designed to downplay the dangers of the men's lives, like calling a raid a 'do' and a 'shaky do' when casualties and damage to the planes are involved. Another is the men's disdain for rhetorical posturing. When the Squadron Leader tries to tell Patricia of his admiration for her husband, he says, 'I hate all this patriotic bilge in the newspapers, but, my God, we do owe these boys something, you know.' Later Teddy is embarrassed to hear himself telling her, 'We've got to win this war somehow, you know', adding, 'God, how *Daily Mail*! I'm glad nobody heard it but you.'

The success of *Flare Path*'s London revival in 2011, when it was acclaimed by critics and audiences with no personal experience of the war, demonstrates the play's dramatic quality. It also testifies to the profundity of the question of fear and the courage required to overcome

* The play was directed by Anthony Asquith, always known as Puffin, whose father was Herbert Asquith, the first Prime Minister under whom Churchill had served before and during the First World War. His mother, Margot Asquith, accompanied her old friends Churchill and his wife to the performance.

it. To a wartime audience made up of men and women who had survived the blitz and with family members serving with the armed forces, it would have sent a direct message: that, whatever their situation, they must master their fear and carry on. As its run continued, they would have been aware of its direct links to real life. When the show opened on Broadway Rattigan had to miss the first night because he was under orders from the RAF to ferry an aircraft across the Atlantic, while the young actor who played Teddy Graham, and who was also serving in the RAF, had to be replaced during the play's run when he was posted out of London.

Flare Path ran for some six hundred and seventy performances and transformed Rattigan's career. His previous two plays had failed badly. In the view of his biographer Geoffrey Wansell, if *Flare Path* had suffered the same fate, 'he might never have risked writing for the stage again, taking refuge instead in screenplays'.[9] It relaunched his career and established him as one of the most successful commercial playwrights of the mid-twentieth century.

Cold War

Lord of the Flies by William Golding, 1954,
and *On the Beach* by Nevil Shute, 1957.

The Dead, the Dying and the Damned by D. J. Hollands, 1956.

Lord of the Flies

by William Golding (1954)

On the Beach

by Nevil Shute* (1957)

The end of the Second World War was followed almost immediately by the outbreak of the Cold War between the Soviet Union and the countries it controlled in the Communist bloc on the one hand and the Western Alliance led by the United States on the other. Initially the United States enjoyed a monopoly of nuclear weapons, but in 1949 the Soviet Union successfully tested an atom bomb. By the mid-1950s, when both Britain and the Soviet Union had acquired hydrogen bombs and China too had become a nuclear power, a full-scale war involving any two of them would have wreaked damage on an unprecedented scale. A paper considered by the British Cabinet in 1954 estimated that ten bombs dropped, one each on selected cities, in this country would cause anything up to twelve million casualties, depending on their strength.[1] Without knowing the details, which were closely

* A pseudonym. His real name was Nevil Shute Norway. He was a professional engineer and adopted a pen-name to protect himself from publicity.

guarded secrets, the general public was aware that a nuclear war would destroy not just the fabric of British society, but perhaps even eliminate life itself on the planet. The nightmares of H. G. Wells and Baldwin's warnings about the end of civilization, described in earlier chapters, had become a potential reality.

Two books published during the 1950s stand out for the extent to which they both reflect and fanned the fears of the time: *Lord of the Flies* by William Golding in 1954 and *On the Beach* by Nevil Shute in 1957. Both were bestsellers in Britain and abroad and their influence was further enhanced when they were turned into films. The former was a first novel that launched a career that culminated in a Nobel Prize for Literature and remains the book for which Golding is best known. The latter was by an established author who already had a large body of work to his credit.

They could not be more different, with each playing on a different aspect of people's fears. *Lord of the Flies* is a parable set among children about the breakdown of civilization and a reversion to barbarism. *On the Beach* is about how the last remaining survivors of a nuclear war prepare for their inevitable deaths. Both draw extensively on imagery and attitudes that would have been familiar to contemporary readers from the Second World War.

The action in *Lord of the Flies* takes place on a deserted tropical island in an unnamed ocean where an aeroplane carrying British schoolboys being evacuated from the war zone has crashed. There are no adult survivors and no girls. The boys have had no previous connection with each other. The oldest are about twelve and the youngest, as far as one can gather, about six. Other than the fact that an atom bomb has been dropped, the reader is told nothing about the war itself. The book is devoted to how the older boys respond to the situation and how they relate to each other.

When he wrote it, Golding was teaching English and Classics at a grammar school in Salisbury, which gave him an intimate understanding of how pre-adolescent boys spoke and thought at that time. He had also been deeply affected by the war, which had convinced him that, if social sanctions and prohibitions break down, most people, whatever their nationality, are capable of committing the sort of atrocities perpetrated by the Nazis. It is all a question of circumstances. Some of the views that are today freely expressed on the unregulated social media platforms and the threats made against individuals and minorities bear witness to the dark forces that lurk beneath even the most stable and sophisticated societies and lend credence to that view.

In *Lord of the Flies* Golding develops this idea by showing how, as the conventions within which they had formerly lived drop away, the boys become murderous gangsters. There are three key characters: Ralph, Jack and Piggy. When the boys, dazed and disorientated, gather together for the first time after the crash Ralph, a natural head boy, takes charge. The fat, bespectacled, asthmatic Piggy becomes his sidekick. A little later Jack turns up at the head of group of choirboys, who behave with almost military discipline, and puts himself forward as the overall leader. A vote takes place. Everyone except the choir supports Ralph and Jack grudgingly gives way. A search party is sent out, which establishes that they are on an island. Another meeting then takes place at which, under Ralph's direction, a set of rules is agreed of which the most important is that a fire must be kept alight on a hill at all times in the hope of attracting the attention of rescuers.

As time passes the choirboys become hunters who provide the meat on which the boys subsist by killing pigs that run wild on the island. As this role becomes more important and the group's memories of their previous lives fade, so Jack's resentment against Ralph and his dislike of Piggy become more outspoken. Life gets harder, Ralph's authority frays and tensions erupt over whether hunting or keeping the fire alight is the more important activity. As respect for the rules crumbles, the hunters grow more assertive. Eventually Jack is able to isolate Ralph and Piggy, who are banished from the community. The parallel with the way in which the military had ousted constitutional governments in several European countries between the First and Second World Wars would have been immediately apparent to readers.

With Jack in charge the rules are set aside and the descent into madness and cruelty begins. The boys forget the moral code they had been brought up with before leaving home. Violence for its own sake takes hold of their emotions and, like a lynch mob, they develop a fearsome rhythmic chant: 'Kill the beast! Cut his throat! Spill his blood!' While under its influence the group becomes so carried away that one of the boys is semi-accidentally killed. Under the new regime another is subjected to brutal punishment. And then Piggy is murdered.

Ralph is warned by a sympathizer that 'they're going to do you'. He tries to hide, fails and is hunted down like a pig. As he flees across the island the fire, no longer receiving proper attention, bursts out of control. At the end of his tether with the flames and his pursuers closing in on him he finally collapses on the beach expecting the blows to come raining down on him. Instead he is confronted by a British naval officer, who, complete with escort, has been sent ashore to investigate from a passing ship that has seen the fire.

As soon as the officer takes charge, the boys revert to type. Ralph pulls himself together and acts as their spokesman while Jack fades into the background; an unmistakeable reprise to contemporary readers of what had happened in 1945 when the victorious powers took control in Germany and the Nazis sought to disappear into the general population. As the island is consumed by fire the boys, sobbing with emotion, are taken off in a cutter to the warship lying offshore.

On the Beach has no such happy ending. Its story is inspired by the concluding lines of T. S. Eliot's poem *The Hollow Men*: 'This is the way the world ends/Not with a bang but a whimper'. It is set in 1963, six years into the future from when the book was published. In the previous year there had been a cataclysmic nuclear exchange between the Soviet Union and the West followed by another between the Soviet Union and China – a perfectly imaginable sequence of events at that time and eerily reminiscent of those envisaged by H. G. Wells in *The War in the Air* and *The World Set Free*.

All life in the Northern Hemisphere has been extinguished and a fatal radiation cloud is moving inexorably southwards. In Melbourne, the world's southernmost large city, people await their fate as the radio reports each day on how one by one the countries and cities in the cloud's path 'go out', like so many candles. Shute actually wrote the book while living not far from Melbourne, having emigrated from Britain in 1950, which invests his book with a sense that there is no hiding place, regardless of how far from the theatre of war a person flees or where they might happen to be.

The book's focus is on a small group of characters: a naval officer, his wife and their baby, their relations and friends, including the American commander of a nuclear submarine that escaped the holocaust and which he has placed under Australian command. When the story opens life in Melbourne and its environs is continuing very much as normal. Although the cloud is already over the northern part of Australia, shops are open, people go to work, the radio broadcasts and government functions. Scientists suggest that as the cloud moves south the radioactivity in the atmosphere might be weakening and that the southernmost parts of the globe might survive. An intermittent radio signal from a United States naval base at Edmonds on the American west coast gives rise to the hope that perhaps in some places life is hanging on.

The American submarine with the Australian naval officer and a scientist on board is sent on a Pacific cruise to investigate. It calls at various places. Some have been badly bombed. Others, when the commander peers through his periscope, look normal and untouched, except that there is nobody to be seen. At Edmonds an officer in protective clothing goes ashore to find the source of the radio signal. He is confronted by a modern Herculaneum – everything as it was at the instant the radiation struck with corpses at a desk, another sitting on the lavatory and a group gathered together at a party. At the transmitting office he finds that a loose window banging against an overturned Coca-Cola bottle on the transmitter is sending out the signals.

The scientist, meanwhile, conducts various tests, which show that the radioactivity in the atmosphere is as strong as ever. So no hope is left and the commander reports back to Melbourne accordingly. While all this is happening a sailor whose home is at Edmonds manages to escape through a torpedo hatch. The following day the commander sees him through the periscope fishing from a boat. They speak through a loud hailer and the seaman explains that as he is going to die anyway he wants to do so in his home town, among his own people and doing what he likes best.

After the submarine returns to Melbourne, the various characters, each in his or her own way, concentrate on making the best of the time left to them – tending their garden, caring for their baby, organizing and participating in a sports car race, drinking their way through their club's wine cellar and conducting a flirtation. A public debate takes place over whether the opening of the trout fishing season should be brought forward by a month, which it is, so that anglers can enjoy a final fling. The nearer the cloud gets the more they immerse themselves in their own interests. Their unemotional stoicism and their belief that that is the only way to get through the crisis recalls a somewhat idealized wartime Britain, except that there, even during the worst of the bombing, there was hope while in Australia there is none. In the background riotous parties take place, the supply of goods and services breaks down and people stop going to work.

Society, however, remains fundamentally orderly. People don't flee from one place to another in search of safety. As everywhere is doomed, it is better to prepare to die 'tidily' where one is. The American commander takes his submarine out to sea and scuttles it. For those who don't want to wait or to endure the unpleasantness of radiation sickness before dying the government makes suicide pills freely available.

There is no sex among the characters in either *Lord of the Flies* or *On the Beach*, which would have been inconceivable if they had been published at any time after the 1950s. In *On the Beach* the American submarine commander has a platonic affair with an Australian woman. She would like to sleep with him, but he is determined to go on living as if his family in the United States is still alive, buying presents for his children and remaining faithful to his wife. He asks the woman whether she thinks this is crazy. She replies that she doesn't. Everyone has to find their own way of coping with the inevitability of death. Those engaged in the riotous parties may well have sex, but we are not told about it. In *Lord of the Flies* there are no sexual relationships or activity of any kind. The nearest approach to any sexual reference occurs when the hunters giggle, after killing a sow, about how one of their spears has gone 'Right up her ass!', after which they mime her efforts to avoid it.

The quality of Golding's and Shute's writing is such that their scenarios are entirely convincing. And perhaps they are not so very far removed from how, in the situations they describe, people might have behaved.

A chilling example of the kind of violence that occurred in private schools at that time is to be found in the memoirs of my old friend Richard Luce, the former Governor of Gibraltar and Lord Chamberlain to the Queen.[2] He recalls how at Wellington College, in the early 1950s, a boy like Jack once tied his dressing gown round his neck and suspended him over the bannisters from an upper floor, a memory that has remained with him for the rest of his life. I never witnessed anything remotely comparable, but at my own prep school, King's College Choir School in Cambridge, to which I went at the age of seven in 1944, boys underwent a ritualized 'bashing up' in their second term. I remember my fear when it was my turn to be bashed and how I was just as nasty as the rest when it was the turn of others.

In her memoirs, the author Elizabeth Jenkins[3] describes events that lend credibility to some of the reactions of characters in *On the Beach*. In May 1940, as German tanks rampaged through France and the British Army retreated to Dunkirk, she and other Jane Austen enthusiasts gathered at a house near Austen's former home at Chawton in Hampshire to form the Jane Austen Society. There, while the threat of invasion loomed, they busied themselves with such matters as who should be the honorary secretary and what the subscription rate should be. In an echo of a bygone war they asked the Duke of Wellington, as a county grandee, to be their President. He replied that he was delighted to hear about the formation of the society and added, 'Thank you for making so much of me.' Today that society is among the most successful of its kind and has spawned a network of associated bodies across the world – an example of how, short of a nuclear holocaust, even the worst situations can lead to good and lasting initiatives.

The Dead, the Dying and the Damned

by D. J. Hollands (1956)

The Cold War between the Western Alliance led by the United States on the one hand and the Communist bloc led by Soviet Russia on the other, that began soon after the end of the Second World War in 1945, meant that Britain could not revert to its normal peacetime practice of relying on professional volunteers for its armed forces. It was still a major world power, one of the 'Big 3' in the jargon of the time, with the United States and the Soviet Union. It had imperial commitments in Asia, the Middle East and Africa and a key role to play in the defence of Western Europe. The regular forces by themselves could not have coped in the event of another war, which for a long time seemed quite possible, and the country needed both a large standing army and a large reserve of trained manpower.

To fill the gap a system of National Service was introduced under which, between 1945 and November 1960, over two million young men were conscripted into the armed services, initially for a period of eighteen months and from 1950 for two years. All men born between 1928 and September 1939 (coincidentally the month the Second World War began) were liable. Some were deemed medically unfit, a few were able to escape for educational or other reasons and a tiny minority were conscientious objectors, but, until the system began to run down towards the end, the vast majority served. About two-thirds went into the army, the rest into the Royal Navy or the Royal Air Force. For nearly all it was by far the most important event in their lives up to that point. For men from working-class backgrounds it was usually the first time they had ever left home.

For most, regardless of social background, it remained a defining experience for the rest of their lives, as it has for me. After it ended numerous novels were written about it, often dealing with the absurdities and futilities of service life as they appeared to men who, in their own minds, remained civilians throughout their time in uniform. It also features extensively in memoirs and autobiographies written in the 1990s and early 2000s by men looking back to a distant youth. But during the years that it lasted very few books were written about it.

One of the first, published in 1956, was D. J. Hollands' *The Dead, the Dying and the Damned*, an autobiographical novel set against the background of the Korean War in which he had served in the army as a second lieutenant in the 1st Battalion of the Duke of Wellington's Regiment* and been awarded a Military Cross for gallantry. That war, which lasted from 1950 until 1953, was by far the largest and most important conflict in which conscripts were involved; two hundred and eighty-six were killed and one thousand and fifty-six wounded. There were other engagements – the failed Anglo-French invasion

* A battalion is the basic infantry formation. Those serving in Korea generally comprised about thirty officers and six hundred and thirty non-commissioned officers and men. Officers, who hold the Sovereign's commission, range from second lieutenant up to field marshal. National Servicemen very rarely rose above second lieutenant. Non-commissioned officers (NCOs) range from lance corporal to regimental sergeant major. At the very bottom are the men with the rank of private in the infantry. The generic term for all those who are not officers is 'other ranks'.

of Suez in 1956 and operations against independence movements and other opponents of British rule in Malaya, Kenya, Aden and Cyprus – but the Korean War was in a class of its own. It began when North Korea, backed by the Soviet Union, invaded South Korea and a United States-led United Nations force, including a British and Commonwealth contingent, went to the defence of the South.* To many it seemed like a prelude to a Third World War and when China came in on the side of the North the United States contemplated a nuclear response. In the end, it petered out in a stalemate and the Korean peninsula has since remained divided between the two Korean states with the armistice line where the fighting stopped acting as the frontier between them.

Those National Servicemen who fought in Korea and the various colonial uprisings against British rule were the unlucky ones. Most never heard a shot fired in anger. Some never left the United Kingdom while others, including me, served in West Germany in the huge British Army of the Rhine ready to withstand a Soviet attack from the East. It never came, but we treated the threat and the training we undertook to prepare for it seriously.

The Dead, the Dying and the Damned has no great literary pretensions though it sold well when it came out. It reads easily, the characterization is good and the extensive battle scenes highly convincing. Through the prism of a small group – Second Lieutenant Peter Blake and some other officers and men in a single infantry battalion – it provides a microcosm of what life was like in most branches of the army at that time. The relationships between the different ranks, their attitudes to each other and their respective codes of behaviour are clearly delineated and in line with my memories of my service from 1955 to 1957.

---

* At this time the Soviet Union was boycotting the United Nations, which enabled the United States to carry a motion condemning the invasion and establishing a UN force under American command to repulse it.

Except in one respect: in keeping with the publishing proprieties of the time the book doesn't contain a single four-letter word. Yet among the NCOs and men no sentence was complete without one and 'fucking' was used as an all-purpose adjective at a time when the word was much less common in general conversation than it is now. Nor does the book record the imaginative verbal abuse with which drill sergeants and sergeant majors exhorted recruits marching back and forth across the parade ground, such as: 'If you don't sharpen up, Tugendhat, I'll put my fucking pace stick up your arse and turn you into walking lollipop.' Or: 'What happened when you were born, you horrible little man? I'll tell you. They threw away the fucking baby and kept the fucking afterbirth and that's you, a horrible mess of afterbirth. Now repeat after me "when I was born ...".' In my experience, the only insult that could never be directed at a man by his superior was the word 'bastard' because it might be true.

The great majority of National Servicemen joined up at eighteen. With very few exceptions all the army's recruits, regardless of class and educational background, were then knocked into shape by drill sergeants and sergeant majors during a few weeks of basic training. For nearly all of us that experience was the first time we had ever encountered contemporaries from another social class on a basis of equality.

Thereafter the road forked. In practice only those who had been to public schools and to some extent grammar schools could go on to become officers. By no means all of them passed the necessary tests and survived the additional training at officer cadet school to achieve that status.* Many did not, but nobody else could aspire to become an officer and the privileges that went with it. The contrast between the

* In the Royal Navy and the Royal Air Force, with their more demanding technical requirements, it was more difficult for National Servicemen to become officers than in the army. In some of the army's specialist corps, such as the Royal Army Pay Corps and the Army Catering Corps, class and rank distinctions were less clearly drawn. The Royal Air Force was also more relaxed.

comforts of the officers' mess with a room of one's own, eating better food and being waited upon by servants, including a personal servant, known as a 'batman', with the barrack room life of the ordinary soldier was total.

Officers in the British Army had traditionally been drawn from the more privileged and prosperous classes, those who in earlier epochs had customarily employed servants. During the two world wars the gates had had to be widened to enable men with the right qualities but the wrong backgrounds to pass through, but during the period of National Service traditional criteria were again much in evidence.

The public and grammar schoolboys were far better educated than those who had been to ordinary state schools and left to start work at fifteen. They had remained at school until they were eighteen with most entering the armed forces within a few weeks of the end of their last term, although some went to university first and deferred their military service until they had secured their degree.* Though less well educated in the formal sense than their public school contemporaries, those from state schools often knew more about life. They had earned a living and been free to enjoy sex lives that boys cooped up in single-sex public schools could only dream about.

This could create problems for young officers trying to maintain the morale of men under their command, as Peter Blake discovers. A not uncommon cause of depression among young soldiers was the arrival of a 'Dear John' letter from their girl back home announcing the end of a relationship or even of an engagement. When one of his men on the front line in Korea later receives a 'Dear John' the virginal nineteen-year-old Blake is at a loss as to how to offer comfort

* Medical students were able to defer until they had qualified when they would enter the forces as medical officers. Once the end of National Service had been announced most of those with university places took them up immediately and deferred their National Service in the knowledge that it would be over by the time they graduated.

or advice. Subsequently he falls in love with a Japanese woman who takes him in hand while he is on leave in Tokyo after which he receives one himself.

Military hierarchy and discipline were such that regardless of age and experience there was never any question as to who was in charge in any given situation. It was always the man with the higher rank. So, when I, as a newly minted second lieutenant, took command of my platoon in the 1st Battalion of the Essex Regiment in Germany the chain of command was clear. I was answerable to my company commander and, above him, my battalion commander, and responsible for the thirty or so men in the platoon under my command. But rank and experience were two very different things. My platoon sergeant and second in command was about twice my age and had served in the Second World War and Korea. He and I and the rest of the platoon all understood perfectly well that he knew infinitely more about soldiering than I did. I drew extensively on his wisdom and he showed great tact in proffering advice. We weren't tested in battle like Hollands and his men. The nearest we got to it was being on standby to join the Anglo-French invasion of Suez in 1956.

I have often wondered about what might have happened if we had become involved in serious fighting there. My sergeant had served in Egypt and claimed to know the people well. 'Don't ever let yourself get captured,' he warned the platoon. 'The Gyppos will hand you over to the women who'll cut off your balls.' My men believed him and, though I was sceptical, I had no basis on which to contradict him, let alone to be believed. What would have happened, if, after some hard fighting, we had taken Egyptian soldiers prisoner with my men believing what my sergeant had told them?

In his memoirs, Richard Luce, to whom I referred in relation to *Lord of the Flies*, records his experiences serving as a second lieutenant in Cyprus during the uprising there while I was in Germany.

'Certainly, prisoners were tortured to gain information,' he writes. 'But in an emergency and facing violence it is difficult not to get angry with people who shelter terrorists.'[4] A man with whom I many years later served on a corporate board told me of his experiences when fighting as a second lieutenant in the French army during the Algerian war of independence. His platoon had taken a rebel prisoner and he had agreed when his experienced sergeant said, 'Leave him to me, I'll find out what he knows.' The prisoner had died. This had weighed on my friend's conscience ever since with the weight growing heavier as he grew older. There is no mention of prisoners in Hollands' book.

Some of his most striking passages show how, despite the experience of being under fire together, the social gap between a man who had served as an officer and one who had been under his command remained unbridgeable for as long as both were under the influence of the army. At the end of the book Blake and another National Serviceman who had risen to the rank of sergeant are passing through London on their way home to the north. They like and respect each other. In the army, the sergeant would have addressed Blake as Sir. Now, civilians once again, he says Mr Blake while Blake calls him by his nickname.

Whatever their other differences of rank and character, almost all National Servicemen had one big thing in common. They couldn't wait to leave the army and get on with their own lives. 'Roll on demob' was the phrase we used. This didn't mean that the National Servicemen performed any less well than their regular comrades in battle. In Hollands' book the only young officer to be overcome by fear while under fire is a regular and Blake is warned against a particular regular sergeant who might let him down when out on patrol. All the evidence suggests[5] that the National Servicemen of all ranks were as good as the regulars and sometimes more resourceful. A number, like Hollands, were awarded medals for gallantry.* But it did mean that they sometimes had a different approach from the regulars to disciplinary issues.

Hollands provides two telling examples. One involves a soldier under Blake's command, who has, without realizing the implications of what he was doing, signed a document indicating that, if asked, he might be willing to extend his service. When he is ordered by senior officers to sign on again, Blake, to their uncomprehending fury, advises him that he is not legally obliged to do so and he refuses. Another occurs when Blake himself refuses to accept his senior officer's explanation of why he and his men had been subjected to a prolonged bout of 'friendly fire' during an engagement and asks to be removed from that officer's command, a breach of military etiquette. The senior officer exacts an unscrupulous revenge that could easily have resulted in him being killed in action.

For their part, the regular officers and NCOs couldn't wait to see the back of National Service. They looked forward to returning to the traditional British practice of a professional volunteer army. If ever there was a case of 'beware of what you wish for' this was it. National Service enormously increased the size of the army thereby increasing the regulars' promotion opportunities. It also created jobs running training programmes and dealing with the administrative burdens of new intakes coming in and old ones going out at fortnightly intervals. The removal of these tasks meant that many of the regular officers and NCOs who had carried them out found themselves being 'bowler hatted', to use the euphemism of that time for early retirement, when National Service came to an end.

* The highest, a Distinguished Service Order (DSO) for gallantry, second only to the Victoria Cross (VC), was awarded to Second Lieutenant William Purves of the King's Own Scottish Borderers, whom I knew well in later life when he was Chairman of the HSBC bank and I was Chairman of Abbey National.

The demobilization of the last National Servicemen, including those who had signed on for an extra year to get the additional pay that went with it, represented a landmark for the country as well as the armed services. When they returned to civilian life in 1962 and 1963 the roll call of veterans extended back through the two world wars to a small number of octogenarian survivors of the Boer War at the turn of the twentieth century. Never since has such a large proportion of the male population shared a common experience, except for the ephemeral thrills of great British sporting successes.

Imperialist Complexities

Heart of Darkness by Joseph Conrad, 1902.

Our Island Story by H. E. Marshall, 1905,
and *Scouting for Boys* by Robert Baden-Powell, 1908.

A Passage to India by E. M. Forster, 1924,
and *Altogether* by W. Somerset Maugham, 1931.

The Last September by Elizabeth Bowen, 1929.

Remote People by Evelyn Waugh, 1931, and *So Rough a Wind: The Kenya Memoirs of Sir Michael Blundell*, 1964.

Heart of Darkness

by Joseph Conrad (1902)

Joseph Conrad's *Heart of Darkness*, published in 1902,* runs to only thirty-eight thousand words. It is a short story or novella rather than a novel. Yet it is one of the most influential texts of the twentieth century. It deals with the moral issues that arise when, thanks to technology and superior strength, people of one nation acquire unrestrained power over another, issues that lay at the heart of imperialism when it first appeared and still cast a long shadow over our historical perspective of that period. In the words of his most recent biographer, the American historian Maya Jasanoff: 'Conrad's book has become a touchstone for thinking about Africa and Europe, civilization and savagery, imperialism, genocide, insanity – about human nature itself.'[1]

It is about the exploitation of Africans by Europeans and to some Conrad's use of the words 'niggers' and 'savages' in describing Africans is so objectionable as to outweigh the book's qualities. The Nigerian novelist Chinua Achebe dismisses him as a racist. Yet, offensive as they are, those words did not carry the same meaning for Conrad as they do today. They were the ones in general use at the time, which is a reflection

---

* It first appeared as an article in *Blackwood's Magazine* in 1899. A final revised version first appeared in book form in 1902 as one of a number of stories by Conrad in a volume entitled *Youth*.

on the age rather than the man. As a student the future President of the United States, Barack Obama, was able to see through them to Conrad himself. When rebuked by a fellow student for reading a racist tract, he replied: 'See, the book's not really about Africa. Or black people. It's about the man who wrote it. The European. The American. A particular way of looking at the world.'[2] He saw that the point of *Heart of Darkness* is that people of all races share a common humanity and that evil is no less evil when the sufferers are black than when they are white.*

In this respect Conrad was way ahead of his time. In the United States the lynching, often carried out with great savagery, of black men by white mobs was a common occurrence in the Southern states of the United States – more than a hundred in 1901 alone – while the European empires in Africa and Asia were based on the assumption of white racial superiority.

It is not only in terms of our understanding of the past and of human nature that Conrad's story is memorable. It has also exercised considerable literary influence. Among the authors to have derived inspiration from it are T. S. Eliot and Graham Greene, while Francis Ford Coppola's film *Apocalypse Now*, set during the Vietnam War, draws heavily on it. In 1932, Graham Greene wrote in his diary of *Heart of Darkness*: 'It makes me despair of the book I am finishing, of any book I am now likely to write, but at the same time filled me with longing to write finely.' Another admirer was the French author and Nobel Prize-winner André Gide. He dedicated his own *Travels in the Congo* (1927) 'To the Memory of Joseph Conrad' and wrote, 'I am re-reading *Heart of Darkness* for the fourth time. It is only after having seen the country that I realize how good it is.'

---

* It is interesting to compare the attitudes of Achebe and Obama with those of the Nigerian novelist Chimamanda Ngozi Adichie who has described Graham Greene's novel *The Heart of the Matter*, which is set in colonial-era Sierra Leone and makes frequent use of the n-word, as 'close to my idea of the perfect novel. It is beautifully written and has a wonderful grave quality.' See Parul Sehgal, 'A Conversation with Chimamanda Ngozi Adichie', *Tin House*, summer issue, 2013.

The story opens with the narrator, Philip Marlow, like Conrad a retired master mariner on the last generation of sailing ships, sitting with a group of friends on the deck of a boat moored in the Thames estuary. As the sun goes down on a scene of utter tranquillity Marlow embarks on a tale of violence and horror about a voyage he had once undertaken on the River Congo, which at that time flowed through a territory owned and run by a company controlled in a personal capacity by King Leopold II of the Belgians. The company, like other imperial enterprises, claimed to have a civilizing mission, but its operations had acquired a reputation for avarice and cruelty on a monumental scale. Marlow's voyage, which was based on one that Conrad himself had undertaken a few years earlier, had brought him face to face with the worst of the atrocities. The contrast between the surroundings in which the story is told and those to which it relates creates an hallucinatory effect in the mind of the reader. One feels one is experiencing a nightmare, but without wishing to awake as the prose is so mesmerizing.

The purpose of Marlow's voyage as captain of a riverboat was to find and bring back Kurtz, the company's star agent, who it is feared is sick or perhaps even dead. As he proceeds upriver so the yawning gulf between the company's ostensible civilizing mission and its actual practices becomes apparent. When he stops at the first of its trading stations he is shocked to see Africans lying about in various grotesque positions – 'black shadows of disease and starvation' – as, no longer fit for work or of use to the company, they await death. The scene he goes on to describe is eerily similar to the eyewitness account of the Nazi death camp for Jews at Belzec in the memoirs of the Polish resistance fighter Jan Karski.[3] In both what chills the reader's blood is the contrast between the dying lying hugger-mugger on the ground, shorn of any semblance of human dignity while the SS men and company officials go casually about their business untouched by the suffering around them.

From the moment he arrives in Congo Marlow is told by those he meets of Kurtz's remarkable qualities – how he 'sends in more ivory than all the others put together', how he 'is an emissary of pity and science and progress' and how he is destined to rise to the top of the company. Marlow also learns that, 'All Europe contributed to the making of Kurtz.' His mother was half-English, his father half-French and he was partly educated in England; he is the personification of the great imperial powers. So great is his reputation that he has been entrusted by the International Society for the Suppression of Savage Customs with the preparation of a report for its future guidance.

Which makes the reality of his activities and his abuse of power all the more dreadful. Far from suppressing the customs the society regards as savage, Kurtz has been perpetrating the most savage practices of his own. A white man, a Russian, whom Marlow encounters as he sails upriver, explains how Kurtz came to the Africans with 'thunder and lightning', how 'they had never seen anything like him' and how 'very terrible he could be'. 'There was nothing on earth to prevent him killing whom he jolly well pleased.' The Russian himself was forced to hand over his ivory on pain of being shot. Yet so charismatic is Kurtz that he still fell under the man's spell when he spoke to him of his dreams and of love.

When Marlow finally arrives at Kurtz's station he is confronted with the reality of the man's power. What had appeared from a distance to be ornamental knobs on pillars around his house turn out to be the severed heads of those he has had executed. By virtue of the strength of his personality and the power and machinery at his disposal he has acquired both a physical and a psychological domination over the local population. The chiefs crawl when they approach his presence and he has the status of a demon god. Sick and bedridden though he has become, they are fearful of what may befall them without him to rule over them. When Marlow takes him away they lament his departure with exotic expressions of grief.

On the return voyage Kurtz becomes delirious. His dreams of the good he might have done and his belief in the importance of always having the right motives mingle with his terror as he faces up to what he actually did. He asks for the shutter to be closed so that he can't see the passing jungle. 'I can't bear to look at this,' he cries. Marlow is gripped by the expression on his face of 'sombre pride, of ruthless power, of craven terror – of an intense and hopeless despair'. His last words, now famous for defining his legacy and the message of the novella are: 'The horror! The horror!' Marlow is deeply moved by the fate of a man, who, because he understands the difference between good and evil and chose the latter, is overwhelmed by the horror of what he has done.

On his return to Europe Marlow goes to the company's headquarters in Brussels, 'a city that always makes me think of a whited sepulchre', a term which in biblical language implies hypocrisy. Its representatives press him to hand over commercial information they believe he has received from Kurtz. They are not interested in the circumstances of his death or the events surrounding it. He also visits the woman Kurtz had intended to marry in order to give her a packet of personal papers. When he hears her talk of Kurtz, 'of all his promise, and of all his greatness, of his generous mind, of his noble heart' and of how 'his goodness shone in every act' he feels he must spare her the truth and confirm her illusions. Those illusions are genuine and represent the dream of what in the right hands colonialism might achieve. The exclusive concern of the company's representatives with commercial information represents the reality.

The lesson of Kurtz, Marlow reflects, is of how, in the absence of restraints, a man with unlimited power can give way to 'the gratification of his various lusts'. What the absence of restraints can lead to is a recurring theme in the book. At the outset of his story Marlow recalls that the Thames must once have seemed as savage to the Romans as the Congo does to him and his contemporaries. He reflects on how, when they came to Britain, 'they grabbed what they could get for the sake of what was to be got'. He tells too of meeting a group on his voyage upriver called the Eldorado Exploring Expedition. 'To tear the treasure out of the bowels of the land was their desire, with no more moral purpose at the back of it than there is in burglars breaking into a safe.' In both cases, the Romans and the Eldorado, 'They were conquerors and for that you want only brute force – nothing to boast of, when you have it, since your strength is just an accident arising from the weakness of others.' In the age of empire, when the white races held sway over all others and many among them believed it to be ordained by God that they should do so, these were deeply unconventional sentiments.

But then Conrad was a deeply unconventional man. Marlow is portrayed as an easily recognizable type of seafaring Englishman. But his creator hailed from a totally un-English cultural and intellectual tradition. Joseph Conrad, whose original name was Józef Teodor Konrad Korzeniowski, was born in 1857 to Polish parents living in a part of their traditional homeland that was then occupied by Russia. They conspired against Russian rule for which they were exiled to a remote province, taking him with them, when he was four years old. Both parents died while he was still a child, leaving him in the care of an uncle. He nursed the extraordinary ambition for one born in such a landlocked territory of going to sea and in 1874 left home for Marseilles, as French was his second language, to join the French merchant marine as a steward. In 1878 he switched to the British service, perhaps because, as a Russian citizen, he needed the permission of the Russian consul to serve under the French flag. Serving on British ships he in due course gained his master's certificate, acquired British nationality and changed his name. When, while still at sea, he began writing novels in English it was his third language. He is said to have wished he could have been a French novelist and to have regretted being unable to make the change.

Many books written by British writers during the first sixty years of the last century were set abroad in the empire and elsewhere; Somerset Maugham, E. M. Forster, Graham Greene and Lawrence Durrell come to mind. But, however cosmopolitan their characters and settings, and whatever their own attitude to imperialism, these men saw the world through British eyes and their judgements inevitably owed much to the culture in which they had been brought up. They took it for granted that the terms on which white people interacted with others would be set by the whites. Conrad would have understood this to be the reality as well as anyone, but he would also have had a different perspective. As a Pole he knew from personal experience what it meant to be a member of a subject people – a people very unlike the victims in *Heart of Darkness*, but, like them, at the mercy of an arbitrary and unrestrained overlord.

Our Island Story

by H. E. Marshall (1905)

Scouting for Boys

by Robert Baden-Powell (1908)

The purpose of these two books, published in the first decade of the twentieth century, was to foster a sense of common identity and shared interest among young people throughout the British empire. Their message was that, wherever they might be living, if they had roots in the United Kingdom, which at that time included the whole of Ireland, they were part of one large family. In *Our Island Story*, published in 1905, H. E. Marshall, always known by her initials rather than as Henrietta, puts the emphasis on this worldwide kinship while treating other races as colourful background, like extras in a film. In *Scouting for Boys*, published in 1908, Robert Baden-Powell adopts a different approach. He wants to encourage boys in this country to draw inspiration from the way men live in the wilder parts of the empire so that they are equipped to defend Britain against an invader. He also wants to inspire them, whether they live here or in the colonies, to uphold British rule over other races.

Both books enjoyed phenomenal sales and have been reprinted many times over. As the basic text of the scout movement that originated in this country, each new edition of *Scouting for Boys* was adapted to take account of changing circumstances and social mores and of the spread of scouting across the world. The overtly racist and militaristic characteristics that are so prominent in the original edition were toned down and then edited out. By contrast the original text of *Our Island Story* remained unchanged from one edition to the next with new chapters being added to bring the story up to date. The most recent re-publication was in 2005 with a foreword by the popular historian Antonia Fraser, after which it enjoyed something of a revival with a further boost in 2014 when the then Prime Minister, David Cameron, said when he was a boy, 'it really captured my imagination'.*

Our Island Story begins in Australia, though this is not explicitly stated, with a father telling his two children that he is opening a letter 'from home'. As they are in their own house, they don't understand what he means by home. He explains: "I mean 'the little island in the west' to which we belong, and where I used to live". The children respond that they live in a big island, so how can they belong to a little one? The father replies that 'the big island and the little island belong to each other'. The children want to know more and the book is the story they are told.

At the outset Marshall makes clear that her book is 'not a history lesson, but a story book' and that some of the stories 'are only fairy-tales and not history'. The text, however, rarely distinguishes between the two. Both, she argues, are part of *Our Island Story*. The result is a charming, discursive and clearly written chronological account of British history from mythical origins in the mists of time until the beginning of the twentieth century. Fact and legend are interwoven to create an idealized narrative of how the English, Welsh, Scots and Irish came together. The battles by means of which the English largely brought this about are mentioned, but unpleasantness is glossed over

* In a speech campaigning against Scottish independence as reported in the *Guardian*, 7 February 2014.

and the end result is all for the best. Thereafter the country, combining the four nations in a common allegiance to the Crown, goes on to build a worldwide empire.

Reading *Our Island Story* is like coming across familiar paintings in an art gallery or wandering round the Houses of Parliament and looking at the pictures there that illustrate significant moments in our national history, like the plucking of the red and white roses to mark the start of the Wars of the Roses or the departure of the pilgrims for North America. It includes all the old familiar tales, such as King Alfred burning the cakes, the Scottish king, Robert the Bruce, defeating the English at the Battle of Bannockburn and Francis Drake finishing his game of bowls before boarding his ship to take on the Spanish armada. Besides aiming to inform and hold her readers' interest, Marshall has one overriding objective. She wants them to feel that wherever they live in Britain or the empire they have an equal stake in the great continuing national saga.

This involves omissions and interpretations, some of which now look distinctly weird. One would, for instance, never suppose from reading *Our Island Story* that within a couple of decades of it being written the Irish would revolt against the United Kingdom and establish their own separate state.* Her handling of events in South Africa at the time of the Boer War between Britain and the Afrikaans-speaking settlers of Dutch origin, known as Boers, and the peace treaty in 1902 that ended it is concerned only with the two white groups. She doesn't refer to the black South Africans, who outnumbered both, whose interests were ignored and whose battle against oppression would, in due course, become the dominant feature of South African politics as the century progressed.

In this Marshall was typical of her time. Whether in Africa or elsewhere, she mentions indigenous peoples only insofar as they temporarily impede the spread of Britain's beneficent influence through

* The Irish Free State was established in 1922 and in 1949 the present Republic of Ireland was declared.

the acquisition of their territories. She accords them no rights or interest in how they are governed. She ignores their injustices. Nor does she take much account of the influence of economic and social factors in how Britain and the empire evolved. History for her is made by great men, and occasionally women, and epochs defined by ruling dynasties. That is how history was still taught when I started school in the 1940s. As that approach changed, and as the empire was wound up in the late 1950s and early 1960s, so the book went out of fashion. It owed its revival not to a return to early twentieth-century attitudes, but to a resurgence of interest in a chronological, as distinct from a thematic, approach to history and to the clarity and charm of its narrative.

Scouting for Boys is a completely different sort of book. Its subtitle is *A Handbook for Instruction in Good Citizenship*. As such it provides us with an insight into what constituted that concept in the reign of Edward VII. Its aim, conveyed through a sequence of 'Camp Fire Yarns', was to teach boys how to become responsible citizens primarily by learning how to look after themselves in the wild, or at least the British countryside, as members of organized scout troops led by an adult. This involved mastering such practical arts as tracking, woodcraft, signalling, marksmanship, lighting fires and first aid. It also meant subscribing to a Code of Honour and refraining from such bad practices as smoking, eating and drinking too much and cruelty to animals. The sense of being part of a disciplined elite group engaged in adventurous activities that appeals to so many boys is powerfully conveyed. Even so, it is hard to imagine how this worthy but prosaic agenda could have had such an impact that within a year of the book's publication the Scout Movement had attracted over a hundred thousand members.

The answer lies in the immense prestige of its author, the Boer War hero Lieutenant General Robert Baden-Powell. Like his younger contemporary Winston Churchill, Baden-Powell had embellished his military career with self-promoting journalism so that when the Boer

War broke out he was already well known. The war then turned him, like Churchill, into a celebrity.* He was in command of the town of Mafeking when the Boers laid siege to it in 1899. His defence and ultimate victory after two hundred and nineteen days was the first British triumph in a hitherto unsuccessful war and led to immense national rejoicing. The book draws on what happened during the siege and on the ingenuity of the defenders, including a cadet corps of boys that 'did very useful work'.

Baden-Powell asserts his book's patriotic purpose at the outset with the statement, 'I suppose every British boy wants to help his country in some way or other. There is a way in which he can easily do that and that is by becoming a scout.' He then presents scouting as being in a direct line of descent from such heroic figures of the past as the fictional King Arthur and his knights, Richard Cœur de Lion and the Crusaders, Francis Drake and, a particular favourite of his, Captain John Smith,† who played a leading role in the foundation of Virginia, England's first North American colony, in the early seventeenth century. The exploits in India of Rudyard Kipling's character Kim in the novel of that name are invoked as an example of what an individual boy can singlehandedly achieve to further the imperial cause.

Inspiration is also drawn from the empire. The way of life of big-game hunters, trappers and explorers in its wilder reaches is held up as an example to be emulated. So too are colonials in general for being more 'open and cheery' than stay-at-home Britons and because 'in the Colonies boys think more about shooting than their games, because the shooting is for their *country* the games for themselves'. The character of John Buchan's hero Richard Hannay‡ is prefigured in Baden-Powell's eulogy of the qualities engendered by colonial life.

---

* See essay on *My Early Life* by Winston S. Churchill.

† Claimed by Baden-Powell's mother to be an ancestor.

‡ See essay on *The Riddle of the Sands* by Erskine Childers and *The Thirty-Nine Steps* by John Buchan.

Colonial means white. Scouts are enjoined to learn from Zulus, Native Americans and others about tracking, hunting and how to live in the wild. But white racial superiority and the importance of maintaining it are recurring themes throughout the book. Scouts are urged to practise the technique of imposing their will on subject people by means of staging plays. In one example John Smith, through sheer force of character, persuades a Native American chief in Virginia to accept British rule. In another a middle-ranking British official humiliates an Indian prince who had failed to show proper respect by keeping his shoes on when he came into the official's presence.

The assertion of white racial superiority is combined with a deep underlying unease about the future. Thanks to the improved statistics that were becoming available at that time the political class was being made aware, as they had not been before, of the poor health of the great mass of the population. They tended to assume that it was a recent phenomenon whereas in fact it had existed since time immemorial. To Baden-Powell the conclusion was clear. 'Recent reports of the deterioration of our race ought to act as a warning,' he wrote in *Scouting for Boys*. The healthy outdoor life of scouts, he suggested, was part of the solution.

Another cause of concern in the early years of the twentieth century was the extent to which Britain had found herself isolated during the Boer War with public opinion on the Continent and in the United States favouring the Boers. This was mainly because the Boers were perceived to be a gallant David up against an overbearing Goliath rather than a manifestation of active hostile intent towards the United Kingdom. Nonetheless, Baden-Powell was reflecting a widespread public unease when he wrote: 'We have many powerful enemies round about us in Europe who want very much to get hold of the trade in our great manufacturing towns, and of the vast farmlands in our colonies.' He thought it 'quite likely that England will some day be attacked just as Mafeking was, unexpectedly and by a large number of enemies'.

Scouting, he contended, could help to counter this threat. In a Camp Fire Yarn about signalling, scouts are told, 'if it should ever happen that an enemy got into England, the Boy Scouts would be of the greatest value if they have practised this art'. Under the heading 'How the Empire Must Be Held', they are told, 'Don't be disgraced like the young Romans, who lost the empire of their forefathers by being wishy-washy slackers without any patriotism in them.' In an extraordinary passage he writes, 'we ought really not to think too much of any boy, even though a cricketer and footballer, unless he can also shoot, and can drill and scout. That is the fellow who is going to be useful if England is attacked.' 'So,' he urges, 'make yourself good scouts and good rifle shots in order to protect the women and children of your country if it should ever become necessary.'

The call to arms and overt racism of the original edition of *Scouting for Boys* are a far cry from what the scouts came to stand for in Britain and abroad as the twentieth century progressed. As times changed and the Scout Movement gained in popularity across the globe, including in countries that were not exclusively white, so each new edition was modified. The imperialistic and paramilitary aspects, which had featured so prominently at the beginning, were played down and eventually disappeared. The camp-fire camaraderie and moral code aspects were brought to the fore. Over time, scouting came to be regarded simply as an enjoyable way for boys, particularly from urban backgrounds, to learn social skills and self-reliance and to be kept out of trouble while camping in the countryside. Meanwhile, girls were catered for separately in the Girl Guides, founded as early as 1910, with first Baden-Powell's sister and then his wife at their head.

In their original form, *Our Island Story* and *Scouting for Boys* reflect two sides of the same coin. The former represents the glory, grandeur and self-confidence of the British at the high noon of empire, which is generally how we look back on the Edwardian era; the latter displays the anxieties gnawing away beneath the surface and the belief that it was from the colonies that strength and inspiration could be drawn to save it. Neither Baden-Powell nor Marshall lived to see the end of empire. Both died in 1941; he with a knighthood, a peerage and other honours, she unsung and largely forgotten.

A Passage to India

by E. M. Forster (1924)

Altogether

by W. Somerset Maugham (1934)

The British Empire was a huge enterprise. At its greatest extent after 1919* it covered a quarter of the earth's surface and a fifth of its population. There were two distinct forms of membership. On the one hand there were what were then known as the 'self-governing dominions' – Canada, Australia, New Zealand and South Africa – which between the two world wars became fully independent states linked to Britain by a shared allegiance to the Crown. On the other there were numerous colonies and dependent territories of various kinds, of which by far the most important was India. There the British sovereign ruled as Emperor with a Viceroy in Delhi, once the seat of the Mughal emperors. In schools throughout Britain there were maps and globes, large portions of which were coloured pink to show that they 'belonged to us'. They formed the basis of my earliest geography lessons.

* When, as part of the peace settlement, several former German colonies and other former enemy territories were awarded to Britain under the guise of mandates from the League of Nations.

The Dominions were populated largely, but not exclusively, by people who had emigrated from this country, except for South Africa, where a majority of the whites were Afrikaners of Dutch and Huguenot origin and Africans formed the overall majority. In most of the rest where the British went to work rather than to settle, people from this country were few and far between. According to the 1931 census, there were some three hundred and fifty million Indians.* Yet the Indian Civil Service, which administered the country on behalf of the imperial power, never numbered more than about twelve hundred men. The total number of British officials of all kinds and of British troops in the subcontinent was generally of the order of twenty thousand. Again according to the 1931 census, all the British in India – that is to say businessmen, professionals, tea planters, missionaries and those providing services of various kinds plus their families as well as the officials and their families – totalled less than a hundred and fifty thousand with men outnumbering women by two to one.

It was a source of wonderment and envy to both Hitler and Stalin that such a small number of British officials and military should be able to dominate such a large territory as India with its huge population.[4] That they were able to do so is tribute to the efficiency and beneficence of their administration, notwithstanding their racial prejudice. It also reflected the extent of the numerous divisions that existed within Indian society, of which that between Hindus and Muslims was only the most conspicuous.

In Britain's other Far Eastern territories, such as Burma (now Myanmar), which was run as an adjunct to India, Malaya (not then part of Malaysia) and Ceylon (now Sri Lanka) the British were similarly

---

* The India over which Britain ruled comprised India as it is today plus what is now Pakistan and Bangladesh, which broke away from Pakistan in 1971. The British administration of Myanmar, formerly Burma, was also subordinate to the Viceroy's government in Delhi.

thin on the ground and scattered over a wide area. When the twenty-eight-year-old Leonard Woolf (Virginia's future husband) became an Assistant Government Agent in Ceylon in 1908 he was in charge of a district of a thousand square miles with a population of a hundred thousand people. His nearest fellow countryman was twenty miles away through the jungle.[5]

In different ways E. M. Forster's novel *A Passage to India* and Somerset Maugham's Malayan short stories in *Altogether*, both set in the 1920s, are about the effect it had on individuals to conduct their working lives in circumstances in which they were at the same time members of a ruling caste, overwhelmingly outnumbered and temporary rather than permanent residents. With rare exceptions, all the British in the East during this period went out when they were young, around the age of twenty, and returned home to retire, which in the case of the Indian Civil Service was between the ages of forty-seven and fifty-eight.

The men spent their initial years as bachelors and would meet their wives either when they returned to Britain for a 'home leave'* or from among the young women who went out in search of husbands in what were known as 'the fishing fleets'. All those who could afford to, which includes the characters in these two books, sent their children back to Britain to be educated. Before the era of air travel it was impossible for the children to return for the holidays so parents and children would, in most cases, not see each other for years at a stretch. Each generation started out afresh and family life in the sense of parents and children living together was confined to the earliest years of childhood up to about seven. It is no wonder if subsequent generations should find people living in this way eccentric and strange.

Forster made two prolonged visits to India, the first in 1912–13, with introductions from a young Muslim aristocrat, Syed Ross Masood,

---

* In the 1960s I dated a girl whose mother had many years earlier established a marriage bureau, as dating agencies were then called, aimed at this market.

to whom he dedicated the book. During the second in 1921 he served for six months as the private secretary to the Maharajah of one of the princely states that enjoyed limited autonomy within the framework of British rule. So, on both occasions he was in India largely under Indian auspices and thus able to move on both sides of the social wall that divided the British, or Anglo-Indians as they were often known, from the 'natives'. This was unusual. Most Britons would have been firmly on the British side and able to meet Indians socially only under contrived and artificial circumstances.

It is an attempt by two visiting British women to break free from this convention that sparks the sequence of events that form the story of *A Passage to India*. One is Adela Quested, who, having met the City Magistrate of Chandrapore, Ronny Heaslop, in Britain has come out expecting to marry him. The other is her chaperone, Heaslop's mother. They want to see the 'real India' and to socialize with Indians as they would with people at home. They are told that is not the way things are done. All that can be arranged is a 'Bridge Party'. Indians are forbidden to enter the British club and so are invited to tea on its lawn where they can be suitably patronized and later mocked after their departure. This is not enough for the ladies who, to the massive disapproval of their hosts, accept an invitation from a young Muslim, Doctor Aziz, to go on a picnic to the nearby Marabar Caves.* This ends in disaster when Adela Quested alleges she has been the victim of an attempted assault without being able to say who by.

The deepest prejudices of the British community are aroused. Without any evidence or even a warrant, Aziz is arrested. The case provokes a crisis in communal relations that threatens to become a political cause célèbre with consequences far beyond the city. Everything hinges on the outcome of the trial: the British are determined to make

* Based on the real-life Barabar Caves in the Jehanabad district of Bihar.

an example of Aziz while the Indians want to win a great victory over the imperial power. But while the crisis builds Adela Quested has increasing doubts about what actually happened, whether she can go ahead with her marriage and whether she can bear to become the wife of a British official. She breaks down on the witness stand, admits her doubts about the accusation and the case collapses. The British are horrified and the Indians exultant. The marriage is called off and she leaves the country.

It is not, however, these events nor their dramatic denouement that lie at the heart of this enthralling and beautiful novel. They are the backdrop against which Forster develops his central message, which is that for as long as the British control India it will be impossible for Britons and Indians to understand each other as human beings or to form real friendships. He illustrates this through the relationship between Aziz and the schoolmaster Fielding, the most sympathetic of the British characters, who want to like and trust each other but whose efforts to do so are constantly thwarted by circumstances.

There is also a poignant recollection by an elderly Indian of how, in his youth, he had felt part of an English family who had befriended him when he was studying in England, but now that their grown-up son has come out to India he dare not approach him for fear of being snubbed and suspected of taking advantage of the earlier relationship. Heaslop's mother asks her son why she can't seek to be pleasant and make friends with Indians in Chandrapore as she would if she had arrived at somewhere new in England. He explains: 'We're not out here for the purpose of behaving pleasantly … We're out here to do justice and keep the peace … We're not pleasant in India and we don't intend to be. We've something more important to do.'

Forster is just. He shows that Heaslop works hard and does his best to administer justice in a society in which Hindus and Muslims, different castes of Hindu, other sects and landowners and peasants are all constantly striving to take advantage of each other. He portrays

Indian society as deeply divided and his judgements foreshadow the division of British India some twenty-five years later into India with a Hindu majority and Muslim Pakistan. He reveals flaws in his Indian characters and deplores the ruthlessness with which they take advantage of Aziz's acquittal to humiliate Adela Quested. But above all as a Briton, he is horrified by the distorting effects that being the ruling caste has on the minds and attitudes of his compatriots – the sense of racial superiority over the Indians and disdain for their culture that it engenders; the suspicion of their motives and contempt for their characters that it breeds. In short, what today is called racism.

Much of the action among the British characters takes place in their club, what George Orwell, who served in the Burma Police, described 'as the spiritual citadel, the real seat of British power, the Nirvana for which native officials and millionaires pine in vain'.[6] It was where men and women could rant about their surroundings, where prejudices were reinforced, characters assessed and standards set. When a crisis erupted in a district, it was where the local Anglo-Indian community gathered to form a united front.

The constant references by the British characters in *A Passage to India* to the Indians 'hating them', in fact far too strong a word, to how useless the Indians are and to their own indispensability come across not as self-confidence, but as the refrain of people aware of their own vulnerability and needing to justify their own existence. The women are particularly intolerant and damning of the Indians, which is why Fielding rarely goes to the club. 'He had discovered that it is possible to keep in with Indians and Englishmen, but that he who would also keep in with Englishwomen must drop Indians. The two wouldn't combine … He found it convenient and pleasant to associate with Indians and he must pay the price.'

In his novel *Burmese Days*, based on his experiences serving in Burma, Orwell also describes the reactions of the members of a British club to a local crisis that pits the British against the locals. There are similarities between the two accounts and Orwell too has a character who runs into trouble with his compatriots because of his friendship with an Indian, but Orwell's British characters are more hostile to the 'natives' and their racism is expressed in stronger language than those in Forster's novel, perhaps reflecting the fact that *Burmese Days* is set in a more isolated and out-of-the-way location.

Unlike Forster, who set his novel in a town, Maugham focuses on people living on isolated rubber plantations and in remote administrative outstations surrounded by servants and employees, often without seeing another white face for weeks or more at a time. He made two visits to Malaya, each of several months, with his lover Gerald Haxton and made no secret of the fact that he was looking for material, which he acquired partly by extensive travel and partly from the hours he and Haxton spent in bars and clubs. As both were good listeners and those they met were flattered to be in the presence of a famous writer, they were told a good deal. Although he fictionalized what he heard, his characters were based on real people. When his stories were published his local readers recognized what they read and denounced him not for inventiveness but for disloyalty and betraying his hosts. Maugham didn't care. In her biography of him, Selina Hastings quotes him as saying: 'If they didn't like the way I honestly thought them to be, then to hell with them.'[7]

Loneliness and boredom and how to maintain some connection with 'home' are recurring themes in the stories. In this connection newspapers and periodicals, though delivered six weeks or more late, played an important role. So did food. The impression conveyed by these stories is that most of the British insisted on their cooks producing English meals, however inappropriate to the climate and however much it involved relying on tinned rather than fresh ingredients. Some took the ritual of meals a step further. The principal character in 'The

Outstation' is an official who always wears evening dress for dinner, although he is often alone for months on end.

Class and background were very important. Officials were acutely aware of where in the social hierarchy in Britain their colleagues hailed from. Those who had been to the smartest public schools, like Winchester and Harrow, were always at pains to advertise the fact. In the aftermath of the First World War the regiment in which a man had served became important. But the trump card was to be able to demonstrate a connection, by family or friendship, with the aristocracy.

By far the biggest problem arising out of loneliness was sex. As most young men spent their first years in Malaya as bachelors it was common for them to take a 'native' mistress, which frequently led to the fathering of mixed-race children. Though officially frowned upon, this practice was widely condoned. A man was expected to send his mistress and children back to their kampong, or 'native' quarters, when another white person came to visit, but it was understood that few young men would wish, or be able, to remain celibate and alone in the circumstances in which they lived. This frequently led to horrible misunderstandings when young wives found out what their husbands had been up to as bachelors.

One of the saddest stories is 'Force of Circumstance', which tells of a wife newly arrived from England, who rejects the husband she loves when she learns that he had had a mistress and actually sees the woman with her children living not far from her own home. She cannot bear the prospect that they should continue in such close proximity. Although she recognizes that her husband was lonely and without any emotional or intellectual support, she cannot forgive him and, to the great distress of them both, they part. Selina Hastings writes that the problem of wives only discovering about their husbands' bachelor days after their arrival in the country was of sufficient concern among the white community as to be openly discussed in their newspaper, the *Malay Mail*.[8]

Neither a mistress nor the children were accorded any rights or status. While some men made financial provision for them others did not and, whatever their financial circumstances, the children generally had to grow up as outsiders on the margins of society. Occasionally, in an earlier period before the colour bar became as established as it did in the 1920s, a man might send his mistress or children back to Britain to be looked after by his family there.

One of the stories, entitled, with malicious irony, 'The Yellow Streak', is about just such a child, who, after being educated at Harrow and serving in a smart regiment during the war, returns to Malaya to take up a career as an official. He is popular and successful and, thanks to his school and regiment coupled with his own charm, enjoys an impregnable social position. But he is obsessed by the fear that one day his antecedents will be exposed and his life ruined. Eventually, as a result of a moment of panic and cowardice during an accident on a river and his attempt to cover up what really happened, a South African with whom he is travelling guesses the truth. The story ends with the reader left not knowing whether the secret will be revealed to others or not.

The scarcity of white women and the monotony of plantation and administrative life inevitably led to affairs, a source of endless fascination to Maugham. Two of his stories are about murders that resulted from them. Both, he writes in the preface to *Altogether*, 'were told to me and I had nothing to do, but to make them probable, coherent and dramatic'. One, entitled 'The Letter', involving a woman who shoots her white lover because he had thrown her over for a Chinese woman and then concocts a story that he had tried to rape her, is based on a trial that actually took place in 1911. She was found guilty, for which, given the law at the time, she should have hanged, but she was granted a reprieve. In his story Maugham draws on the details but alters the outcome by having the husband buy a letter from the Chinese woman's family that would have destroyed her defence, thereby enabling her to escape justice.

In 'Footprints in the Jungle' Bronson invites his old friend Cartwright, who has lost his job, to stay with him and his wife at their plantation until he finds another. The Bronsons are childless and when Mrs Bronson becomes pregnant by Cartwright they arrange the husband's murder in such a way as to make it appear that he has been killed by his own workers. The police investigation runs into the sand and in due course the case is closed. After a lapse of time new evidence comes to light that convinces the local Police Chief of Cartwright's guilt, but it is too degraded to be credible in a court of law. Some years later the Police Chief is transferred to a small town where, as a matter of course, he joins the local club. Mr and Mrs Cartwright, as they have become, are already members and they become his regular bridge partners.

Maugham's stock-in-trade as a writer was the vagaries of human nature while Forster's was the clash of irreconcilable values and interests. Both found much to engage them in the peculiar circumstances in which British people pursued their careers in the British empire in Asia. When, at the end of those careers, they returned 'home' they often found it hard to settle down. They were shorn of their status and role, conditions were so different from what they were used to and nobody who had not been involved in the empire was interested in what they had done. Many of those who had looked forward for many years to returning 'home' found themselves disappointed by what they found.

The Last September

by Elizabeth Bowen (1929)

When great empires begin to crumble they generally do so first at the edges, as happened to the Roman, Ottoman and, most recently, Soviet empires, to name but three. The British empire was an exception. The first province successfully to challenge the imperial power was Ireland, the one closest to the centre, which achieved independence as the Irish Free State in 1922, two years before the publication of *A Passage to India*, twenty-five years before India and some forty years before the empire finally came to an end in the early 1960s.

In some respects, the breach with Ireland was the most painful. There were so many with a foot in both camps. Erskine Childers, whose experiences are described in an earlier chapter, was one.* The writer Elizabeth Bowen was another. In *The Last September*, published in 1929 and set in 1920 at the height of the Irish rebellion, she draws on her own experience to show what that rebellion meant for the British landowners in Ireland, who had been settled there for centuries and become known as Anglo-Irish.

Her family was typical of that group. They were descended from a Welsh colonel who had served under Oliver Cromwell during his

---

* See earlier essay on *The Riddle of the Sands*.

pacification of Ireland in the 1650s. As a reward for his services the colonel was granted land in Co. Cork confiscated from its original owners. In 1776 his descendants built a house there called Bowen's Court, which had passed down from father to son until Elizabeth herself inherited it after the events described in this novel.* Many other such 'Big Houses', as they were known, were to be found all over Ireland belonging to families whose Protestant ancestors – English, Welsh and Scottish – had taken part in the various incursions by English rulers into Ireland. Their descendants remained Protestant and the houses dominated the rural Catholic communities around them.

These families had put down roots of their own in Irish soil and identified both with their British heritage and with their Irish surroundings and backgrounds. They stood to lose more than anyone from the rebellion against British rule. But at the heart of Bowen's novel is their ambivalence in confronting it. Irish nationalists disdained this duality. They regarded the 'Big Houses' as the physical manifestation of alien rule. During the War of Independence, a largely guerrilla or terrorist affair, the Irish Republican Army, commonly known as the IRA, burned a large number to the ground, though not Bowen's Court.

The Last September is not about that war as such. It is a study of the war's impact on the Anglo-Irish and how they reacted to it. The setting is a 'Big House' in Co. Cork called Danielstown that is derived from Bowen's Court. The principal characters are the owners, Sir Robert and Lady Naylor, their nineteen-year-old niece, Lois, their guests and British officers in the neighbouring garrison. Lois is a couple of years younger than Bowen was at the time the book is set and, like her creator, falls in love with a British officer. In both cases aunts step in to

---

* A description of Bowen's Court and an account of its history and that of the Bowen family may be found in *Bowen's Court* by Elizabeth Bowen, first published by Longmans, Green & Co. in 1942. A second edition with an afterword was published in 1964 and republished by Vintage in 1999 along with a memoir of her childhood in Dublin entitled *Seven Winters* and an introduction by Hermione Lee.

halt the romance, but whereas Bowen was sent to Italy to get over her attachment, Lois' boyfriend is killed before she can be sent away.

The Last September is an outstanding novel imbued on the one hand with a sensitivity derived from Bowen's own feelings and memories and on the other with the objectivity of the London literary figure that, by 1929, she had become. The literary critic and Oxford academic Maurice Bowra praised her for combining 'a historian's impartiality with a novelist's commitment'.* Her description of the emotions, absurdities and dilemmas of the Naylors, a family emblematic of their caste, shows how painful and difficult it was for the Anglo-Irish landowners to grasp that their world and their hegemony were collapsing until finally forced to face up to reality when their house is consumed by flames.

Until then they try to minimize the horrors going on around them. At one moment Sir Robert says, 'There should be less of this ambushing and skirmishing and hey-fidadding now that the days are drawing in', as if they were merely some kind of summer madness. At another Lady Naylor complains that the parents of the girls Lois had been at school with in England won't send them over to stay because 'something said in the English press has given rise to an idea that this country is unsafe'.

When neighbours and some officers and their wives come over to Danielstown to play tennis the conversation over tea turns to a recent attack on a nearby police barracks that had left several policemen dead. One of the officers' wives seeks to reassure the Anglo-Irish round the table that 'we're here to take care of you' and is disconcerted at the lack of a grateful response. To the Anglo-Irish the atrocity is more in the nature of an embarrassment to be passed over as quickly as possible. When an incident touches themselves, they seek reassurance by seizing on any explanation except the most likely. So, when a house guest at Danielstown reports that a raid has taken place at the neighbouring Castle Trent, the

* Quoted by Victoria Glendinning in her introduction (p. 6) to the Vintage edition of *The Last September*, published in 1998.

Trents' explanation that it was done by a gardener's cousin who hates the family rather than by the IRA is accepted. 'He left a quite unnecessary message behind with a skull and crossbones,' says the woman who conveys the news, adding, 'he sounds to me a rather silly man'.

In theory, the position of the Naylors, their family and friends should be clear. The rebels are trying not just to establish an independent state, but to subvert the existing social order as well. The army, the police and the notorious auxiliaries sent over to Ireland by the British government, called Black and Tans, are defending the status quo of which their houses and way of life are a prominent part. The Naylors and their neighbours also entertain the army officers and their wives in their homes and are entertained by them at the military base. Yet, in practice the Anglo-Irish see the situation in more complicated terms. They want life to return to normal, but they also worry about how the forces of the Crown are harassing and causing suffering to their tenants for whom they feel responsible and have known all their lives. Nor do they see the behaviour of the two sides in clear-cut terms. The disorderly and unpredictable behaviour of the Black and Tans is such that they fear being stopped by a Black and Tan patrol when they leave their estates as much as by the rebels.

This conflict of loyalties is poignantly illustrated by the relationship between the Naylors and their tenants, the Connors. When Lois asks after Michael Connor's wife and whether they have yet heard from their son, Peter, who is away from home, both she and Connor know Peter is a rebel on the run, but neither refers to that fact. A short time later, while at lunch with the Naylors, Lois' boyfriend, Lieutenant Lesworth, announces proudly that while on patrol the previous night he raided the Connors' house and arrested Peter. He expects to be congratulated for capturing a terrorist. Instead Sir Robert says how sorry he is; he knows Lesworth must do his duty, but Peter's mother is dying and this will be a terrible blow to her. In a futile and almost feudal gesture, he adds that he must send the family some grapes. Lesworth is left gasping: 'I had no idea these people were friends of yours.'

Even in the case of strangers the Anglo-Irish behaviour, as depicted by Bowen, is ambivalent. While out for a walk Lois and a woman house guest come across a man sleeping in the woods. He wakes, points a pistol at them and asks who they are and what they've seen. When they tell him where they're from he warns them to 'keep to the house while y'have it' and to stop their walks. He then lets them go. They promise not to tell anyone about seeing him and stick to their undertaking when they get home rather than reporting the incident to the authorities.

When, a short time later, Lesworth is killed in an ambush one wonders whether this man might have been responsible. Lois makes no such connection, but Sir Robert immediately thinks of 'Peter Connor's friends – they knew everything, they were persistent: it did not do to imagine ...' He feels powerless in the face of events that have run beyond his capacity to comprehend.

A big part of the Naylors' problem and of others like them was their social isolation. They were part of a caste of closely related and intermarried families who knew each other intimately, but other people scarcely at all. They had friends and relations who had gone out into the wider world and achieved success in the professions and other fields in Ireland, England and the empire, but those who had stayed within their own demesnes, as their estates were called, had become cut off from the changes that were transforming society on both sides of the Irish Sea. Their contacts with their tenants, those who worked for them and the local trades people were conducted on the basis of an impenetrable deference and politeness that masked the fundamental changes taking place beneath the surface.

As hereditary landowners, they looked down on the officers and their wives from suburban and Home Counties backgrounds with a snobbish disdain and, behind their backs, mocked their social solecisms. Discussing with a friend the fact that Lesworth comes from Surrey, Lady Naylor says,

'One cannot trace him ... Practically nobody who lives in Surrey ever seems to have been heard of, and if one does hear of them they have never heard of anybody else who lives in Surrey.' She wonders whether his 'people are in trade', but 'I should never say a thing like that without foundation'.

After the establishment in 1922 of the Irish Free State, the forerunner of today's republic,* those 'Big Houses' that survived became increasingly hard to maintain. Over time, with a few exceptions, they and the way of life based on them faded away. Many were sold. Some of the previous owners stayed in Ireland. Others departed for Britain or to the six counties of Ulster that remained part of the United Kingdom. Elizabeth Bowen was based in London when she inherited Bowen's Court in 1930. She visited it regularly and entertained her London literary friends there. In 1934 these included Virginia Woolf, who found it very run-down and recorded in her diary that it was 'pompous & pretentious & imitative & ruined'.[9] Bowen tried hard to keep it up, but eventually the struggle proved too much. In 1959, she sold it to a local farmer, who demolished it in the following year. She felt that to be 'a clean end. Bowen's Court never lived to be a ruin.'[10] In later years, after Ireland had become prosperous, some of the other former 'Big Houses' were converted into country house hotels, a fate she would have hated to befall Bowen's Court.

Bowen herself embodied the duality of the Anglo-Irish as she demonstrated during the Second World War when she travelled regularly from London to Ireland reporting back to the Ministry of Information on the situation there. This has since been condemned by Irish nationalists as spying. Yet in London, where Irish neutrality was widely resented, she championed Ireland's right to be neutral as a means of achieving national self-respect after centuries of British domination.

---

* The Irish Free State was established as a Dominion owing allegiance to the King, like Canada or Australia. In 1937, it adopted a new constitution with an elected non-executive President as head of state. In 1949, it was officially declared a republic when it also formally left the Commonwealth and severed all formal ties with the British Crown.

Remote People

by Evelyn Waugh (1931)

So Rough a Wind

by Sir Michael Blundell (1964)

When I read history at Cambridge in the late 1950s I took an optional course entitled The Expansion of Europe. It dealt with the mass migration of people from Europe over the previous four hundred years and their creation of new states in North and South America, Australasia and Africa. It dwelt much more on the achievements of the Europeans in their new habitats than on the fate of the indigenous peoples, who were either subjugated, sidelined or largely eliminated. It was a popular course because of its topicality: we could see that this long historical process was suddenly and painfully coming to an end.

In Algeria, where a large French population had been living for generations, the French army was fighting a bitter war that was shortly to end in defeat and the withdrawal of the settlers. In Kenya the British were simultaneously putting down a revolt by a section of the African population while defying the wishes of the colony's white settlers by promoting political reforms designed to lead to African majority rule. In the Central African Federation, made up of Southern Rhodesia (now Zimbabwe), Northern Rhodesia (now Zambia) and Nyasaland (now Malawi), British ministers were trying to bring about a settlement between whites and blacks that recognized the rights of the black majority. This was to lead to a revolt by the whites in Southern Rhodesia, who in 1965 established an illegal state that lasted until black majority rule was finally achieved in 1980. In South Africa the white minority government was clamping down on the growing assertiveness of the black majority by means of the oppressive and discriminatory apartheid regime.

These conflicts put Africa and the issue of decolonization at the forefront of British politics. The left and younger people on the right were generally in favour of African advancement while older people and the Conservative right wanted the British government to support those in the colonies and South Africa who were trying to resist it. The debate was sharp and bitter because the white people in Kenya and Rhodesia and many of those in South Africa were, in the phrase of the time, 'our kith and kin'. They were British by race and retained strong family and other links with this country. In January 1961 the Prime Minister, Harold Macmillan, wrote in his diary of his fear that, 'From the party point of view Kenya is going to create a big problem. We might even split on it. Lord Salisbury and Lord Lambton could easily rally a settler lobby here of considerable power.'[11]

According to one view, the settlers in Kenya and Rhodesia deserved support because they were British. According to the other they had to be opposed because they were acting in defiance of the principles of democracy and equality before the law on which our society is based. Besides which, in realpolitik terms – and this was crucial – they were holding up the conversion of the colonial empire that Britain could no longer afford into a commonwealth of independent nations, a policy that became a major British priority in the 1950s.

So Rough a Wind, published in 1964, is the autobiography of Michael Blundell, a leading white politician in colonial Kenya who had arrived there as a young man from Britain in 1925. It traces the evolution of his thinking from an assumption of white mastery through the idea of partnership between Africans and Europeans, as the British settlers* described themselves, to an acceptance of black leadership as the only way in which white people would be able to remain. In his travel book *Remote People*, published many years earlier in 1931, the novelist Evelyn Waugh records his impressions of a visit to Kenya when the settlers were in their heyday. He applauds their way of life and their desire for the colony to be run in their own interests. He also expresses his support for the idea of white, in particular Anglo-Saxon, racial superiority. Yet in the same breath he forecasts, in defiance of all expert opinion at the time, that the colonial venture would not last beyond the 1950s.

Michael Blundell's journey across the political spectrum earned him a knighthood from the British government, but the enmity of his fellow settlers. Many in the white community ostracized him and accused him of being a traitor. On one occasion when he returned from a conference in London he was greeted by a European crowd at Nairobi airport with shouts of 'Judas' and thirty silver coins were thrown at him. In later years, after Kenya had become independent, the wheel turned full circle as those Europeans who had remained often looked to him to intercede on their behalf with the African government.

As he looks back over his career Blundell shows understanding of the aspirations and dilemmas of both races as well as of the traders and businessmen from the Indian subcontinent who had settled in the colony and become objects of suspicion to black and white alike, despite

---

* A few were Scandinavian, including Karen Blixen, the author of the famous book *Out of Africa*, who was Danish. My wife, whose father was a colonial administrator in the neighbouring territory of Tanganyika, went to boarding school in Nairobi, the capital of Kenya, where her best friend was the daughter of Swedish settlers in that country.

their indispensable role in running the economy. Yet, as one reads his account, with the benefit of both his and history's hindsight, it is hard to escape the conclusion that there were three rocks on which the project of a permanent place for the white settlers was always bound, sooner or later, to founder. One was the question of to whom did the land rightfully belong. The second was that the blacks outnumbered the whites by a hundred to one or more. The third was the enduring racism of the white community.

In the nineteenth century the land question would have been settled by force of arms as it was in the United States, Australia, South Africa and other areas of white settlement. In those places where the indigenous people were weak, as in the first two, they were left on the margins of society with scraps of land the white people didn't want. Even where they were strong enough to put up a significant fight, as in South Africa, they lost out badly. In all cases they were denied political rights. As late as 1910 Britain granted self-government to South Africa with power being handed over exclusively to the white minority without much regard to the interests of the black majority.

It was against this background that white settlers began to move informally into Kenya in the 1890s. In 1902 the British government initiated a consistent settlement policy awarding incoming whites land that had been appropriated from the Africans. After the First World War army veterans were granted land under the British government's Soldier Settlement Scheme. This was followed after the Second World War by another scheme for ex-servicemen to settle on land reserved exclusively for Europeans. All these settlers, and others who arrived independently, believed they were putting down roots in a territory that would remain under British control for as far ahead as they could see. Indeed, the post-1945 scheme was explicitly designed to run for forty-four years. They assumed too that those parts of the country, notably the highlands, that were reserved for Europeans would remain so. In the nineteenth century their interests would have prevailed against all others. Their mistake was to believe that this would still be case in the twentieth.

The early settlers had to create everything from scratch. When Blundell began he worked for another settler, lived in a mud and wattle hut and helped to build his boss' house before going on to acquire a farm of his own. They were as much pioneers as those who opened up the American West. Later arrivals sometimes, but not always, acquired farms that were already going concerns. They too had then worked hard to develop them in conditions where the vagaries of the climate and the fluctuations in the price of their products on world markets made for a very uncertain life. They believed they had a right to what they owned both because it had been legally granted to them and because of the work they had put into it. They also believed that they had a right to look to the British government for protection.

For their part the Africans believed that the land rightfully belonged to them and that it had been taken from them against their will by force backed up by legal means that at the time they did not fully understand. They further believed, and not without reason, that over the years government policy and subsidies had favoured European over African farming and that it was, in any case, outrageous that parts of the country should be reserved exclusively for Europeans. They also resented the presence of the large Indian community in the colony. They too believed that they had a right to look to the British government for redress and that, as they constituted the overwhelming majority of the population, their will should prevail.

Blundell was among the first Europeans to grasp that the war marked a watershed in the relationship between the races. Before 1939 African nationalism was weak and the bulk of the African population had neither the skills nor the confidence to challenge the white supremacy. After 1945 this had ceased to be the case. The Africans were no longer willing to be treated as a 'junior partner' in their own country.

He commanded African troops serving initially in Ethiopia against the Italians and later in India. He saw how their experiences outside their own country led the men serving under him to question their old assumptions. 'They asked why only Europeans were officers in the East African Army and why the food scales were different as between white and black soldiers. They learnt that courage, fear, hunger and physical exhaustion were common to men of all races.' And they began to apply the Allied wartime propaganda about fighting for freedom and democracy to their own situation. In 1945 he read a letter from an African soldier that made a big impression on him. After describing the many disadvantages under which Africans laboured in their own country it ended 'with a passionate and bitter cry "Long hair, long hair (i.e. European hair) has stolen my country away." I was face to face with the smouldering thoughts of a new Africa.'

Even so it took Blundell some time to adjust his ideas to the new reality. In 1948, when he first stood for election to the colonial legislature, he still argued in favour of 'European leadership, reservation of the European highlands and a communal or racial role for election purposes', a device to ensure that the European minority would always have as many seats in the legislature as the other races combined.

Sir Philip Mitchell, the colony's Governor from 1944 to 1952, helped to change Blundell's mind by posing the question: 'What then is the wise course for a European population of some 45,000 set among 100,000 Asians and 5,000,000 Africans? … If it insists on separation and special rights and refuses genuine co-operation with other races, it will isolate itself, stimulate African nationalism and almost certainly drive Asians into that camp.' To persist in that course, the far-sighted Governor warned, would lead the whites to rebel against Britain, as would later happen in Southern Rhodesia where the whites could rely on the support of neighbouring South Africa, an advantage the Kenya whites did not have.

It was because he faced up to this reality ahead of most other Europeans that Blundell came 'to realize that the role of the white man must change from undisputed leader to associate and friend of the new forces which were emerging in our country'. In 1960, by which time there were sixty thousand Europeans to six million Africans, he had reached the point, under pressure from the British government, of accepting that 'Kenya was destined to be an African country'.

Which raises the question of why other Europeans had such difficulty in coming to the same conclusion. As Blundell puts it, 'They believed firmly in the benefit of British rule to the African and were proudly conscious of what they had achieved in turning chunks of raw Africa into smiling farms and prosperous valleys.' In a speech in London in 1960, he himself claimed that it was a 'country we had created', without mentioning the contribution of Africans and Asians. But at bottom, as he admits, lay their enduring racial prejudice – 'the dark chasms in the minds of the (white) electorate over race'. The issue lurks beneath the surface of the book without ever being tackled head-on. For that one must turn to Evelyn Waugh.

In *Remote People*, published in 1931, Waugh is enchanted by the Kenya settlers; in his view, 'perfectly normal, respectable Englishmen' trying to re-create 'the traditional life of the English squirarchy', that was going out of fashion in their own country. He praises the endeavour and regards it as perfectly natural that they should want to reserve the colony for people like themselves and not be required to share power or amenities with either Africans or Asians.

That those other races, regardless of an individual's sophistication, education or wealth, should be denied political rights and not allowed to use the same hotels and restaurants or travel in the same part of a bus or train as white people seemed to him, as to the settlers, to be part of the natural order of things. It was, after all, the practice not only in neighbouring South Africa, but also in the Southern states of the United States, as well as Washington DC.

In a passage that makes for painful reading today, but accurately reflects the attitudes of the period, Waugh points out with characteristic bluntness that wherever Anglo-Saxons lived in close proximity with other races – he cites India and Virginia as examples – 'the reality of racial antagonism' exists. 'It is not a matter one can be censorious about. Gentle Reader, you would behave in just the same way yourself after a year in the tropics.' He then suggests that because it is so widely felt, 'It is just worth considering that there may be something valuable behind the indefensible and inexplicable assumption of superiority by the Anglo-Saxon race.'

To hold such views in the 1930s was commonplace. They were among the assumptions on which the empire was based. By the 1950s they had become lethal to the settlers' own long-term interest, but the pace of change had been too fast for many of them to realize this. They wanted to continue to live as nearly as possible as they always had. They could not understand the insistence of British ministers that the only way to avoid bloodshed was to bring the colony to independence on the basis of black majority rule. Nor did they grasp that, although a vocal minority in Britain spoke up for them, the majority did not care what happened to them.

This was the outcome foreseen by Waugh. He concludes his discussion of racial attitudes in *Remote People* by suggesting that 'it is uncertain whether the kind of life the Kenya settlers are attempting to re-establish is capable of survival; whether indeed the European colonization of Africa will survive in any form; whether there may not be in the next twenty-five years a general Withdrawal of the Legions to defend Western civilization at its sources'. Whether that would be because of those attitudes or despite them he does not say. Either way it was a remarkable prognostication.

Provincial Life

Anna of the Five Towns by Arnold Bennett, 1902, *The Condition of England* by C. F. G. Masterman, 1909, and *The Ragged-Trousered Philanthropists* by Robert Tressall, 1914.

Love on the Dole by Walter Greenwood, 1933, and *Saturday Night and Sunday Morning* by Alan Sillitoe, 1958.

Room at the Top by John Braine, 1957, and *This Sporting Life* by David Storey, 1960.

Anna of the Five Towns

by Arnold Bennett (1902)

The Condition of England

by C. F. G. Masterman (1909)

The Ragged-Trousered Philanthropists

by Robert Tressall (1914)

Despite the fear of war and the general sense of insecurity described in the chapters on the build-up to the First World War, the period between the death of Queen Victoria in January 1901 and the outbreak of the First World War in August 1914 is suffused in British folk memory with a golden glow. It is regarded not just as the calm before the storm but as a period of serenity and contentment epitomized by the plump and pleasure-loving figure of King Edward VII, who ruled for most of it. The struggles turning to violence of the suffragettes, the industrial disputes and strikes, and the extent to which politics was embittered by the dispute over Home Rule for Ireland are overshadowed by the horrors of what followed. In later years the memoirs of those who survived the war tended to describe their lives before it broke out in idyllic terms. Popular television dramas such as *Upstairs, Downstairs* and *Downton Abbey* have embellished these recollections and embedded them in the public mind.

But those whose memoirs were published were nearly always members of the prosperous and privileged classes. The television dramas also focus on those classes and their retainers. For the aristocracy, the rich and the well-to-do the Edwardian age was indeed a wonderful time to be alive. Their love of luxury and self-indulgence has become the stuff of legend and contributed disproportionately to our image of the age. These three books – an outstanding novel by Arnold Bennett, a political tract in the guise of a novel by Robert Tressall* and a comprehensive survey of the state of the nation by the Liberal MP and journalist Charles Masterman – deal with men and women who do not appear in the memoirs of the period. They are set in different parts of the country and among different types of people. Together they show how harsh life was for most people and how severe the penalties for failure and misfortune.

Masterman researched and wrote his book soon after the election of a reforming Liberal government in 1906. By the time it was published in 1909 he had become a junior minister. His title invoked a famous phrase coined in 1839 by the historian and philosopher Thomas Carlyle to describe the working class during the Industrial Revolution, which has since become a generic cliché to describe books that set out to analyse contemporary politics, economics and society. His aim was to influence public opinion in favour of the government's reforms.

His report on the countryside is particularly striking. Far from being the unspoilt arcadia of popular imagination, it was, to paraphrase the hymn 'Jerusalem', no 'green and pleasant land'. Conditions there were

---

* His real name was Robert Noonan. He signed the original manuscript as Robert Tressell, which is how it appeared on later editions. But it was printed as Tressall on the first edition, published in 1914, which is why I have adopted it here.

in fact worse than in 'the dark satanic mills'* of the great industrial cities. 'Rural England,' he writes, 'beyond the radius of certain favoured neighbourhoods, and apart from the specialized population which serves the necessities of the country house is everywhere hastening to decay.' The main underlying reason for this was the opening up of North and South America and Australia in the latter half of the nineteenth century and the development of fast steamships and refrigeration that enabled their produce to be delivered to Britain at prices with which local production could not compete. This had created a crisis for the rural economy.

Masterman has little to say about these causes, which is understandable as the Liberals were in favour of continued free trade while the Conservatives wanted to introduce tariffs that would have helped the rural economy to recover but at the cost of higher food prices. This was one of the big political issues of the day. Rather he blames everything on the large landowners and farmers. He points out that much of the landowners' wealth, whether aristocrats or the newly rich, derived from investments in trade, industry and finance. He berates them for deserting agriculture in favour of parks and avenues with woods devoted to the breeding of game birds for shooting and stretches of land left open for hunting. He sees these as both the cause and the symbol of what had gone wrong. He is equally scornful of 'the great farmers' who had bought up their less successful neighbours, enclosed and taken over common land and created large fields surrounded by hedges to achieve economies of scale.

These developments were draining the life out of the countryside, 'with village after village in which no new cottages have been built for a hundred years; crumbling walls falling into decay; crowded families with all the starved life and degradation inevitably associated with such overcrowding; the whole presenting an aspect of fatigue and decline'.

* 'Jerusalem' by William Blake.

The more energetic either went off in search of work in the cities or emigrated to Australia, Canada or the United States. Those who remained were at the mercy of the landowners, who not only employed them but, for the most part, also owned the cottages in which they lived. To lose a job, therefore, usually meant losing the home that went with it. Being rendered homeless was an ever-present fear, especially for elderly men and women faced with the prospect of ending their days in the workhouse where husbands and wives were generally separated. Masterman describes the rural population as being so cowed as to resent the intrusion of politicians and trade unionists campaigning for better conditions for fear of retribution from their landlords.

To illustrate his point, he recounts a recent incident in Oxfordshire where a Liberal MP had persuaded villagers in his constituency to go to court to resist the enclosure by the landlord of a right of way. 'The resistance was sustained, and the village preserved its ancient privilege. But all six witnesses were dismissed from their occupations and driven from the district. And indignation fell, not on the landlord who thus revealed his power, but on the member of Parliament who revealed his impotence.' For all its good intentions and, despite pioneering old age pensions and unemployment benefit, the Liberal Party had no answer to problems of this kind, whether in agriculture or industry, thereby leaving the way open for the emergence of the Labour Party sponsored by the trade unions.

Robert Tressall's *The Ragged-Trousered Philanthropists* was one of the Labour Party's earliest inspirations. Writing in 2011, the former Labour Cabinet minister and icon of the left Tony Benn described it as 'a major Socialist novel that has influenced thousands of readers since it was published in 1914'.[1] From the other end of the political spectrum the World Economic Forum in Davos in 2016 listed it among nine novels 'that have changed society' because of the influence they had on 'the drive for social reform at the start of the last century'.[2] It fully achieves its author's aim, set out in his preface, to produce 'a readable story full of human interest and based on the happenings of everyday life' to convey his message that socialism was the answer to injustice and exploitation. Its policy prescriptions have long since lost their relevance, but its account of working-class life in the early years of the twentieth century retains all the clarity of a photograph.

The author was the illegitimate son of a prosperous Dubliner, who received a good education before it was cut short when his father died, after which, resenting his mother's marriage to another man, he emigrated to South Africa. On returning to Britain he became a signwriter and house painter in Hastings, where the novel is set. The original version was eighteen hundred pages long and it was not until three years after his death from tuberculosis that his daughter secured the publication of a shortened version of three hundred and ninety-one pages. Later editions include more of the original text, but it was the shorter version that established the book's fame and it remains the most readable. The title was meant to be a sardonic reference to the way in which poor men gave away their labour to richer men for much less than it was worth, thereby colluding in their own exploitation. His renaming of Hastings as Mugsborough drives the point home.

The action is set among a group of employees of a building firm called Rushtons who are working on the renovation of a large house known as The Cave. The central character, Frank Owen, is, like the author, a signwriter and house painter, a socialist, an atheist and suffering from the early onset of tuberculosis.*

The men's lives are dominated by debt. It overshadows every aspect of their existence. All owe money for food, clothing or furniture and

---

* In her autobiography *Walking in the Shade* (p. 88) Doris Lessing writes of staying in a hotel in Hastings in the 1950s that was reputed to have been the house on which Tressall based The Cave. There she was shown 'a beautiful ceiling' that was said to be 'a possible work' by him.

often for all three. To be in arrears on their rent is normal and their possessions move in and out of the pawnbrokers as need dictates. When they are in work they pay down their debts. When they are out of work their debts increase. Their heads are never above water as whenever they approach the surface another setback pushes them under. Their ever-present fear at a time when there was no unemployment benefit* is of being out of work, which they frequently are. By its very nature the building trade is seasonal so that work was harder to find in winter than in summer and, as soon as a big job like The Cave finished, they were likely to be laid off until their current employer, or one of the others in the town, won another big contract.

Their wives are responsible for managing the family's finances, which means facing up to the rent collector and shopkeepers to whom they owe money, juggling the debts and eking out what is left. What that meant in practice is shown when one of the characters called Easton and his wife review their situation after he has been taken on at The Cave at twenty-five shillings a week (about £133 in contemporary money)† compared with the eighteen shillings, taking good times with bad, that he had averaged over the previous year. They find they are four weeks in arrears with their rent, which amounts to twenty-four shillings, face a demand for rates‡ of nearly twenty-five shillings, owe twelve shillings for furniture bought on hire purchase, and about thirty shillings to the grocer, butcher, baker, milkman and greengrocer. Easton rebukes her for mismanagement, only to get into the habit of going off to the pub with his mates after receiving his weekly wages instead of taking them home to her, a not uncommon phenomenon. The Eastons were not long

---

* It was introduced in 1911, the year the author died.

† Until the decimalization of the currency in 1971 the pound was divided into twenty shillings, which were in turn divided into twelve pence. For the sake of simplicity I have only used shillings in respect of the men's finances. A guinea was worth one pound one shilling.

‡ A property tax, the nearest equivalent to which is today's council tax.

married with only one child. Other couples with the large families that were normal at that time would have faced greater challenges.

These mountains of debt put men at the mercy of those with the power to hire and fire, towards whom they behave with fawning obsequiousness and loathing in their hearts. Yet those managers and foremen were themselves at the mercy of the men who owned the building firms and were under constant pressure to cut costs in order to win contracts. If they failed, they too would lose their jobs. One of the most poignant episodes in the book is the suicide of the manager who tyrannizes the workers at The Cave when, in a fit of despair, he can no longer make his figures add up. Because of the constant pressure on costs the work is always being 'scamped' instead of properly done, with too few coats of paint being applied and inferior materials substituted for those in the contract. When one of the men takes too much trouble over a task and so too long to finish it, he is sacked. Safety is ignored with the result that a man dies falling from an upper storey because a frayed rope hasn't been replaced. At the inquest his workmates perjure themselves rather than reveal the cause of the accident for fear of reprisals from their employer if they tell the truth.

Better educated and more articulate than the others, Frank Owen veers between fury with them for their passivity in the face of such conditions and sympathy for their inability to understand what's wrong and to rebel against it. During their lunch breaks he explains how the system works whereby the benefits flow disproportionately to the owners of the businesses while those who do all the hard work earn so little and are discarded when no longer needed. In a memorable chapter entitled 'The Money Trick', he at last manages to rouse their indignation, but the moment is lost when the bell rings to summon them back to work. Otherwise they listen to him with amusement or scepticism and in some cases, notably the foreman, impatience for being too clever by half for an ordinary working man.

The idea of thinking about how industry or society might be changed doesn't interest them or, at least, not for more than a few moments at a time. In the mines, the docks and the railways trade unions had already become powerful and strikes were endemic in the years leading up to the outbreak of war, but in less organized industries, such as the building trades and agriculture, men like Owen found it hard to convince their colleagues to organize so that their combined strength could be used to secure better terms and conditions. Because his workmates like him, they let him speak, but when a group of socialists arrives in the town to canvass support they regard them as troublemakers and drive them out.

It is not only at work that the men and their families are exploited. Tressall shows how as ratepayers they lose out too through their employers' control of the local council. The owner of The Cave arranges for the council to pay for linking its drainage to the municipal system and the members of the council line their own pockets through arranging the merger of the local gas and electricity companies while paying off the officials who facilitate the process on their behalf. The fifty guineas, or 1,050 shillings, that one receives for his help in this matter stands in stark contrast to the weekly wages of the workers.

Tressall's strongest anger is reserved for the Nonconformist Shining Light Chapel where the great men of the town preside and parade their Christian principles by taking the Sunday school and in other ways. The pastor is hand in glove with them. Owen is nauseated to hear him telling the underfed and ill-clothed children of the workers to thank God for having been 'made happy English children' while their parents are expected to contribute to the chapel's upkeep. They are also asked to subscribe to a fund to enable the pastor to have a holiday in the South of France, which raises a sum of money that could have made a huge difference to the poorest of the parish. The preacher who stands in for him is paid at the rate of eighty-four shillings a service whereas the chapel's widowed caretaker receives a derisory six shillings a week with which she has to feed her son, who as an apprentice works for almost nothing, as well as herself.

At the end of the book, when the tuberculosis is taking hold of Owen and he fears he may soon die, he agonizes at the prospect of his wife and son being left 'alone and defenceless in the midst of the "Christian" wolves who were waiting to rend them as soon as he was gone'.

Arnold Bennett took a similarly jaundiced view of the Methodist brand of Nonconformism practised in the Staffordshire pottery towns where he was brought up and where *Anna of the Five Towns* is set.* The novel has two interweaving themes. One is the ruthlessness displayed towards each other by the town's leading businessmen and how far it diverges from the doctrines they espouse and preach at the chapel of which they are all members. The other is the mastery of men over women. The two are brought together in the relationship between the eponymous Anna and her father, the miser Ephraim Tellwright. Bennett is particularly good at portraying women and conveying the dilemmas they faced as a result of their subordinate status. He understood how the conventions of the time made it so difficult for them to turn independent thought into action against the will of a dominant man, regardless of their legal rights.

Anna and her younger sister, Agnes, live with the widowed Tellwright, whose 'surly and terrorizing ferocity' dominates their lives. He was a man who 'could recall the fearful timidity of his mother's eyes without a trace of compassion' and, in a telling phrase, 'belonged to the great and powerful class of house-tyrants, the backbone of the British nation'. When, on her twenty-first birthday, Anna inherits a portfolio of shares and properties worth £50,000 (about £6,000,000 in contemporary money) from her maternal grandfather she cannot

* There were in fact six towns, which in 1910 were incorporated into a new county borough called Stoke-on-Trent, which became a city in 1925.

help but allow him to continue to administer it. She then has to watch helplessly as, in her own financial interest but against her wishes and her conscience, he drives a tenant who owes her money to financial ruin and suicide. As the screw tightens we do not condemn her for being weak; we sympathize with her for her inability to be strong.

It is not just her conscience that suffers; her emotions are engaged as well. She had fallen in love with the tenant's son, Willie Price, after witnessing his courage in standing up for his father against her own. But because of the circumstances that have brought them together, and because a woman could not possibly take the initiative in declaring such an emotion, she fails to act. Instead she allows herself to be manoeuvred by kindly neighbours into committing herself to their highly suitable, but, as yet, impecunious young cousin, Henry Mynors, whose business success will be assured with her money behind him. 'She had sucked in with her mother's milk the profound truth that a woman's life is always a renunciation, greater or less. Hers by chance was greater.' Her thoughts, after marriage, 'often dwelt lovingly on Willie Price', who, following his father's death, had told her he was off to Australia. She had given him £100 in a sealed envelope not to be opened until he reached his destination. What she will never know is that instead of emigrating, his shame at his family's disgrace had led him to commit suicide by throwing himself down an abandoned mine shaft.

The novel is about the life of a community Bennett knew intimately and, besides the dramas of its plots, it contains some memorable scenes of life within it. When Mynors shows Anna round his works, which he had designed himself, it is to him a thing of beauty and to her a source of wonder. The reader sees it through the eyes of both and there can rarely have been a more lyrical description of an industrial process. Another is the revivalist meeting and the fervour with which the preacher calls on God to save the congregation's souls and on the congregation to give generously to the collection. In the chapel 'the atmosphere was electric, perilous, over-charged with spiritual emotion' as, one after another, seventeen people left the pews to go forward to be saved.

A third is the special tea at which the family who brought Anna and Mynors together celebrate their engagement. 'Such a meal as could only have been compassed in Staffordshire or Yorkshire', the array of delicacies is described in loving detail, from 'the fowl which had been boiled for four hours' at one end of the table to 'a hot pork pie, islanded in liquor' at the other. This was the world she was moving into and the contrast between its lavishness and the fate of those whose businesses failed is stark.

Anna of the Five Towns was Bennett's third novel and established his reputation as one of the leading and most prolific novelists of his generation. After his death in 1930 it went into a decline from which – unfairly in my view – it has never recovered. He was a great bon viveur who loved grand hotels and is now remembered, if at all, mainly for the Omelette Arnold Bennett,* a delicious concoction that the chef at London's Savoy Hotel named in his honour. It may still sometimes be found on the menu at traditional establishments and, whenever I come across it, I order it.

* Its ingredients are egg, smoked haddock, a hard cheese such as parmesan or gruyère, milk, butter and flour.

Love on the Dole

by Walter Greenwood (1933)

Saturday Night and Sunday Morning

by Alan Sillitoe (1958)

Love on the Dole, published in 1933, and *Saturday Night and Sunday Morning*, published in 1958, stand in relation to each other like the before and after images in an advertisement for washing powder. Both are about working-class life in a community that revolves around a great manufacturing company. In the former it is the Hanky Park district of Salford, now part of Greater Manchester, beginning in 1926 but mainly in the Depression-hit early 1930s. In the latter it is Nottingham in the mid-1950s shortly before the then Prime Minister, Harold Macmillan, famously claimed that 'most of our people have never had it so good'.*

How right he was! The contrast between the lives of the characters in these two books is immense and shows the extent to which the way of life of the British industrial working class was transformed during the twenty-five years between their publication. Those in *Love on the Dole* live in extreme penury with every aspect of their existence dominated by

* Speech 20 July 1957 at Bedford.

the impact of long-term unemployment. In their wildest dreams they would not have been able to imagine the lavish spending and freedom from insecurity enjoyed by Arthur Seaton, around whose life *Saturday Night and Sunday Morning* revolves. Their lives are much closer to the pre-First World War conditions described in *The Ragged-Trousered Philanthropists*,* although unemployment benefit – the dole – and means-tested relief had somewhat mitigated the hardship of unemployment.

This great transformation had taken place despite the Second World War and was the result of both international and domestic factors. Just as the problems of the 1930s had above all been caused by the collapse of the world economy, so the prosperity of the 1950s was primarily the result of the rapid expansion in the world economy that began after the war. All industrialized countries benefited. Britain in fact grew richer at a somewhat slower pace than some others while doing sufficiently well to ensure full employment. On top of this there was the welfare state, introduced by the 1945–51 Labour government, which benefited all classes, but above all those who had previously been the least well off.

Both authors were writing about their own people. Greenwood, born in 1903, lost his father when he was nine, his mother worked as a waitress and he left school at thirteen. By the time he was thirty, when *Love on the Dole* was published, he had worked at a variety of low-paid jobs without ever earning as much as £2 a week (about £130 in today's money), alternating with long periods of unemployment. His book was drawn directly from life, which makes his descriptions of urban poverty and the dialogue of his characters so realistic.

Sillitoe, born in 1928, also experienced extreme poverty. After his father lost his job the family was reduced to transferring their belongings from one refuge to another in a handcart. After leaving school at fourteen he was for some time a piece worker in the bicycle

* See previous essay.

factory in which the central character in his novel, Arthur Seaton, later works. His life was transformed by a prolonged period of convalescence from tuberculosis while doing his National Service. Unpleasant though this must have been, it provided him with the opportunity to read widely and to return to civilian life with a small pension that enabled him to devote his time to writing.

The two authors differ from other writers with whom they are often classified. In Greenwood's case that is George Orwell, an infinitely more accomplished writer whose classic *The Road to Wigan Pier** has come to be regarded as the definitive account of working-class life during the Depression while *Love on the Dole* is largely forgotten. But as a middle-class radical intellectual, Orwell was writing from the point of view of a visitor from another social planet not as a 'native'. He was, moreover, following in Greenwood's footsteps.

The distinction between Sillitoe and the other writers with whom he is often grouped as part of the 1950s working-class movement, such as John Braine, David Storey† and Stan Barstow, is more subtle. As none of them had been to a public school they regarded themselves, and were regarded by others, as outsiders in the literary world. But, unlike Sillitoe, they had been educated at perfectly good grammar schools. These lacked the social cachet of public schools, but in educational terms were often just as good and in some cases better. Sillitoe, by contrast, was largely self-educated.

Love on the Dole is about the hopelessness of the Hardcastle family, typical members of the community in which they live in the sense of always being victims of circumstances beyond their control. This derives from the impossibility of ever finding sufficient regular work to bring in enough money to secure more than a subsistence existence and the

* Published by Victor Gollancz in 1937.

† See following essay on John Braine's *Room at the Top* and David Storey's *This Sporting Life*.

constant fear of losing even that. The father, an ex-miner whose pit has closed, is consumed with shame at being unable to provide for his children. The mother defies his injunction never to get into debt in order to buy their son, Harry, the suit he yearns for. Harry later loses his job at the local engineering works as the firm always sacks young men as soon as they finish their apprenticeship and qualify for an adult wage, in order to replace them with other apprentices able to work for a lower rate. Shortly afterwards his girlfriend, Helen, becomes pregnant and they have to marry with minimal means of support.

The answer to these problems is provided by his beautiful sister, Sally. She had been hoping to marry the local Labour Party organizer with whom she was in love, but when he dies as a result of a combination of pneumonia and being roughed up by the police while leading an unemployment march (based on one that actually took place in October 1931), she agrees to become the mistress of the local bookmaker in order to save the family. As the richest and most influential man in the neighbourhood, he secures jobs for her father and brother with the local bus company and provides her with a financial settlement. Such a plot could easily descend into maudlin melodrama, but the rawness of their language and dialect and the brutal realism with which the characters confront their lot save it from doing so.*

Hanky Park was representative of conditions throughout the industrial North of England and the significance of *Love on the Dole* derives from the light it casts on the daily life of the urban poor. The abuse of the apprenticeship system by employers is one such example. Another is the central role played by the pawnshop in the life of the community, just as it had a generation earlier as described in *The Ragged-Trousered Philanthropists*. It provided a service whereby women – and

* Links are sometimes drawn between Greenwood's descriptions of life in Hanky Park and L. S. Lowry's paintings of the same period of life in Salford on which the novel was based.

it is always the women – can hand over clothes, or other household goods for which they have no immediate need in return for cash and then redeem them for a slightly larger sum when they are in funds. A normal practice was for a wife to take in her husband's suit on Monday to get money to tide them over to payday on Friday when it could be redeemed for the weekend. Money, such as it was, was always the wife's responsibility. On payday the convention, not always observed, of course, was for those members of the household in receipt of wages or benefits to hand them over to her to deduct what she needed for housekeeping before returning the small change remaining for spending money.

Some households were extremely large. Helen has eleven siblings all sharing a four-room dwelling with their parents. In such conditions privacy was impossible and there could be no secrets. When the young men in the community talk about sex they joke about what they've seen and heard their parents do. It is above all in order to escape from hearing her parents having sex in the next room that Helen wants to leave home.

This aspect of communal living has rarely been dealt with in literature.* In drawing attention to it Greenwood brought home to his middle-class readers the horrors of poverty in a particularly forceful manner. He did not, however, mention the incest between fathers and daughters to which the overcrowding sometimes gave rise. That would have been going too far. Yet, as I recount in a later chapter, the campaigner for women's rights and future Cabinet minister Margaret Bondfield had explicitly drawn attention to the problem in 1910 in her report to the Women's Labour League on conditions in the Yorkshire woollen industry.

Arthur Seaton, the twenty-two-year-old anti-hero of *Saturday Night and Sunday Morning*, would have been born at about the same time as Harry's and Helen's child, but by the time he has grown up the Hardcastles'

---

* Another example is Graham Greene's novel *Brighton Rock*, published by Heinemann in 1938. Its central character, Pinky, a brutal teenage murderer, is haunted by memories of what he witnessed his parents do in bed.

miseries are a distant memory. He is aware that his parents' generation have had difficult lives from which they still bear scars and is somewhat awed by the experiences of one of his aunts, but, like anyone else of his age, he lives in the present. At a time of full employment, he takes his job for granted and thinks about it only in terms of how to manipulate the piecework system by which he is paid in order to maximize his earnings. He is on terms of guarded equality with the foreman, who supervises his work; a big change from the pre-war years and those of *The Ragged-Trousered Philanthropists* when, as a man with the power to hire and fire, a foreman inspired fear among those who worked under him.

While at work Seaton's thoughts are on the two older married sisters, Brenda and Winnie, with whom he is having affairs, where to get drunk at the weekend and what clothes to buy and wear. His life is devoted to self-indulgence interspersed with random acts of violence against those who annoy him. When a small car nearly runs into him, he and his brother turn it over. When an old woman in the street where he lives gossips about him, he wounds her by shooting her with an airgun. He rejects all authority and accepts no obligations or responsibilities, except to his extended family and to giving pleasure to women he is sleeping with. 'Make a woman enjoy being in bed with you – that's a big part of the battle – then you were well on the way to keeping her with you for good. Christ, that's the best thing I've ever done,' he soliloquizes. Eventually, however, retribution catches up with him when Winnie's soldier husband comes home on leave and with a mate beats him up in a dark alley. By then he has met Doreen, a girl younger than himself who takes him in hand and to whom, in a chastened mood, he becomes engaged.

The book received a sensational reception for two reasons that cast light on the social attitudes of the time. One was the portrayal of Arthur, who came to be regarded as an iconic figure of what was called 'working-class literature'. The other was the graphic account of

Brenda's successful attempt to terminate her pregnancy by the time-honoured method of lying in a bath of very hot water while drinking her way through a bottle of gin. This passage is thought to have played some part in influencing public opinion in favour of the legalization of abortion that came a few years later. Subsequent generations must also be struck by the furtiveness and embarrassment involved in those days in the purchase of contraceptives, which, of course, led to many unwanted pregnancies, backstreet abortions, illegitimate babies and forced marriages.

There are several other insights into what it was like to live in the 1950s. The acquisition of a television set is still something to be very excited about and it is still rare for anyone in Arthur's circle to own a car. Nobody yet goes abroad on holiday. The army casts a long shadow. Winnie is lonely and open to Arthur's charms because her husband is away serving in Germany in the British Army of the Rhine. Arthur's earlier two years of National Service in the army and the two weeks each year for some years after that which he is required to spend at Territorial Army camps are the only times in his life that he ever leaves home.

That there might be another war is a recurring subject of speculation and leads to passages in the book that are completely at variance with the heroic terms in which the war is conventionally portrayed. Being tall, Arthur was drafted into the Royal Military Police, or Redcaps, but this in no way diminished his anarchic tendencies. He looks back with admiration on the exploits of his older cousins, who had deserted during the war rather than fight: 'Tall grinning army deserters caught time and again by Redcaps or police, but always escaping, on the run, in hiding, living with whores, thieving for food and money because they had neither ration-books nor employment cards. A shaky game … But they had been right, he knew that, because they were still here, alive, at work, earning a good living in spite of the army.' They had said why should they fight after the years of unemployment and hardship they had endured before the war. He is resentful because he is paid much less when on military service than in his factory. 'But let them start a war, he thought, and see what a bad soldier I can be.'

I have no idea how widespread such sentiments were. During the weeks of my National Service basic training in the Royal Armoured Corps I shared a hut and all my waking hours with some thirty men from different parts of the country with backgrounds like Arthur's and met many more. Yet I never heard anything remotely along these lines. Some rancour and resentment and plenty of homesickness, but nothing incendiary. During the Korean War and in the various colonial engagements with which the army was involved National Servicemen fought well.*

During the Second World War the desertion rate never reached even one 1 per cent a year, although, given the enormous size of the armed forces at that time, that still amounted to a significant number of men. By 1945 the total number of men on the run as deserters is estimated to have reached nearly a hundred thousand.† Some suffering from traumas of one kind or another wanted only to hide. Others became involved in crime, often violent, and the twenty thousand deserters estimated to be at large in London were a major source of trouble to the police.

In another respect too, *Saturday Night and Sunday Morning* differs from other records of the 1950s. It was published in the same year as the Notting Hill race riots in London and when, as described in a later chapter, racial discrimination was rife in the capital.‡ Yet a sergeant from the Gold Coast (now Ghana), whom one of Seaton's cousins had met in the army, is invited to spend Christmas with his family and

---

* See essay on *The Dead, the Dying and the Damned.*

† Figures taken from sources at the National Archives and reproduced in David French, 'Discipline and the Death Penalty in the British Army in the War Against Germany During the Second World War, *Journal of Contemporary History*, October 1998, Vol. 33, No. 4, p. 541.

‡ See essay on *The Lonely Londoners* by Sam Selvon and two novels by Colin MacInnes.

receives a warm welcome. This could perhaps be attributed to military solidarity, but the presence of an Indian man as a permanent lodger in Doreen's mother's house without anyone seeming to mind suggests that, so far as individuals at least were concerned, racial discrimination was still quiescent in the circles Sillitoe was writing about.

Both *Love on the Dole* and *Saturday Night and Sunday Morning* were first novels which, after being rejected by a number of publishers, achieved instant success and were later turned into films. Their authors went on to write a good many other books and, in Greenwood's case, plays and television scripts, without achieving anything like the same success. Sillitoe was acclaimed in the Soviet Union, which would have liked to use him for propaganda purposes as a voice of the British working class. Far from responding, he became a critic of Soviet human rights abuses and campaigned on behalf of political prisoners in the Communist bloc countries and individual Jews who were prevented from leaving for the West.

Room at the Top

by John Braine (1957)

This Sporting Life

by David Storey (1960)

John Braine's *Room at the Top*, published in 1957, and David Storey's *This Sporting Life*, published in 1960, have much in common with Alan Sillitoe's *Saturday Night and Sunday Morning* in the preceding essay. All are first novels by young men with no literary training or experience that enjoyed instant critical acclaim and commercial success that was further compounded by hugely popular films. Their heroes are working class and they are set in surroundings their authors knew well from personal experience. Taken together, and along with others of the same genre, they opened the eyes of many middle- and upper-class readers to an unfamiliar world with different values from those they were accustomed to read about. They are as readable today as when they first appeared, while the films they inspired remain landmarks of British film-making. They also throw light on the power structure in northern cities in the 1950s and, in the cases of *Saturday Night and Sunday Morning* and *Room at the Top*, on a surprising attitude towards the war.

They cover a wider canvas than *Saturday Night and Sunday Morning* because their heroes, Joe Lampton in *Room at the Top*, and Arthur Machin in *This Sporting Life*, break away from their social backgrounds, albeit only temporarily in the latter case, while Arthur Seaton in *Saturday Night and Sunday Morning* is content to remain in his. As a result, through their eyes and experience, we gain vivid and unvarnished glimpses into the power structure as well as the social life in northern industrial towns in the now forgotten era when their woollen mills and manufacturing industries were still large employers. This was before much of their economy had fallen under the control of multinational companies and large London-based combines; an era when the companies that ran those industries were largely locally based while the men who owned and controlled them lived in the big houses on the hills above the towns – the Top, or 'T'Top', as they say in Yorkshire – and dominated much of the life in the communities around them. The workers were at the bottom near the works and social prestige could be measured by where on the gradient one lived.

Before writing *Room at the Top* John Braine was a librarian at the Public Library in the Yorkshire textile and market town of Bingley. The novel begins in 1947 with Joe Lampton arriving in a town called Warley to take up a post at the Municipal Treasury and to lodge not far below 'T'Top' with a master at the local grammar school and his wife. The couple had lost their only son during the war and are pleased to have Joe, who, like their son, had been in the Royal Air Force, to fill the gap left in their lives. Joe is thrilled. Having come from a poor working-class background in a neighbouring city, Joe has never been in such a well-appointed house before and is determined to use his new professional and social position as a launch pad to rise still further. He describes his ambition to himself as being 'as clear and compelling as the sense of vocation which doctors and missionaries are supposed to experience, though in my instance, of course, the call ordered me to do good to myself not others'.

Joe's initial jump from the backstreets into the professional class had been brought about in circumstances that are hard to imagine today. It was the result of having been shot down while on a bombing raid over Germany and spending three years there as a prisoner of war. During that time, under the auspices of the International Red Cross, he was able to qualify as an accountant and to accumulate £800 in back pay, a modest capital that he would never otherwise have been able to acquire. Food was short in the camp and he remembers how hungry he had been, but he has no doubt that captivity had been his lucky break.

When he is upbraided for not having tried to escape, like Jack Wales, the son of one of the local grandees who had earned a gallantry medal, he responds in a powerful passage that is totally at variance with how the war and being a PoW are conventionally portrayed: 'It was all right for him to escape. He had a rich daddy to look after him and to buy him an education. He could afford to waste his time. I couldn't. Those three years were the only chance I'd get to be qualified. Let those rich bastards who have all the fun be heroes. Let them pay for their privileges. If you want it straight from the shoulder I'll tell you: I was bloody well pleased when I was captured. I wasn't going to be killed trying to escape and I wasn't going to be killed flying again.' Even by the standards of Arthur Seaton's admiration in *Saturday Night and Sunday Morning* for those of his relations who had deserted from the armed forces to engage in the black market, this is very far removed from how it is now thought people in the 1940s thought and spoke about the war.

Taking and passing exams while in captivity was not unusual. Anthony Barber, who served as Chancellor of the Exchequer in Ted Heath's government from 1970 to 1974, was among those who did so. Before the war he was an articled clerk in a provincial solicitor's office. While in captivity from 1942 to 1945 he achieved a first-class law degree from London University through the good offices of the International Red Cross. As a result, when finally liberated he was awarded a grant to go to Oxford from which he went on to become a barrister in the Inner Temple; a less transformational rise than Joe Lampton's, but still something he would have been unlikely to have achieved in peacetime. Unlike Joe, however, Barber combined his studies with attempts to escape* and helping others to do so, for which he was mentioned in dispatches, the next best thing to a gallantry medal.

The vehicle by means of which Joe pursues his ambition is again very much of its time. He joins the town's amateur dramatic society, an institution which in those pre-television days flourished in provincial towns and cities. In this respectable milieu, bound by its very nature to forge bonds between the participants, he is brought into contact with a wide range of people: fellow professionals in different walks of life and their wives, women in search of an interest outside the home and Susan Brown, the rather childish and innocent nineteen-year-old daughter of one the town's important industrialists and influential members of the town council, Councillor Brown.

She becomes his target. Marriage to her and with it a position in her father's firm will, in one bound, take him straight to the Top. He faces two great obstacles, one emotional the other practical. The emotional is that having embarked on a 'no commitments on either side' affair with Alice, one of the married women in the group, he falls in love with her and she with him. The practical is that Susan's parents want her to marry Wales and don't regard him as at all a suitable match. The terms in which they and Wales snub, patronize and belittle him on social occasions are illustrative of the social mores of the time. Joe's boss warns him that if he crosses Councillor Brown it could damage his career while, if he gets on the right side of the Councillor, it will be to his benefit; a warning that would deter most young council employees from

---

* One of the attempts in which he was involved inspired the film *The Wooden Horse*, according to the *Oxford Dictionary of National Biography* account of his life by Denis Kavanagh.

pursuing the Councillor's daughter. But Joe perseveres while continuing his affair with Alice until a denouement is reached when he all but rapes Susan, who then triumphantly tells him he won't need Alice any more.

Soon after, he is summoned by Councillor Brown to the local Conservative Club, portrayed as the luxurious inner sanctum of the rich and powerful, a far cry from the seedy decay of so many of the provincial Conservative clubs of today. Brown offers to set him up in business and to provide him with customers if he will leave Susan alone. When Joe refuses, Brown immediately changes tack, says he 'wanted to see what you were made of' and tells Joe that he and Susan should marry right away. It then emerges that Susan is pregnant and that she hadn't told Joe because she hadn't wanted him to marry her 'out of a sense of duty'.

As Brown makes clear, it is not the way in which he had hoped his daughter would marry, but he is easily reconciled to the fact. He recognizes that Joe is an able and ambitious young man who is worth backing anyway. He also recognizes something of himself in Joe as he too had come from nothing and furthered his own career by marrying into his wife's established county family. The one condition he imposes, not unreasonably, is that Joe should sever all connection with Alice.

At this point tragedy intervenes. While Joe is still revelling in his success, he hears that soon after he and Alice had had their acrimonious final meeting she had gone on a drunken binge, crashed her car into a wall and died a lingering death. Her best friend, whose flat he and Alice had borrowed for their love-making, accuses him of being responsible and tells him how much she had loved him. He knows that to be true, and himself goes on a drunken binge during the course of which he narrowly escapes being beaten up. When friends find him, he blames himself for murdering Alice and when they say she would have ruined his life and 'nobody blames you' their sympathy intensifies his remorse.

Big-hearted, impetuous, unable to understand the feelings of others, let alone manipulate them, and given to violence, Arthur Machin, the hero of *This Sporting Life* is the polar opposite of Joe Lampton. He is a professional rugby league player. Among the toughest of team sports, rugby league football, not to be confused with rugby union, is in this country a North of England sport. In the 1950s it was an integral part of working-class culture there and it remains a distinctive regional feature dividing north and south. David Storey had himself been a professional rugby league player, though a most unusual one, as he had combined playing for Leeds Rugby League Football Club with studying at the Slade School of Fine Art in London. It is hard to imagine a man straddling a wider cultural divide. His book is the only literary novel written by a professional player of any form of football and, as such, something of a literary curiosity.

The opening lines put the reader at the heart of the action: 'I had my head to Mellor's backside, waiting for the ball to come between his legs. He was too slow. I was moving away when the leather shot back into my hands and before I could pass, a shoulder came up to my jaw. It rammed my teeth together with a force that stunned me into blackness.' The trainer takes him off and tells him his front teeth are broken, despite which he returns to the pitch to finish the game.

Arthur is a valued player. As soon as the game is over Weaver, a local magnate, and one of the two men who control the club, whisks him off in his Bentley to the dentist and then, to add lustre, to his Christmas party at his house at the Top. Arthur still works as a lathe operator in Weaver's works, but as a football star he transcends class – for as long as he is on form and in favour. As he soon discovers, however, for Weaver and his partner-cum-rival, another big local industrialist called Slomer, the club is 'their mutual toy. They bought and sold players, built them up and dropped them, like a couple of kids with lead soldiers.'

Arthur's fate, like that of most other professional sportsmen at that time, was always to remain one of the lead soldiers. Without the education or ability to use his temporary fame and earning power to create a long-term career for when his playing days come to an end, his only assets are his youth, skill and strength. In the pre-television age rugby league was too local a sport and the wages and celebrity status of its stars too circumscribed for a player to earn the sort of money that could transform his life.

Even football stars with a national and international reputation were infinitely less well off than they are today as their wage rates were capped in the interests of the clubs that employed them. One of the greatest players of the 1950s was Tom Finney, still regarded by some as the most complete footballer ever to have played for England, who was knighted in 1998, thirty-eight years after his retirement. In 1952 he was earning £12 a week and in 1960 £20 – the equivalent to about £340 and £450 in today's money. He had been apprenticed as a plumber before becoming a professional footballer and after his retirement ran his own plumbing and heating firm in his home town of Preston.

This was exceptional. The lucky ones might take over a pub, a possibility Arthur discusses with one of his team-mates. Others, for the most part, reverted to being wage earners of one sort or another. The question at the heart of *This Sporting Life* is whether, in the circumstances of its time and place, the temporarily glamorous life it describes was worth the pain and the price involved.

The parabola of Arthur's career is traced through episodes on and off the field. At the outset there is an excruciating act of violence when an older player on his own side, jealous of his talent, sets out to starve him of the ball. Arthur awaits his chance. Then, while they are both heads down in the scrum and the referee can't see, 'I swung my right fist into the middle of his face. He cried out loud. I hit him again and saw the red pulp of his nose and lips as my hand came away.' The referee blames a player in the opposing team and the man leaves the field with a broken nose. Thereafter Arthur plays a blinder and, though they have a fair idea of what happened, the club officials sign him up as a professional.

When he is established in the first team and so fit that he can come off the field 'fresher than when I went on', he recalls an incident when he scores a try. 'I went straight for the full-back, and when he came in I gave him the base of my wrist on his nose. The crack, the groan, the release of his arms, all coincided with a soaring of my guts. I moved in between the posts keeping my eye on the delight of the crowd as I put the ball down.' Towards the end of his career the roles are reversed. He is trying to prevent an opponent scoring, misses his man, falls and, as the crowd roars 'its pain like a maimed animal', is left to 'stare unbelievingly at my legs, which had betrayed me'. In the dressing room afterwards, Arthur watches the new young star being ceremoniously doused under the cold water tap to celebrate his success while his own ankles are being strapped and he is putting his false teeth in. He knows his glory days are over and that he has nothing to fall back on.

In the town, which is too small to be Leeds and may be based on Storey's home town of Wakefield, Arthur in his prime is a celebrity. He is recognized wherever he goes, welcome in the clubs and restaurants frequented by the local elite and, with Weaver's help, able to buy his car and a television at a discount. It gives him self-confidence and a swagger but cuts him off from his parents and creates a barrier between him and the woman he falls in love with, a young widow in whose house he lodges. He gives her a fur coat and a television and takes her and her children for trips in his Jaguar to expensive restaurants. She sleeps with him but worries about becoming overwhelmed and a mere appendage. When she tries to explain her doubts about committing to him, 'I couldn't think why she should say all this, and the shortest way of stopping it was to hit her. I cracked her hard across the face, and I wanted to apologize when I saw the mark.' What works on the football field doesn't with her. She throws him out of her house. Later, when she contracts a fatal illness, he pays for her to have private treatment but her death leaves him again with nothing.

A tantalizing aspect of the rivalry between Weaver and Slomer, and of the attitude of others towards them that Storey touches on but fails to elaborate upon, is the position of Catholics in the town. At an early stage in their relationship Arthur mentions to the widow that Slomer has a lot of money. 'And you're satisfied with that sort of money? He's a Catholic,' she replies, as if the mere fact of his religion makes his money disreputable. Arthur wonders, 'how far that should affect me … a Catholic more or less represented a foreign agent. They might be on your side. On the other hand they might not. It was better to treat them all as enemies, then you could be sure.' Later Slomer asks Arthur if he has ever thought of becoming a Catholic: 'It's got a lot of advantages for a young man like you. It has organization for one thing,' he explains. Arthur doesn't pursue the matter and there is no further reference to it. In Scotland the sectarian divide was deeply embedded and expressed through football* until well into this century; to a lesser extent, that was true of Liverpool as well. But that Storey, drawing on his own experience, should represent it as influencing power struggles within a Yorkshire rugby league club and social attitudes within the local community during the 1950s is surprising.

After achieving great success with their first novels the careers of John Braine and David Storey went in opposite directions. Braine, who died in 1986, never repeated his initial triumph. By contrast, Storey, who died aged eighty-three in 2017, went on to write many successful novels and to become a distinguished playwright and screenwriter as well. In his later years he returned to painting and drawing and an exhibition of more than four hundred of his works was held in Wakefield a year before his death.

---

* Catholic Celtic vs Protestant Rangers in Glasgow and, less well known, Protestant Heart of Midlothian vs Catholic Hibernian in Edinburgh.

Early Feminism

Suffragette Sally by Gertrude Colmore, 1911,
Testament of Youth by Vera Brittain, 1933,
and *A Life's Work* by Margaret Bondfield, 1948.

A Room of One's Own by Virginia Woolf, 1929,
and *Three Guineas* by Virginia Woolf, 1938.

The Golden Notebook by Doris Lessing, 1962.

Suffragette Sally

by Gertrude Colmore* (1911)

Testament of Youth

by Vera Brittain (1933)

A Life's Work

by Margaret Bondfield (1948)

History is written by the victors, or so the saying goes.† Of no subject is this more true than the battles fought on many fronts, political, in the workplace and in the home, for women's rights and aspirations in the early years of the twentieth century. It is the suffragettes' campaign for the right to vote in parliamentary elections that dominates the national memory. It is their exploits – the violence they perpetrated and the suffering they endured – in the years immediately before the First World War that have been recorded and dramatized in countless

* A nom de plume. Her real name was Gertrude Baillie-Weaver.

† It is attributed to different authors, including Winston Churchill, but I have not been able to discover who used it first or when.

books, documentaries and films. It is the statue of their leader, Emmeline Pankhurst, that has stood in Victoria Tower Gardens beside the Houses of Parliament since 1930. In his great classic on pre-1914 politics, *The Strange Death of Liberal England*, George Dangerfield writes that Mrs Pankhurst and her followers must be 'enrolled among the makers of history'.*

Millicent Fawcett, the doyenne of campaigners for women's suffrage, who abhorred the violence of the suffragettes, which she regarded as damaging rather than helpful to bringing about reform, was, until the installation of her statue in London's Parliament Square in 2018, a largely forgotten figure. Yet her life had been devoted to campaigning for women's suffrage since 1865, when, as a young woman, she had helped to gather signatures for the petition that in 1866 first put the issue onto the political agenda. In 1913 the National Union of Women's Suffrage Societies (NUWSS), which she led and which sought to bring about change by constitutional methods, enormously outnumbered the Women's Social and Political Union (WSPU), the official name for the suffragettes. Figures vary, but some estimates give the former up to one hundred thousand members compared with two thousand for the latter.

Still forgotten, and in many ways still more remarkable, is Margaret Bondfield, who in 1929 became the first woman Cabinet minister. While Emmeline Pankhurst and Millicent Fawcett were securely anchored in the prosperous middle class, she was a working-class woman with little education and nothing but her wits and her energy to support her. When she began work as a shop assistant in 1887 shop assistants were among the most exploited of working women. Her campaigns, initially on their behalf, and, later, on behalf of women in other industries,

* George Dangerfield, *The Strange Death of Liberal England*, Harrison Smith and Robert Haas, 1935, p. 147. This was in New York where it quickly went out of print. It only achieved fame when republished in the United Kingdom in the following year, since when many other editions have been issued.

helped to pioneer effective trade union action on behalf of women; action which brought about tangible improvements in their lives and working conditions long before the vote, and the political clout that went with it, was achieved.

The significance of these battles in the political and industrial arenas during the late nineteenth and early twentieth centuries can now be appreciated. At the time they were far removed from the concerns of women trying to break free from their traditional role within their own families. Among the most outstanding twentieth-century autobiographies, and one of the finest chronicles of the First World War, is Vera Brittain's *Testament of Youth*. Published in 1933, it became an instant bestseller and is still widely read today. Between the wars she was an inveterate campaigner for the League of Nations and other anti-war causes. Yet in her account of her early years before 1914 she barely mentions the political debate about whether women should have the vote and the activities of women trade unionists completely passed her by. Her ambitions were solely directed at persuading her parents to allow her to go to Oxford, an extremely unusual aspiration for a young woman from a prosperous provincial background at that time, and to passing the exams required to get there.

Vera Brittain was born in 1893. By the turn of the century it was no longer unusual for girls from well-to-do families to attend school though many were still being educated at home. During the previous thirty years or so a tiny minority had gone on to university. A few had even become academics and doctors; Britain's first woman doctor was Fawcett's sister, Elizabeth Garrett Anderson. Most professions, however, other than school teaching and nursing, which did not require university degrees or similar qualifications, were still closed to women. In the prosperous classes parents neither wanted nor expected their daughters to earn their own living and saw no need for them to acquire qualifications; rather the reverse. It was widely believed that if a woman was too well educated it would harm her marriage prospects and distract her from the domestic duties that were held to be her true vocation.*

Vera Brittain's family were typical in not taking her education seriously and in wanting her to grow up 'as an ornamental young lady'. While her father regarded it as axiomatic that her younger and less intellectual brother should go to university, he was adamantly opposed to his daughter doing so. He was happy to buy her a grand piano and to spend money on music lessons but begrudged every penny that went on her tuition. Her school friends regarded her ambition with incomprehension while the women in her parents' social set in the Derbyshire town of Buxton considered it to be 'ridiculous' and described her in the contemptuous term of the time as a 'bluestocking'. To overcome such a battery of conventions and prejudices required courage and determination. Her measured account of how she gained her parents' acquiescence, found out what exams she had to take and worked to pass them explains why so few tried and the nature of the constraints on a young woman in even a loving and prosperous home.

Tragically, no sooner had she reached her promised land than war broke out. The authorities at Somerville College, Oxford, exhorted their undergraduates to continue with their studies and not allow the war to distract them. Most did so. Brittain again defied convention by volunteering to become a nurse and only returning to Oxford when peace was restored. By then her fiancé, her brother and her two other closest men friends had all been killed.

As I write, more than half the young people going to university in this country are women. The days when they had to overcome a wall of parental prejudice and other obstacles to get there seem like a distant memory. In fact, they continued until well into the 1960s. Some of the most intelligent and intellectually active women that I know in my own

---

* See later essay on *A Room of One's Own* by Virginia Woolf for more on this subject.

generation were not allowed to go to university by their parents in the belief that it wasn't the right thing for a girl to do. Finishing schools and secretarial colleges were deemed to be more appropriate. Fathers, like Margaret Thatcher's, who, in the 1940s, determined that she should go to Oxford, remained very much the exception until well into the 1970s, shortly before Mrs Thatcher herself became Prime Minister.

Suffragette Sally, published in 1911, is a very different sort of book. Its aim was to propagandize on behalf of the suffragette movement and to encourage recruits to join its ranks. Though a novel, it is hard to separate fact from fiction. The demonstrations and confrontations between the suffragettes and the police that it describes are taken from life, as are the horrific experiences of those women who were sent to prison and suffered in other ways. The women described as the movement's leaders in the book, are clearly Mrs Emmeline Pankhurst and her allies lightly disguised. Of the three main characters, the aristocratic Lady Henry Hill is derived from Lady Constance Bulwer-Lytton while the working-class Sally Simmonds and the upper-middle-class Edith Carstairs are composite figures drawn from the author's experience.

As a piece of propaganda *Suffragette Sally* scores highly, portraying the suffragettes as a dedicated group drawn from every social class battling on behalf of all women and open to women of all classes. Class distinctions are dealt with very subtly. Far from being eliminated they provide inspiration and reassurance. Sally herself, a former maid of all work, is inspired to find herself working for the same cause as, and coming into personal contact with, Lady Henry while Lady Henry's charm and position give Edith Carstairs the courage to oppose her family's wishes and even to stifle the mockery of her brother.

One of the book's most trenchant messages was that, whatever her class, a suffragette would often find that the most intense opposition she had to face would be from her own relations and social circle. When Edith Carstairs, after finally overcoming her doubts, participates in a demonstration, she is arrested. Her mother is horrified and deeply hurt. Her clergyman uncle and aunt forbid her to enter their house because she has brought disgrace on the family. This reaction reflected the way many respectable people reacted to the suffragettes' methods. The great majority of women, whether in favour of the vote or not, disapproved of and were indeed often shocked by their methods, which was why the other women's groups campaigning for the vote, known as suffragists, thought the suffragettes' tactics were counter-productive. The ridicule, insults and social ostracism to which Edith Carstairs and Sally were subjected varied in tone but not in intensity from one class to another.

The book conveys in graphic detail both the nature of the suffragettes' protests and the punishments they received. The former ranged from demonstrations and marches in the streets, disrupting political meetings and harassing individual politicians to stone-throwing, breaking windows, vandalizing golf courses and setting fire to empty buildings. The usual punishment was a short prison sentence. To protest against being imprisoned for, as they saw it, demanding the right to vote rather than for a crime, a number of those who were arrested went on hunger strike. This led to a form of forced feeding that amounted to torture.

The authorities were, however, determined that no embarrassing accident should befall women from the upper classes. As a result, while 'common' or 'working women' were subjected to this harrowing experience as a matter of course, 'ladies' were often given a medical examination on the basis of which they would be discharged. In an incident based on the real-life experience of Lady Constance, Lady Henry exposes this injustice by getting herself arrested under a pseudonym and then publicizing her experiences after her release from prison, which helps to bring about a change of policy. Lady Henry recovers from her ordeal, but Lady Constance's health was broken, as happened to many others. Sally herself dies after a prolonged illness caused by being kicked in the stomach by a policeman during a demonstration.

A point that does not emerge from *Suffragette Sally* is the precise nature of the franchise for which the WSPU was campaigning. In fact, it was not arguing for the vote for all women and Sally herself would have been excluded from the franchise its members were campaigning for. At that time, the vote was not only restricted to men; there was a property qualification as well that excluded a significant proportion of working-class men. What the WSPU wanted was votes for women on the same basis as men. They were not arguing for a universal adult suffrage.

This brought them up against the redoubtable Margaret Bondfield, who chaired the Adult Suffrage Society. Her view, as explained in her autobiography, *A Life's Work*, was that if only well-to-do women won the right to vote, it would tip the political scales still further against the workers by strengthening the power of the rich and powerful. 'I have never been able to approach the question [of women's suffrage] from the standpoint of women's rights,' she wrote. What she wanted was for all men and women above the age of twenty-one to be given the vote.

She was one of the most remarkable women of her age and it is surprising to me that she is not more honoured in the feminist pantheon. Born in 1873, one of eleven children of a Somerset lace-maker and his wife, she left school and started work as a shop assistant at fourteen. In 1929, after a lifetime campaigning on behalf of the poorest and most disadvantaged women, she became the first ever woman Cabinet minister. Her autobiography, published in 1948, is badly constructed and difficult to read, but is nonetheless an important historical record of how much effective campaigning and political activity some women were engaged in, long before getting the vote.

Her first campaign was on behalf of shop assistants like herself, who were subjected to the rigours of the 'the living in' system whereby unmarried staff were obliged to live in single-sex dormitories owned and run by the employers. Their wages were reduced accordingly to cover the cost. The food and hygiene were notoriously bad and, as she describes in her book, the overcrowding was dreadful. The practice enabled the employers to control every aspect of their employees' lives. When she was living in, she worked 'for about sixty-four hours a week for which she was paid between £15 and £25 per annum' (£2,000 and £3,200 in today's money), which could at any time be arbitrarily reduced if she broke any one of the numerous rules for which her employer could impose a fine. She gives examples of these gleaned from a number of different firms in London and elsewhere – being late for work or for meals, not serving a customer quickly enough, addressing a customer as Miss when it should have been Madam, not using paper or string with economy, sleeping out without permission and using candles when the bedroom gas is turned off.

Instead of knuckling down under what she regarded as 'humiliating and degrading' conditions, she joined a trade union,* which brought her into contact with women who told her about working practices in other firms. Under the pseudonym Grace Dare she began writing short stories for the union journal, *Shop Assistant*, about the conditions under which its members worked. She did this at night by candlelight behind a towel while her room-mates were asleep and relied on them not to give her away. Had she been discovered she would have been summarily dismissed.

As it was, she went on to be recruited by the privately funded Women's Industrial Council, which carried out covert investigations into women's working conditions, the results of which were published in a national newspaper as part of a campaign to change the law. In 1901 this led to her giving evidence before a select committee of the House of Lords, an early step on the road to becoming a public figure.

* The National Union of Shop Assistants, Warehousemen and Clerks (NUSAWC).

Thereafter, the campaign with which she had been associated began to bear fruit. In 1904 the Shop Hours Act limited shop-opening hours while in 1907 the first steps were taken to end the practice of 'living in'.

Her career thereafter shows how politically active and effective it was possible for an exceptional and determined woman to be, even without the right to vote. She became a professional campaigner as organizing secretary of the Women's Labour League and a member of the Women's Co-operative Guild, which exposed her to what was happening across the industrial landscape. In 1910 when she enquired into conditions in the woollen textile industry in Yorkshire she was shocked by the incidence of incest in the overcrowded slums where the workers and their families lived. Among the examples she quotes: 'One family [that] consisted of a mother with two girls, a boy of nineteen and a boy of twelve, all lying in the same bed. Both girls had children to brothers.' She had long campaigned for a minimum wage and for equal pay for women. This experience led her to widen her agenda to include demands for maternity and child benefit and measures to reduce child mortality.

She also became involved with the international aspects of the Labour movement. In 1910, she visited the United States to tell women's organizations there about the work of the Women's Labour League. In 1915, she went as a member of the Women's Peace Council to a conference in Switzerland organized by the Women's International of Socialist and Labour Organizations to call for a negotiated peace to end the war.

In 1923, she became the first woman to chair the Trades Union Congress (TUC) and one of the first three Labour women to be elected to Parliament. In 1924, she joined the short-lived first Labour government as a junior minister and five years later, after the 1929 election, became a Cabinet minister in the second Labour government. Her political career came to an end when that government fell in 1931, after which she continued to be active in the trade union movement until 1938. Despite all her achievements, when she sets out a list of her siblings and their careers in her book she describes herself simply as 'Spinster. The writer of this book.'

The principle of votes for women was decided by the First World War. Their contribution to the war effort made it impossible to deny their claim any longer, but it was granted only partially and grudgingly. The Representation of the People Act of 1918 extended the right to vote in parliamentary elections to all men aged twenty-one and over, whether or not they owned property, while women had to be aged thirty and to meet a residual property qualification. Only in local elections were both sexes allowed to vote on equal terms at age twenty-one without a property qualification. In 1928 this arrangement was extended to parliamentary elections and women finally achieved the same rights to vote as men.* Margaret Bondfield rejoiced in these victories, but other battles, including equal pay, were still far from won when she died in 1953.†

---

* The qualifying age has since been lowered to eighteen.

† I possess a souvenir of her life in the form of a copy of John Maynard Keynes' book, *The Economic Consequences of the Peace* (see later essay), with her ownership inscription on the flyleaf.

A Room of One's Own

by Virginia Woolf (1929)

Three Guineas

by Virginia Woolf (1938)

Who's Afraid of Virginia Woolf is the title of a well-known play by the American Edward Albee first performed in 1962. It's about the complexities of a marriage and has nothing to do with Virginia Woolf herself, but the words of the title convey her daunting reputation and the way people tend to think of her. Her name has come to personify the most rarefied intellectualism and sensitive aestheticism. Her ethereal face with its large, expressive eyes provides their physical manifestation.

Her fame derives both from her books and from the circle in which she moved. Her most famous stream-of-consciousness novels, *Mrs Dalloway*, *To the Lighthouse* and *The Waves*, which deal more with what's happening in their characters' minds than with what they are doing or what is happening around them, are among the key books of the modernist movement. Like the works of James Joyce and Marcel Proust, all serious readers feel they ought to have tackled them and tend to be apologetic about admitting it when they haven't or gave up the attempt.

A Room of One's Own and *Three Guineas* pose no such problems. They are extended essays and easy to read. Together they provide the foundation on which her reputation as one of the century's pioneering feminist (a word she hated) thinkers and writers is built. Hermione Lee, the Goldsmiths' Professor of English Literature at Oxford and biographer of Woolf, describes *A Room of One's Own* as 'probably the most influential feminist essay of the twentieth century'.[1] *Three Guineas* is less famous, but marks a point at which women, having achieved the vote and enhanced educational opportunities, began to turn their attention to breaking down the barriers against them in the professions.

As described in the essay on Lytton Strachey and *Eminent Victorians*, Virginia Woolf with her sister, the artist Vanessa Bell, formed the hub around which the famous Bloomsbury Group of writers, artists and intellectuals gathered before, during and after the First World War. Besides Strachey and such well-known individuals as the great economist John Maynard Keynes and the artists Duncan Grant and Roger Fry, it included her husband, Leonard Woolf.

He was crucial to her success as a writer. Throughout her adult life she was prone to mental instability and breakdowns, which some believe may have been exacerbated by abuse she suffered as a child at the hands of her half-brothers, George and Gerald Duckworth. When she was afflicted Leonard sustained her; when depression threatened he helped her to deal with it. He also founded the Hogarth Press, a private venture which published many of her books as well as those of other leading writers of the period. Given her delicate mental balance and the stress bringing a book to publication always caused her, it must be doubted whether she would have been able to produce the body of work that she did if her husband and his press had not been there to ease the strain. Despite his care and help, life eventually became too much for her to bear. In 1941, at the age of fifty-nine, with worries about the war adding to her mental distress, she gave up the struggle and drowned herself in a river that ran by their country cottage at Rodmell in Sussex.

The Woolfs and their friends were people of independent means, not rich and certainly not lavish spenders, but ultimately not dependent on what they earned for how they lived. Virginia Woolf's advocacy of women's rights kept within the comfort zone of her social class. She did not write on behalf of the great mass of women at that time working in factories, shops and domestic service or struggling to feed numerous children on a working man's wages, or less if their husbands were unemployed; the women for whom Margaret Bondfield campaigned. Her focus wasn't on the gap between rich and poor or the problems of the poor. It was on the injustices perpetrated throughout history on the women she describes in *Three Guineas* as 'the daughters of educated men'; in other words, women whose families employed servants.

Within that class, she argued, the single most important reason why women had always been disadvantaged and demeaned by men was their lack of financial independence and the means to acquire it. Not until the Married Women's Property Act was passed in 1882, the year Woolf was born, did married women become entitled to own and control property in their own right. Until then their fathers, before they married, and then their husbands had always controlled the purse strings so that, ultimately, they had to do as they were told. Fathers could prevent their daughters from marrying or, if they insisted, determine who they should marry. Husbands could dictate the way and the values by which they should live. Access to books and the right to write and to express independent views were at the discretion of fathers and husbands. The 1882 Act changed the legal status of married women, but old attitudes persisted well into Woolf's adulthood and beyond while in many families daughters remained as much under parental control as ever they had.

Her indignation and rage against the constricting effect that lack of independence had on women's lives suffuses both books. In a famous passage in *A Room of One's Own* she illustrates the point by imagining the disapproval, frustrations and blighted hopes culminating in suicide that might have faced a fictional sister of Shakespeare, if she had had the same talents and aspirations as him. Prefiguring and demonstrating the need for what are now known as Women's Studies, she writes about what little was known of the lives of a few seventeenth- and early eighteenth-century women writers and of the social significance of the emergence, towards the end of the eighteenth century, of middle-class women writing for money; a development, she argues, that deserves more attention in the history books than the Crusades or the Wars of the Roses.

Two of the best and most famous of the nineteenth-century writers were Jane Austen and Charlotte Brontë. But their success did not enable them to break free from the conventions of their time. Far from it. As an unmarried woman living with her family, Jane Austen had to write her books in the general sitting room. Whenever she heard someone approach she would hide her manuscript under a piece of blotting paper as she would have been embarrassed if servants or visitors or anyone beyond her immediate family should have known what she was doing. Charlotte Brontë's problem was of a different kind. Her father simply forbad her for some years to marry the man she loved and she had to acquiesce.

A Room of One's Own is based on two papers delivered in 1928 to societies at Newnham and Girton, at that time the only two women's colleges at Cambridge and thus the only ones where women could study at that university. It is concerned with creating the conditions that would enable women to attempt to write fiction, whether prose or poetry. To do so, Woolf argues, 'a woman must have money and a room of her own'. By money she means £500 a year, which equates to about

£31,000 a year in today's money. Her own earnings only attained that level in 1926, the year after the publication of *Mrs Dalloway* and eleven years after the publication of her first novel in 1915. Thereafter they increased substantially.

Besides money and a room, she believed that, in order to write, a woman also had to have had an education. Hence her anger, expressed forcibly in both these books, at the way middle- and upper-class families had always spent large sums educating their sons and virtually nothing on their daughters. Girls' schools were still quite a new phenomenon when she was a child and, like many of her contemporaries, she was kept at home where her father, Sir Leslie Stephen, the founding editor of the *Dictionary of National Biography*, took charge of her education and gave her the run of his library until, at the age of fifteen, she attended a few Greek classes under the auspices of King's College London. Hermione Lee argues that 'she would not have been the writer she was, with the subjects she chose, if she had had a formal education'.[2] That must be true, but, as Woolf knew, most girls, whether at school or at home, received much less of an education than their brothers and were correspondingly intellectually handicapped in adulthood.

Woolf illustrates the continuing inequality between men and educated women in her own time by recording a visit to 'Oxbridge' where she has lunch in one of the old colleges that only men could attend. She describes the beauty of the buildings, the perfection of the grounds, the lavishness of her meal and how she is turned away from the library as women could only enter 'if accompanied by a Fellow of the College or furnished with a letter of introduction'. This leads her to speculate about 'the unending stream of gold and silver' in the form of endowments, bequests, gifts and tithes that these colleges had received from rich and powerful men over the centuries on the basis of which 'Oxbridge' has been able to establish chairs, lectureships and fellowships and to stock its libraries and equip its laboratories and observatories.

She ends her day at a women's college where the gardens are bedraggled, the building undistinguished, the dinner plain and resources limited. The first women's colleges were established at Oxford and Cambridge between 1869 and 1875, but women remained second-class citizens for long after that. At Oxford they were only allowed to participate in degree ceremonies in 1920 and at Cambridge not until 1947. Because women in previous generations had not been able to amass fortunes there were no potential female benefactors to call on and Woolf didn't expect men to fill the breach.

The purpose of the essay is, however, more far-reaching than to inveigh against past and continuing inequalities. It is to argue that because all but a tiny fraction of the books that formed the intellectual and cultural basis of the society in which she and her readers lived had been written by men, that society reflected male values, attitudes and assumptions. It not only gave men power over women, it also accorded particular prestige to military prowess, the pursuit of power and the accumulation of large fortunes. If women had been equal rather than subservient, they would have countered these values and cut men down to size. Instead, their subservience led them to nurture and encourage male vanities and ambitions like 'looking glasses possessing the magic and delicious power of reflecting the figure of the man at twice its natural size'. It was because so many women had been brought up to believe that their role in life was essentially to support their menfolk that they often opposed, or at least did not support, reforms aimed at achieving equality between the sexes.

Three Guineas is couched in the form of a response to an 'educated man' who has written a letter to Woolf asking her to support his efforts to prevent a war. She does so by considering, in the light of his letter, which of three organizations that have asked her for money should receive her guinea – an anti-war society, a women's college building fund or a society promoting the employment of professional women.

The essay is diffuse and repetitious and its tone is harsher than *A Room of One's Own*, perhaps because she was mourning the death of her nephew, Julian Bell, in the Spanish Civil War while she was writing it. The absolutism of her pacifism makes no allowance for the seriousness of the Nazi threat facing Britain, which offended a number of her friends, including Keynes, while Leonard thought it her worst book. However, in the opinion of the literary biographer Lyndall Gordon, 'her attack on war as a pastime of men in power'* has in the long run been helpful to her reputation rather than the reverse.

In the essay she makes fun of the way men in power dress up in colourful uniforms and ceremonial robes of office, a particular foible of the British though not confined to them. She suggests that this feeds their sense of self-importance and exclusivity and thus their reluctance to allow women an equal share of life's prizes. Most professions had been obliged to admit women under the Sex Disqualification (Removal) Act of 1919, but as she shows the pace of their advance up the professional ladder had been painfully slow. A few professions even managed to remain closed to women until after her death. The Foreign Office did not accept women until 1946 and, until 1973, obliged them to resign on getting married, while the Jockey Club refused to grant licences to women to train racehorses until a court case in 1966.

Woolf holds up the Church of England as an example of how men could decide among themselves on the basis, in her view, of prejudice and tradition to keep women out. In 1935 it set up a commission to look into the question of women priests. It concluded, she writes, that while there was no inherent reason why women should not be ordained, 'we believe that the general mind of the Church is still in accord with the continuous tradition of a male priesthood'. Not until 1994 were the first women priests ordained.

---

* *Oxford Dictionary of National Biography* entry.

In other fields the whim of an employer could decide whether or not women should even be hired. As late as the 1950s the editor of the *Financial Times*, in other respects a most enlightened man, was reluctant to give women editorial jobs. I joined the paper in 1960 and well remember the stir it caused when this policy began to be relaxed and women to take their place among us.

That these barriers took so long to come down is evidence of how far ahead of her time Woolf was in assaulting them. She was equally, if not more, advanced in challenging the widespread practice of paying women less than men in the same position or doing the same work, a practice often justified on the grounds that a man had a family to support. In response she argued that as tax was levied at the same rate for women as for men they should be paid at the same rate and that in any case unmarried men always received the same salary as those who were married. As in *A Room of One's Own*, she bases her case both on fairness and on the need for women to have the means to escape from the control of their fathers and husbands so as to be able to lead lives of their own.

Looking back from the twenty-first century it is surprising for how long after Woolf's death educated women continued to put up with inequalities at work. The late Diana Athill, a famously successful editor from the 1940s to the 1980s at the André Deutsch publishing house, provides a partial explanation in her memoirs: 'Obviously it is true that indifference to status and pay is not found in all women, but I have seen it in a good many, who, like me, enjoyed their work. All my colleagues in the sixties and seventies admired and sympathized with women who were actively campaigning for women's rights, but none of them joined in as campaigners: we could see the injustice, but we didn't feel the pinch because we happened to be doing what we wanted to do.'[3] It was only when the majority of women ceased at a subconscious level to regard being able to work at what they liked doing as a privilege and started to think of themselves as having the same basic rights to fulfilling careers as men that equality began to come within reach.

Virginia Woolf believed that women had a mission to change and improve society through their writing and by becoming more active in the professions. To do that she wanted them to think of themselves as outsiders and not to adopt existing practices, values and assumptions. In accordance with this principle she refused all honours: to give the prestigious Clark Lectures at Cambridge that her father had once given, appointment as a Companion of Honour and honorary degrees from the universities of Manchester and Liverpool. 'It is an utterly corrupt society,' she wrote in her diary on 25 March 1933, '& I will take nothing that it can give me.'[4] In these two essays, as well as in other writings, she sought to bring about far-reaching change. With women's suffrage and access to the professions achieved, she played an important role in opening up the new front of equal opportunity, albeit that she was concerned only with the interests of 'the daughters of educated men' and not with women from other social classes.

The Golden Notebook

by Doris Lessing (1962)

Doris Lessing's novel *The Golden Notebook*, published in 1962, is one of the most celebrated books of the mid-twentieth century and widely regarded as a feminist bible. In his 1979 anthology, *Ninety-Nine Novels: The Best in English Since 1939*, the author and critic Anthony Burgess described it as 'the most massive statement made up to that time on the position of women in the modern world'.[5] In 2007, when the Swedish Academy awarded Lessing the Nobel Prize for Literature, its citation declared that *The Golden Notebook* 'belongs to the handful of books that informed the 20th century view of the male-female relationship'.[6] In January 2017, shortly before leaving the White House, Barack Obama, in an interview with the *New York Times*, said that it was one of the books he had put on the Kindle he had recently given his daughter Malia.[7]

There can be few books less suitable for reading on a Kindle than *The Golden Notebook*. Not only is it extremely long – five hundred and sixty-seven pages in the original edition – it has a complex and unusual structure that requires frequent cross-checking. As Lessing explains in the preface to the 1972 edition: 'There is a skeleton, or frame, called *Free Women*, which is a conventional short novel, about 60,000 words long, and which could stand by itself. But it is divided into five sections and separated by stages of the four Notebooks, black, red, yellow and blue', that are kept by Anna Wulf, the central character in *Free Women*.[8] After having written one successful novel, Anna is suffering from writer's block. The notebooks with their different coloured covers are a device by means of which she hopes to overcome it. In the black she writes about her life as a writer and in the red about politics. In the yellow she makes up stories derived from her own experiences while the blue is a sort of diary. From out of their fragments comes the new and original golden notebook, which constitutes the catharsis that enables her to come to terms with her life, to give up writing and to become an untrained marriage guidance counsellor.

The result is an enormous canvas, a profusion of characters and several different yet overlapping texts and stories. If Lessing did not write so clearly and so well, the novel would be unreadable. Unless Malia Obama is extremely adept at jumping back and forth on her Kindle, she must at times have found it difficult to keep a handle on the different characters and where they fit into the overall framework. Directly and indirectly *The Golden Notebook* deals not just with the role and aspirations of women, for which it is famous, but also with the end of the Communist dream, life in colonial Africa during the war years and the ideas and attitudes of left-wing intellectuals in London in the 1950s. On all these matters it holds up a mirror to the age in which it was written that is of enduring interest.

Lessing set out to write a classic, but not the one *The Golden Notebook* has become. In her preface to the 1972 edition,[9] she writes that she wanted to describe the intellectual and moral climate of her time as, in the nineteenth century, Tolstoy had done for Russia with *Anna Karenina* and Stendhal for France with *The Red and the Black*. When she embarked on her project in the late 1950s the position and aspirations of women were not in the forefront of her mind. Her main concern was with the disillusionment and emotional crisis through which she and many of her friends and associates were passing owing to the collapse of the moral authority of Communism and, with it, of Soviet Russia, following the exposure of Stalin's crimes by his successor, Nikita Khrushchev. Great tracts of the novel are devoted to their agonizing.

She describes her feelings at the time that she was writing it in her autobiography: 'All around me, people's hearts were breaking, they were having breakdowns, they were suffering religious conversions or – very common, this – formerly hard-line communists were discovering a talent for business and making money, because an obsession with the processes of capitalism was the best of preparations for a career in commerce. The point was, I was seeing people who had put all their eggs in one basket come to grief. What had been shut out of their thinking was rushing in, sometimes in the form of madness.'[10]

The crisis in Lessing's political life coincided with one in her emotional life. In her autobiography she writes that she had 'been dragged to her emotional limits'[11] by two men and was also affected by the growing up of her third and last child. In her own mind at that time breakdown and the self-healing to which it can lead, as exemplified by the golden notebook, was a central theme of the book.

The Golden Notebook was badly received. In the 1972 preface, ten years later, she gives vent to her resentment that 'nobody so much as noticed this central theme'. She also complains that the book was 'belittled' for being about the sex war and that she was accused of being 'unfeminine' and a 'man-hater'.[12] In her autobiography she recalls that 'Women at first certainly did not rush in to approve the book. On the contrary some distanced themselves from it, including personal friends.'[13]

A contributory factor was the frankness with which she wrote about sex – philosophizing on the nature of vaginal and clitoral orgasms, describing the wetness between Anna's thighs when attracted to a man, her analyses of the performance – usually the incompetence – of the various men with whom Anna and other characters go to bed, the casual way in which they decide to do so and the distinction between giving and receiving pleasure. These matters are now commonplace in women's magazines and advice columns as well as in novels. In 1962, only two years after the court case that resulted in *Lady Chatterley's Lover* being cleared for publication in this country, they were still dynamite. Inevitably they distracted attention from other aspects of the book, as I remember well from the way it was discussed at the time.

Another of the book's problems was the absence of general interest in what Lessing regarded as the great historic event of the end of the Communist dream. The trauma afflicting her and her Communist and ex-Communist friends who, as she puts it in her autobiography,[14] had been dreaming of a golden age, which they had thought had been almost within reach, left most readers and critics cold. Her contemporary, the editor and memoirist Diana Athill, spoke for many when, asked by the *Guardian* in 2012, on the 50th anniversary of its publication, what *The Golden Notebook* had meant to her when she first read it. 'I soon became impatient,' she replied, 'with a book full of minute analysis of the dismay and distress of party members when they had to face the ugly truth which had been accepted by everyone else for years. Their situation was interesting, but not so tremendously interesting as all that. Lessing's involvement with it made me think of the Holy Roman Emperor's supposed comment on an opera by Mozart: "Too many notes". On this subject Lessing had written too many words.'[15]

Lessing herself recalls in her autobiography that what transformed the book into a success was its discovery by the feminists in Britain, the United States and Scandinavia, as a result of which it became 'the Bible of the Women's Movement'. This left her feeling in a false position. On the one hand she supported the movement and was pleased to become an instrument for its advancement; on the other she was embarrassed because her book had not been intended as 'a trumpet for Women's Liberation'.

Looking back over the nearly sixty years that have elapsed since its publication it is hard to understand why it should have acquired that role. Apart from the involvement of its female characters in political arguments and activities, *The Golden Notebook* defines women's freedom almost entirely in sexual terms. It asserts their right to the same sexual licence as men had traditionally enjoyed and to be untrammelled by their consciences when they sleep with whoever they want, whether in response to purely physical or emotional needs. In this respect it captured and put into words what many women felt should be the case and were beginning to say. Its timing coincided with the change in sexual mores that marked the beginning of the 1960s and the birth of what came to be called the 'permissive society'.

But there is not a word in *The Golden Notebook* about how essential it is for women to acquire the economic independence without which other forms of independence cannot be sustained. Without work and the income it yields, or at the very least the skills that enable her to work and to earn a living, a woman without money of her own must inevitably be dependent on a man, a theme that runs through Victorian literature. Nor is there anything about a woman's right, not just to work, but to equal recognition, opportunities and rewards. It is as if Virginia Woolf's *A Room of One's Own* and *Three Guineas* had never been written and as if women were not already debating these issues among themselves.

The idea that a woman might wish to be as serious about a career as a man, and to gain from it the kind of self-fulfilment that enables a person to define themselves in relation to their work, as many men have done since time immemorial, is outside *The Golden Notebook*'s frame of reference. This is ironic since Lessing herself was a totally committed professional writer, who defined herself as such and lived entirely from her own earnings. By contrast, the book's two principle characters, Anna and her friend Molly, have no deep attachment to their work and do not regard it as being a significant element in their personalities.

On the evidence available to us, both are financially dependent. Molly lives with her son in the Earl's Court area of London, not as expensive then as it is now, but definitely middle class. She is a small-time actress and her son's school fees are paid for by her ex-husband. At the end of the book, when her son has moved away, she decides, without any pretence of love, to marry a rich businessman who can support her. Anna lives nearby. Her income, we are told, is derived from the declining earnings of her book and rent from a room she lets out in her flat. Yet she is able airily to dismiss the offers she receives for film and television rights regardless of how much difference the money might make to her life.

When her daughter wants to go away to boarding school, Anna agrees and buys the uniform her daughter asks for, even though it is optional, without expressing any anxiety about how the fees are to be paid or whether she can afford them. Either the girl's father is paying, or she must have a private income of some sort, or Lessing doesn't believe such mundane matters merit explanation. Nor does Anna worry about how to reconcile her left-wing principles with sending her daughter to a private instead of to a state school. Many other left-wing people, both then and since, have made the same choice, but usually with a certain amount of soul-searching.

In another respect *The Golden Notebook* reflects one of the characteristics of its time that in retrospect look very odd. Both in *Free Women* and in Anna's notebooks there is a good deal about racial discrimination and the exploitation of Africans in colonial Africa, which draws on Lessing's own experience as a young woman in Southern Rhodesia (now Zimbabwe) and her lifelong sympathy for Africans and the cause of African freedom. Yet there is no reference in any part of the novel to racial issues in Britain, although the Notting Hill race riots of 1958 took place while it was being written and Lessing herself had lived in that part of London. One of the ironies of the period, as illustrated by *The Golden Notebook*, is that, while those on the left and liberal-minded people in general were extremely concerned about

British policy in Africa and the actions of the colonial governments in Kenya, Nyasaland (now Malawi) and Rhodesia, it took a long time for them to take an interest in the plight of black and minority ethnic people in Britain. In ignoring them Anna and her creator were typical of their time.

On another matter, however, Anna was very untypical. As an immigrant to Britain with first-hand experience of a repressive colonial regime, Lessing didn't take British freedoms for granted. In several passages Anna reflects thankfully on the cost-free nature of being, or having been, a Communist in this country in a way it is hard to imagine that someone born and brought up here would have done. In some she compares the position of herself and her friends with what she has heard has happened in the Communist countries of Eastern Europe where disagreements had led to purges, with people in authority finding themselves having to execute former friends. In others the comparison is with the United States where, shortly before the book was written, the notorious Senator Joe McCarthy had carried out his anti-red witch-hunt as a result of which many in the creative industries who had once been Communists or Communist sympathizers lost their jobs and became unemployable. They and other Americans with left-wing leanings often ended up in London. Lessing draws on them for several of the characters who become Anna's lodgers and lovers.

Sex and Relationships

Married Love by Marie Stopes, 1918,
and *Lady Chatterley's Lover* by D. H. Lawrence, 1928.

Maurice by E. M. Forster, 1914,
The Well of Loneliness by Radclyffe Hall, 1928,
and *The Charioteer* by Mary Renault, 1953.

Married Love

by Marie Stopes (1918)

Lady Chatterley's Lover

by D. H. Lawrence (1928 privately in Italy and 1960 in Britain)

Between them these two books have probably provoked more indignation and controversy than any others published in English during the twentieth century. Both are famous for their treatment of sex, primarily from the woman's point of view. Each in its own way was a pioneering work that altered attitudes and, in the case of *Married Love*, the way people lived their lives. The furore they created when they were published speaks volumes about how people thought in those days.

Married Love was published in April 1918 at a critical stage in the war. In the previous month, the Germans had launched a massive attack on the Western Front, which, for a while, looked as if it might carry them to victory. They overreached and the Allies were able to strike back. But in April the outcome of the battle was still uncertain. Despite this national drama, *Married Love* provoked a storm of controversy and became an immediate bestseller. Over two thousand copies were sold within a fortnight. Five further editions had to be printed within the next ten months. By 1931 the book had gone through nineteen editions and sold seven hundred and fifty thousand copies in the United Kingdom. In the same year, it was published in the United States where, until then, it had been banned on grounds of obscenity. Marie Stopes herself became a national celebrity and the nation's first agony aunt, with men as well as women writing to her for advice about their sexual problems.

Nothing like it had been seen before. It was the first book ever published in English by a respectable publisher about sex technique. Although its language now seems coy and archaic, its meaning throughout is absolutely clear. Its purpose was to strip away the prejudice and superstition that surrounded the subject and to inform both men and women about the actions, emotions and sensibilities that would enable them to experience the joy of sex. Its impact on readers may be judged by the reaction of the young Naomi Mitchison, who later became a successful popular novelist. She was married in 1916 and read the book when it came out. As soon as she had done so, she sent a second copy to her husband serving with the army in France with a covering note urging him to 'read this before we meet again'.[1]

At a time when prostitution of every sort was rife and sexually transmitted diseases common, it was widely maintained among the middle and upper classes that respectable women should regard sex in marriage as a duty rather than a pleasure. 'The idea that woman is lowered by sex intercourse is very deeply rooted in our society,' Marie Stopes wrote. She also blamed women's education for 'encouraging the idea that sex-life is a low, physical, and degrading necessity which a pure woman is above enjoying' – attitudes that make it no wonder that their husbands so often resorted to professionals.

Among these classes there was an iron rule that young women should remain virgins until marriage. In many families it was further believed that they should be protected from all knowledge of sexual matters. All too often, therefore, they married in a state of complete sexual ignorance. As a result, Stopes argued, their initiation either became almost tantamount to rape or they were treated with such forbearance as to be left sexually unsatisfied. Either way, she claimed, '70 or 80 per cent of our married women [by which she meant the middle and upper classes] are deprived of full orgasm'. She had no possible means of knowing what the figure was, but, as her subsequent postbag bore out, large numbers were being so deprived owing to their own and their husbands' ignorance.

Rules are one thing, behaviour quite another, especially where sex is concerned. The rules were certainly not universally respected. While still a Cambridge undergraduate a young woman called Amber Reeves embarked on a celebrated affair with the author H. G. Wells, a man many years her senior who fictionalized the experience in his novel *Ann Veronica*. A woman who took matters into her own hands was the mother of the future Cabinet minister Denis Healey. She was a respectable teacher in Gloucester, but when Denis Healey's father, Will, proposed to her in 1914, she insisted that before they finally committed themselves they should first have a trial run on a holiday on the Isle of Man. Her mother was so shocked she wouldn't speak to her for months.[2] At the other extreme was Vera Brittain, whose autobiography, *Testament of Youth*, is discussed in an earlier chapter. She and her fiancé, she recorded, had never even kissed before he left her to fight and die in France.

In any case these niceties were only for those who lived in houses with enough room to allow for some privacy. They had no place in the slums of the industrial cities where large families were packed into tiny houses, as two other books in this anthology make clear: *Love on the Dole*, in which a young woman hates having to hear her parents having sex together, and Margaret Bondfield's account in her autobiography of incest in the Yorkshire woollen towns.

In the preface to *Married Love* Marie Stopes claims, 'in my first marriage I paid such a terrible price for sex ignorance that I feel that knowledge gained at such a cost should be placed at the service of humanity'. That cost, she claimed, included non-consummation, the grounds on which she secured an annulment in 1916 after five years of marriage. This claim was good publicity for the book, as was another, that she had only learned the literal truth about sex in 1913, two years after her marriage, by poring over medical tomes in English, French and German in the restricted access section of the British Museum Reading Room. They are, however, hard to credit. After his death a statement by her first husband was deposited in the British Library which, according to the *Oxford Dictionary of National Biography*, 'tells a rather different, though not necessarily more plausible story'.* Another piece of evidence is a letter written to her only a few months after her first marriage by a clergyman in which he refers to the birth control advice she had offered him while they were travelling together to a scientific congress in Stockholm.

From promoting the joy of sex, Marie Stopes moved quickly on to advocating birth control with the publication of Wise Parenthood in 1919. Thereafter, with the support of her second husband, Humphrey Roe, she devoted much time and energy to the cause. They opened their first clinic in 1921 and others followed.

Her motives in advocating birth control were mixed. Enabling the readers of *Married Love* to enjoy a more liberated sex life was one. Another was to help working-class women escape from the terrible burden of frequent pregnancies and numerous children. A third arose from her involvement with the eugenics movement, which believed in trying to improve the quality of the British race by restraining those with the physical, mental and character defects usually associated with poverty and malnutrition from breeding. This connection led Stopes into the treacherous waters of racial theories, which has cast a shadow

---

* *Oxford Dictionary of National Biography*, entry by Lesley A. Hall.

over her reputation. Her clinics also ran into financial trouble after her death in 1958, but her name lives on as that of the NGO Marie Stopes International, which carries on her work both in this country and abroad.

Married Love and her advocacy of birth control made Marie Stopes famous, but long before embarking on sex education in her late thirties she had built up a substantial academic reputation in a quite different sphere of activity. At the age of twenty-two she gained a first in botany and geology from University College London, after which she became the first woman to be awarded a Ph.D. in botany at Munich University, where she defended her thesis in German. In 1904 she was the first woman to be appointed to the faculty at the University of Manchester and in 1905 she became the youngest Doctor of Science in Britain.

She went on to make a successful career in palaeobotany, the study of fossil plants, undertaking work in Japan and Canada. During the First World War, she carried out research for the government into the composition of coal, arising out of which she co-authored a monograph on its chemical and palaeontological properties for the Department of Scientific and Industrial Research. It too was published in 1918 and led on to a further paper on the ingredients of coal that was published by the Royal Society in 1919. By virtue of the range of her activities as well as their pioneering quality, in science as much as sex education, she was one of the most remarkable women of her time.

Despite the path blazed by *Married Love*, there could be no question of D. H. Lawrence's novel *Lady Chatterley's Lover* being published in Britain, or the United States, when he completed it in 1927 while living in Italy. Instead an Italian bookseller friend of his in Florence, Pino Orioli, produced a handsome edition for private circulation to subscribers. It turned out to be extremely profitable, but inevitably, and to Lawrence's great annoyance, was immediately reissued in a variety of pirate editions. In an attempt to counter them he published a cheap popular edition in Paris in 1930.

The book broke new ground and shocked contemporary opinion at several levels. To begin with it attempted to describe the female orgasm in a way that had never been attempted before in serious English literature and, in so doing, established an imagery on which novelists still draw. It featured a heroine who is liberated by her adultery instead of being punished for it like Anna Karenina and Emma Bovary. It used four-letter words – fuck, cunt, shit – that were regarded as beyond the pale on the printed page. It was also a glorification of sex. As Lawrence wrote in his introduction to the Paris edition: 'And this is the real point of this book. I want men and women to be able to think sex, fully, completely, honestly and cleanly.'

In 1960 Penguin Books published the book in Britain and were immediately prosecuted under the Obscene Publications Act. The trial at the Old Bailey turned out to be a critical battle between the standards of a more straitlaced and inhibited past and the emerging mores of a more permissive future. The jury's verdict of not guilty stands as one of the landmarks of when the so-called 'permissive society' began to emerge. The trial lasted six days and was a great public spectacle as those for and against publication appeared to vie with each other in the absurdity of their opinions. The chief prosecuting counsel, Mervyn Griffiths Jones QC, became a national laughing stock when he asked the jury 'if it was the kind of book you would wish your wife or servants to read'. The celebrated sociologist and lecturer in English at the University of Leicester, Richard Hoggart, provoked astonishment when he called the book 'highly virtuous, if not puritanical'. The trendy Bishop of Woolwich, John Robinson, found himself trapped into saying it was a book all Christians should read.

Reading *Lady Chatterley's Lover* after the trial is something almost everyone of my generation can remember doing; a shared generational memory, like where one was when President Kennedy was assassinated three years later. We did so, of course, for the sex scenes that were unlike anything we had seen, or read, before. It is for these that those who haven't reread the book since will always remember it, which is a pity. The affair between Connie, as Lady Chatterley is always called, and her husband's gamekeeper, Mellors – never Oliver – is the relationship around which the novel revolves and the glorification of sex is its central message. But there is far more to the book than that, in addition to which it casts a penetrating light on the social mores of the 1920s.

Connie's misfortune is that her husband, Sir Clifford, had returned from the war paralysed from the waist down and impotent. Lawrence, who didn't serve in the war, presents him as mean-minded, artificial, possessive and intellectually and socially arrogant; so unpleasant in fact as almost to deserve his wife's infidelity. One wonders what, if they were not too carried away by the sex scenes, contemporaries made of this unsympathetic portrait. All over Britain at that time hundreds of thousands of families – wives, parents and children – were trying to cope with mutilated and disabled men and the effects of their injuries on their characters and on those around them. This aspect of the book has since attracted little attention, but in the 1920s it must have had a good deal of resonance with many women of all classes facing dilemmas similar to Connie's.

The progress of her affair with Mellors is matched by Sir Clifford's own regeneration thanks to the ministrations of his nurse, Mrs Bolton, a relationship that provides some of the book's most interesting passages. Mrs Bolton is a widow, her husband having been killed some years earlier in an accident in one of Sir Clifford's coal mines. Despite this tragedy, restoring Sir Clifford's self-confidence, and thereby enabling him to resume his responsibilities as a coal and land owner, become her mission in life. Yet, all the while that she is helping him she harbours a deep visceral resentment against the ruling class, exults at having the man who owns the neighbourhood dependent upon her and rejoices when she learns that it is a local man from her own village who is cuckolding him.

Not that Mellors is an ordinary local man or an ordinary gamekeeper. During the war he had risen from the ranks and been commissioned as an officer. If he had wished he could have cut himself loose from his background and joined the middle class instead of returning to his origins. Before she embarks on her affair with him, Connie notices and tells her husband that, 'The game-keeper, Mellors, is a curious kind of person … he might almost be a gentleman.' This observation is key to everything that follows.

The nature of their affair and the conversations she has with him are such that it is impossible to believe Connie would have given herself to him, let alone that their physical affair would have mutated into a love so deep that she wants to marry him, if he had been an ordinary working man. Her father and sister are at first appalled that she should have taken up with a servant. The sister feels humiliated by it and the prospect of the scandal involved. But Mellors' social self-confidence and ease of manner when he meets them on their own ground see him through. When he and Connie's father dine together at the latter's club, they are soon on a comfortable footing and her sister too is mollified. Mellors, like Connie, has to secure a divorce, though he has long been separated from his wife, and the book ends with the two of them waiting out the time they have to spend apart that the law in those days required before a divorce could be granted.

Lawrence's reputation since his death in 1930 has had its ups and downs. Initially it went into decline until in the 1950s the Cambridge academic and critic F. R. Leavis, one of the most influential teachers of the day, hailed him as one of the great writers of the twentieth century. Now it is more mixed. *Lady Chatterley* has never been regarded as one of his major novels, like *Sons and Lovers* or *The Rainbow*, but it will ensure that he is never forgotten.

Maurice

by E. M. Forster (completed 1914 and published 1971)

The Well of Loneliness

by Radclyffe Hall (1928)

The Charioteer

by Mary Renault (1953)

'What is the love that dare not speak its name?' prosecuting counsel asked Oscar Wilde when in 1895 he was on trial for gross indecency, by which was meant sex with other men. His impromptu response was: '"The love that dare not speak its name" in this century is such a great affection of an elder for a younger man as there was between David and Jonathan, such as Plato made the very basis of his philosophy, and such as you find in the sonnets of Michelangelo and Shakespeare.'[3] The spectators in the gallery applauded and the jury could not agree on a verdict, but Wilde did not walk free. He was remanded in custody before being released on bail until at a second trial he was found guilty. The phrase, originally the title of a poem by Wilde's lover, Lord Alfred

Douglas,[4] entered the language as a way of referring to sexual relations between men.

Maurice by E. M. Forster, written in 1914 and published in 1971, and Mary Renault's *The Charioteer*, published in 1953, are novels about what it was like to be gay when for men to have sex together was a criminal offence, as it remained until 1967. Lesbianism was not illegal but attracted a similar degree of prejudice and opprobrium. When Radclyffe Hall's lesbian novel, *The Well of Loneliness*, was published in 1928, a government official told the publishers, Jonathan Cape, it was 'inherently obscene ... it supports a depraved practice [and] is gravely detrimental to the public interest'.[5] Sir William Willcox, a distinguished toxicologist at St Mary's Hospital London, told the court that 'lesbianism was a vice which, if widespread, becomes a danger to the well-being of a nation'. Radclyffe Hall, as she was always known, though her first name was Marguerite and in private she liked to be called John, was herself a lesbian, as was Mary Renault, while E. M. Forster was gay.

Despite the law and prejudice there were, of course, many practising gays and lesbians as the biographies of John Maynard Keynes, Somerset Maugham, Benjamin Britten and Vita Sackville West, to name but four, show. Nor were they by any means confined to what might be termed bohemian, artistic and literary circles. Two senior executives in the oil company run by my father lived openly together in the 1940s and 1950s in a large house at Westerham in Kent. In Ongar, the Essex village near where we lived when I was growing up, two women who had served together during the war in the women's branch of the Royal Navy set up house together and ran a small craft shop. There were myriad other such couples sharing their homes and lives up and down the country without running into trouble, although, as in these two cases, plenty of snide comments were exchanged behind their backs.

Men who went in search of new partners and, above all, those looking for adventure and/or paid sex ran great risks. Between 1945 and 1955 the number of annual prosecutions for homosexual offences of various kinds rose from eight hundred to two thousand five hundred, according to the Wolfenden Report published in 1957.[6] In 1952 Alan Turing, the computer scientist whose work during the war had contributed greatly to Bletchley Park's success at breaking the German codes, and in 1953 the celebrated actor John Gielgud were among those prosecuted, found guilty and fined. When Lord Montagu of Beaulieu, later famous for founding the National Motor Museum, and two of his friends were convicted in 1954 they were sent to prison.

The fact that sex between men was a criminal offence meant that those who practised it beyond the restricted circle of those they knew well were at constant risk of blackmail. Besides which both gays and lesbians were aware that they might at any time run up against prejudice and social ostracism. These three authors were all therefore writing from within and about a besieged and, by many, despised community.

Maurice and *The Well of Loneliness* share a common theme. They chart journeys of self-discovery as their principal characters progress from realizing that they are different from the generality of people to understanding the nature of their sexuality. Their reactions differ, but in both cases the nature of their agonizing and the intensity of their emotions, as they grapple with what this means, are bound to seem strange, if not incomprehensible, to those accustomed to living in a society in which sexual relations between people of the same sex has long since ceased to be a taboo.

Clive Durham, with whom the eponymous Maurice has a platonic affair while they are both undergraduates at Cambridge, exemplifies the difference between then and now. He is deeply religious and when he finds that his 'impulse' is homosexual he determines 'that it should not ever become carnal'. He also feels obliged 'to throw over Christianity'. 'He wished Christianity would compromise with him a little and searched the Scriptures for support. There was David and Jonathan; there was even the "disciple that Jesus loved". But the Church's interpretation was against him.' To overcome 'the horrors of the Bible' he turns to Plato's *Phaedrus* in which Socrates and Phaedrus discuss love between men and the distinction between true love and the simple pursuit of pleasure. How different from today when, instead of feeling obliged to throw over Christianity, gay Christians expect the Church to embrace them.

The first part of Forster's novel is dominated by the unconsummated affair between Clive Durham and Maurice Hall. They kiss, cuddle, lie in bed together and exchange love letters, but never actually 'unite'. Initially it is Clive who awakens Maurice's sexuality and later it is he who terminates their affair with a letter announcing, 'Against my will I have become normal. I cannot help it.' His next step is marriage. Maurice is left feeling abandoned and resentful and also, to his horror, recognizing that when a man attracts him it is 'lust' that he feels.

He must, he believes, find a cure for his condition and turns first to an old man who had formerly been his family's doctor. 'I'm an unspeakable of the Oscar Wilde sort,' he explains. 'I want to be cured. I can't put up with the loneliness any more.' The doctor cuts the conversation short. 'Never let that evil hallucination, that temptation from the devil occur to you again,' he responds and calls for his servant to give them both a whisky. Maurice then finds an American doctor, who, through hypnosis, specializes in curing men suffering from what he describes as 'congenital homosexuality' with, he claims, a 50 per cent success rate. Men continued to seek medical advice in such circumstances for long after *Maurice* was written. The distinguished historian Sir Michael Howard recalls in his memoirs[7] how, in 1945, on returning to civilian life after wartime service in the army, he went to see a Harley Street specialist. After describing some possible treatments the specialist told him, 'Frankly I shouldn't worry. There are a lot of people around like you', adding that he should get on with his life. 'Seldom has money been better spent,' writes Howard, as the consultation enabled him to come to terms with himself.

Maurice gets on with his life in more dramatic fashion. While on a visit to the Durhams at their country estate he falls for the gamekeeper, Alec Scudder, and they have marvellous sex together. On his return to London he fears that he has laid himself open to blackmail and Alec indeed sends him a threatening letter. They meet to resolve the matter. One thing leads to another and, after a rapturous night together in a hotel, they declare their love for one another. Alec, who had been planning to emigrate, decides not to, while Maurice announces that he will give up his profession as a stockbroker and leave his family. They determine to live privately together in the countryside defying convention in terms both of their sexuality and class distinctions.

This highly romanticized ending is not how most men in that situation would have behaved. They would have been far more likely to have found a way of continuing with their lives so as to observe the conventions while continuing their connection. Forster's own life is a case in point. He too fell in love with a man from a different class, a policeman called Bob Buckingham, in 1930. Their relationship continued after Bob's marriage and when Forster died in 1970 his ashes were scattered in the Buckinghams' garden. But the relationship between the two men was always kept secret from the general public. When a friend criticized him for this, pointing to the example of André Gide, he replied, 'But Gide hasn't got a mother',[8] a reply that would have resonated with many of Forster's generation and others before and afterwards. Even after his mother's death in 1945 he preferred to remain discreet and did not wish to face the controversy that publishing *Maurice* would have provoked, with the result that the book did not see the light of day until after he too had died.

In the mid-1920s Forster and Radclyffe Hall were the only two writers to have won two of the most prestigious literary prizes of the time, the Femina – Vie Heureuse, a prize awarded to British writers between 1920 and 1940 by the French Hachette publishing group, and the James Tait Black Memorial Prize – he for *A Passage to India** and she for *Adam's Breed*, which had immediately preceded *The Well of Loneliness*. Otherwise they were chalk and cheese. Hall lived openly as an invert, as lesbians were generally called and called themselves (the word was also used for gay men), and she wanted to use her fame 'to encourage inverts to face up to a hostile world in their true colours, and this with dignity and courage'.[9] 'Having attained literary success, I have put my pen at the service of some of the most persecuted and misunderstood people in the world,'[10] she wrote to one of the publishers who turned the book down.

Hall believed herself to be a man trapped in the body of a woman and the hero of her novel, Stephen Gordon, is a reflection of this. She is given a boy's name at birth because her father, a wealthy country landowner, had expected to have a son. As she grows up in Worcestershire she comes to realize that she is not like other girls and wishes she was a boy. She becomes a skilful fencer, excels on the hunting field, starts to wear masculine dress and has an affair with a woman that ends disastrously. She moves to London and, after writing a successful first novel, to Paris, where she joins a lesbian salon. When the First World War breaks out, she serves courageously with an ambulance unit in France and is wounded in the face. She also falls in love with a much younger colleague, Mary Llewellyn.

Hall hoped that her book would encourage understanding and sympathy for those she was writing about. Instead it attracted controversy, obloquy and mockery led by a hate campaign in the *Sunday Express*. Arguing for its suppression, the paper's editor wrote: 'I would rather give a healthy boy or a healthy girl a phial of prussic acid than

---

* See essay on *A Passage to India* and *Altogether*.

this novel. Poison kills the body, but moral poison kills the soul.'[11] People rushed to buy the book before it could be banned as it promptly was by a magistrate's court with the verdict being upheld on appeal. Meanwhile, a spate of lampoons, satires and cartoons made Hall and the cause she was promoting look ridiculous. Despite the seriousness of her purpose, *The Well of Loneliness'* reputation has been indelibly marked by the mockery. I think unfairly, although its style and the author's deeply conservative social values in matters other than sex do not wear well today.

It was not the book's descriptions of what people do in bed that gave offence. There are none. The nearest approach comes in a scene where 'Stephen bent down and kissed Mary's hands very humbly, for now she could find no words any more … and that night they were not divided.' Proust's great multi-volume novel *A la recherche du temps perdu*, English translations of which were being published during the 1920s, deals extensively with lesbianism and homosexuality and is far more explicit. Yet it was never prosecuted. What gave offence in Hall's case was her defiance. She presents lesbians as brave and practical women who did more than their fair share during the war and are treated unfairly and hypocritically by society, while Stephen is portrayed as a heroic figure by turns courageous, tender and self-sacrificing.

So self-sacrificing in fact that, when it becomes apparent to her after the war that for as long as their affair lasts Mary will be identified as a lesbian and thereby denied a normal social life, Stephen makes the ultimate sacrifice of giving her up. She colludes with a man who has fallen in love with Mary to be on hand when Stephen deliberately drives her into his arms by pretending to be unfaithful in a particularly hurtful manner. The book ends with Stephen, lonely and bereft, uttering a private prayer: 'Acknowledge us, oh God, before the world. Give us also the right to our existence.'

Mary Renault, whose real surname was Challens, falls between Forster and Hall. She lived openly with her partner, Julie Mullard, whom she had met when they were both training to become nurses, but did not adopt a public position as a lesbian. She is best remembered for her historical novels set in ancient world, but before turning her hand to those she wrote contemporary novels, for one of which, *Return to Night*, MGM bought the film rights for $125,000 thereby enabling her and Julie to emigrate to South Africa. They were already settled there when, in 1953, *The Charioteer* came out. The publishers, Longmans, Green, were brave to hazard their reputation on a book about homosexuality in the armed forces during the war at a time when prosecutions for homosexual offences were rising sharply. It served as a timely reminder that 'queers', as they were called and referred to themselves, had played their part as much as anyone, and thus made a modest contribution to the campaign for homosexual law reform that was beginning to gather momentum.

Much of the novel is set in a military hospital like that in which Renault herself worked during those fraught months after the British Army's evacuation from Dunkirk in June 1940. Its central character, Laurie Odell, is there undergoing treatment on one of his legs that was badly damaged during the fighting. The naval commander of the small boat that had brought him back to England was the former head boy of his public school, the charismatic Ralph Lanyon, who had been expelled for a homosexual offence. Laurie had hero-worshipped him and carried into action a copy of *Phaedrus* that Ralph had given him before leaving school inscribed with the words, 'It doesn't exist anywhere in real life, so don't let it give you illusions. It's just a nice idea.'

Each holds a mythic place in the mind of the other and when they meet again at a gay party in the town near the hospital the effect on both is traumatic. But by then Laurie, who is aware of his homosexuality, has fallen in love with Andrew Raynes, an innocent young man, who is one of a team of Quaker conscientious objectors working as orderlies in the hospital. The novel is primarily about how that situation is resolved.

Ralph has no hang-ups about his sexuality. His view is 'It's not what one is, it's what one does with it' that matters. What he wants is to give up the promiscuity epitomized by the party for a monogamous relationship with Laurie. Laurie has difficulty in responding. He is emotionally and physically attracted to Ralph and they make love together. But the pure and protective nature of his relationship with Andrew and horror of hurting him pulls the other way. So too does his reluctance to put himself in a position that he feels will mean that the world will define him primarily by his sexuality. Ralph displays considerable forbearance and understanding as Laurie agonizes, and eventually wins out in a dramatic denouement.

As the story unfolds aspects of the gay predicament that continued untouched by the war are illuminated. At an emotional level, Laurie, while coming to terms with the fact that his wound will leave him permanently lame, wants to tell his widowed mother that this is more than made up for by falling in love with Andrew and is deeply hurt by the realization of how shocked she would be if he did. On a practical level, he hears two of Ralph's friends discuss the blackmail of someone they know. One argues that for the sake of their self-respect victims should never give in to it. The other responds, echoing Forster, 'What about his job, what about dependants, what if his mother's got a weak heart and the news will kill her?'

Whether in uniform or not, gays were as much at risk of arrest, and so of blackmail, as before the war. In fact, the annual rate of prosecutions was higher during the war than in the 1930s though lower than in the 1950s. They were also at constant risk of exposure and insult as Laurie realizes when Ralph, in naval officer's uniform, accompanies him to his mother's remarriage and the circumstances of his expulsion from school are about to be revealed before a distraction intervenes.

The Charioteers is about gays and what it meant to be gay. But that aside, it conveys very well the atmosphere during those tense months in the autumn of 1940 when life went on as normal in so many ways while the Battle of Britain raged overhead and invasion seemed imminent. It is particularly good on the conscientious objectors, men who would not bear arms for reasons of conscience and were conscripted to fulfil various functions, such as hospital orderlies, stretcher-bearers and ambulance drivers. They were widely viewed with contempt. When the men in Laurie's ward hear that 'conchies' are to replace the maids, who had previously assisted the nurses, they are appalled. The man in the next bed to Laurie's voices their feelings when he declares that he would prefer German prisoners, who had 'done their duty as they see it, same as us. Not like those creeping-Jesus, knock-kneed conchies.'

When Laurie and Andrew become friends, it is not the possibility of sexual attraction that worries the other men in his ward. It is the fear that Andrew will try to undermine Laurie's military loyalty. Renault, who, as a nurse, would have worked closely with many conscientious objectors, portrays them as brave, trustworthy men standing by their beliefs and working on behalf of others. Some of the passages in which Andrew and Dave, who is in charge of the Quaker team, express their own inner doubts and what drives them are among the most sensitive in the book.

Race and Immigration

The Foundations of the Nineteenth-Century
by Houston Stewart Chamberlain, 1911,
and *The Alien Corn* by W. Somerset Maugham, 1931.

The Story of Art by Ernst Gombrich, 1950,
and *The Buildings of England by Nikolaus Pevsner*, 1951–74.

The Lonely Londoners by Sam Selvon, 1956,
City of Spades by Colin MacInnes, 1957,
and *Absolute Beginners* by Colin MacInnes, 1959.

The Foundations of the Nineteenth Century

by Houston Stewart Chamberlain
(1899 in German and 1911 in English)

The Alien Corn[*]

by W. Somerset Maugham (1931)

Britain has always taken pride in the fact that, unlike some other European countries during the inter-war period, extremist political parties and vicious anti-Semitism never took root here. Oswald Mosley and his Blackshirts, who looked to Nazi Germany and Fascist Italy for inspiration, never progressed beyond the outer reaches of the political fringe. It therefore comes as something of a shock to find that one of the inspirations behind the Nazis, and thus a man whose influence was later to be felt across Europe was British. His name was Houston Stewart Chamberlain[†] and his book *The Foundations of the Nineteenth Century*.

---

* First published in 1931 by Heinemann with five other short stories under the title *First Person Singular*.

† No relation to Neville Chamberlain, Prime Minister from 1937 to 1940, whose father, Joseph, and half-brother, Austen, who were also Cabinet ministers.

On his 70th birthday in 1925 the Nazi newspaper *Völkischer Beobachter* described it as 'the gospel of the National Socialist movement'. In 1927 Hitler and Goebbels visited Chamberlain on his deathbed at the Wagner family property at Bayreuth where he lived with his second wife, the composer's stepdaughter Eva. Three years later Arthur Rosenberg, often described as the principal philosopher of Nazism, published *The Myth of the Twentieth Century* as a homage to Chamberlain, whom he hailed as 'the pioneer and founder of a German future'.*

Described by his biographer Geoffrey Field as 'The Evangelist of Race',[1] Chamberlain initially came to prominence during the reign of Kaiser Wilhelm II before the First World War. On receiving a copy of his book the Kaiser wrote, 'God sent your book to the German people, just as he sent you personally to me, that is my unshakeable conviction.' He went on to praise Chamberlain as his 'comrade-in-arms and ally in the struggle for Teutons against Rome, Jerusalem etc'[2] and provided practical help by organizing subsidies for a popularly priced edition. There wasn't anything particularly new in Chamberlain's book. Others in Germany, Austria and France, where the Dreyfus case that began in 1894 had unleashed a wave of anti-Semitism, were preaching along the same and similar lines. It was the power of his exposition that, in Field's words, 'turned Chamberlain almost overnight into the prophet of race for educated laymen in Central Europe'.

An English translation of *Foundations* was published in Britain in 1911. Lord Redesdale (the paternal grandfather of the Mitford sisters),† a former diplomat, acknowledged authority on international affairs and prominent in artistic and literary circles, provided a eulogistic introduction and it was widely reviewed. The playwright George Bernard

* The references in this paragraph are drawn from the *Oxford Dictionary of National Biography* entry on HSC by Michael Biddiss.

† This connection must have been of some help to Unity Mitford in gaining access to Hitler's circle when she settled in Munich in 1924 with that intention.

Shaw, then at the height of his fame, described it in the left-wing *Fabian News* as 'a masterpiece of really scientific history'.[3] The *Spectator* called it 'a monument of erudition, and the skilful handling of erudition'.[4]

Chamberlain's central thesis was clear. It was that when the Roman empire collapsed it left behind a 'a chaos of peoples', all of whom had become hopelessly mongrelized apart from the Jews, who alone had retained their racial purity. Their counterparts, also pure and undefiled, were the Teutons, who broke into the empire's territories at that time. He rejected the general concept of human progress. Rather, he attributed all that had been achieved since the fall of Rome to the Teutons through 'constant struggle between Teuton and non-Teuton'. As a result, 'Our present civilization and culture are specifically Teutonic, they are exclusively the work of Teutonism ... this is the great primal truth, the "concrete" fact, which the history of the last thousand years teaches us on every page.' Events in other parts of the world did not interest him. His focus was on Europe, an attitude that now seems absurd, but which was not uncommon at the time.

According to his theory all European peoples could be grouped into the Aryan race at the head of which came the Nordic or Teutonic peoples led by 'the most highly gifted group', the Germans. The Latin peoples and the Slavs he regarded as markedly inferior. To explain the genius of historic figures from outside the Teutonic elite he found grounds to endow them with a Teutonic heritage. Thus, Dante and Michelangelo, to take two examples, owed their genius to being descended from the Goths. Christ, who lived before the Teutons appeared on the scene, was, he claimed, despite being Jewish by education and religion, not Jewish by race as 'the national character of the Galileans was essentially different from that of the Jews'.

Perpetually opposed to the Teutons stood two massive and implacable enemies, the Catholic Church and the Jews. The Church he accused of constantly seeking 'to subjugate all our power, freedom, property, bodies and souls and through us (had God not prevented it) the whole world'. However, by the nineteenth century, thanks to two great Germans, Luther and Kant, the Church had been humbled, its pretensions exposed and its power greatly weakened. The Teutons had been 'emancipated' from Rome. But the Jews remained. In Chamberlain's eyes they faced the Teutons as the perpetual other, locked in continuous struggle. Whereas the fight with the Catholic Church was about power, namely the Pope's claims to authority, the fight with the Jews was about race. There was no identifiable *casus belli* and no grounds on which a peace treaty could be negotiated. Rather, two pure races, the oldest and the youngest, were fated to be forever in conflict with each other. The parallel with that between Good and Evil is inescapable.

It followed from this view of the world that Jews could not be trusted as fellow citizens, that they worked only for themselves regardless of the interests of others and that marriages between Gentiles and Jews should not be permitted. Unlike some other anti-Semites at that time, including by 1903 some members of the Russian government,[5] Chamberlain showed no interest in Zionism as a means of resolving the conflict by persuading Jews to migrate from Europe to Palestine. So we shall never know whether he would have approved of Hitler's Final Solution or been appalled by it. His praise for 'the annihilation of the Indians in North America' that paved the way for 'the later development of a thoroughly Teutonic nation upon that soil' suggests he might have approved while giving Americans some food for thought about their own history.

With what we now know about the Holocaust it is hard to believe that the theories propounded by Chamberlain could have been taken at all seriously by people in this country. But in 1911 such an outcome was unimaginable and circumstances were propitious for his book. On the one hand, with the empire at the plenitude of its power, the idea that the white races in general and the British in particular were inherently superior to all others, was taken for granted by most of the population. On the other there was unease about the extent to which newly rich Jewish individuals of foreign origin were becoming prominent in British life.

Edward VII's welcome of such men as Sir Ernest Cassel, Sir Julius Wernher, Lord Rothschild and the Austrian Baron Hirsch into his inner circle had been widely disapproved of. In some parts of the press it was suggested that British soldiers had died during the Boer War to defend the investments of Jewish financiers in South Africa. In 1912 came the Marconi scandal in which two Jewish ministers, as well as others, were accused of profiting from inside information on a government contract. Politics was convulsed and an anti-Semitic outburst triggered in some sections of the press. The temper of the times may be judged from a proposal put forward in 1911 by the popular novelist Hilaire Belloc, who argued that Jews were infiltrating British society while disguising their growing influence by adopting English names. He proposed to counter this by obliging them to enter their names on a national register with false ones being punished by law and to bar them from military service.

The kind of vicious anti-Semitism that could so easily mutate into persecution and ultimately the Holocaust did not take root in Britain. The British variant was of the type that demeaned, mocked and joked about Jews. It also implied, or even asserted, that, however much they might wish to, Jews could never become real Britons or fully integrate into British society. They might join the government, acquire titles or become great landowners, but would always be outsiders vulnerable whenever trouble arose.

In his *Trials of the Diaspora*, probably the most comprehensive study of anti-Semitism in Britain ever published, Anthony Julius[6] cites the example of the then Secretary of State for India, Edwin Montagu, after he had sacked a general responsible for ordering his troops to fire on an unarmed crowd and killing many men, women and children, the infamous Amritsar massacre of 1919. He quotes Montagu's Cabinet colleague Austen Chamberlain, writing in his diary, that to Conservative MPs Montagu's Jewishness meant that the issue had become not a question of justice or discipline, but of 'a Jew, a foreigner rounding on an Englishman and throwing him to the wolves'. More than sixty years later, in 1985–6, when my friend Leon Brittan, as Secretary of State for Trade and Industry, was at the heart of the Westland controversy that briefly threatened to bring down Margaret Thatcher, there was more than a whiff of anti-Semitism behind some of the attacks on him from the backbenches. When Brittan had to leave the government the backbench Conservative MP John Stokes demanded that his replacement should be 'a red-blooded, red-faced Englishman, preferably from the landed interests'.*

Somerset Maugham's short story *The Alien Corn*, set in the 1920s, is about whether integration is possible. Both the title and the text say much about attitudes at that time. It concerns two branches of an immigrant Jewish family. One, headed by Sir Adolphus Bland, always known as Freddy, lives in a lovely Elizabethan house with a large estate in a part of Sussex where he is the local MP. Their way of life and values are those of the landed aristocracy. Lady Bland, Muriel to her friends, refers often to her convent education and their sons go to Eton and Oxford. They want the eldest, George, to make a suitably aristocratic marriage. Everything appears to be as settled and as English as can be. Yet to their friend, the narrator, nothing in the house is quite as it should be – it is all too contrived and has none of the patina of age and inheritance. And there's the rub. The family's name was originally Bleikogel, Freddy was originally Adolph, Muriel was Miriam and the family's ownership of the estate is of recent origin.

---

* As quoted in the *Daily Telegraph* obituary of Sir John Stokes, 30 January 2003. A former Conservative MP has told me of the shock he felt when he heard Stokes utter these words at a meeting of the 1922 Committee of backbench Conservative MPs.

The narrator juxtaposes the Blands with Freddy's uncle, Ferdy Rabenstein, whom he also knows, and his mother, old Lady Bland. Ferdy is a debonair bachelor with a 'fine Semitic profile', who moves easily in the highest reaches of society where he enjoys great success with women while making a point of drawing attention to his Jewishness by telling Jewish jokes and wearing flashy jewellery – 'After all I am an Oriental,' he was in the habit of saying. And 'I can carry a certain barbaric magnificence.' Whereas the Blands want desperately to be indistinguishable from those around them, Ferdy glories in his difference and is welcomed as an exotic outsider. The Blands strongly disapprove of him for retaining his overt Jewishness and for not having changed 'his horrible German name' during the war. They don't want their children to meet him, although George disobeys them and does so. The matriarchal old Lady Bland, Ferdy's sister, speaks with a guttural German accent, calls her daughter-in-law Miriam and wants her grandson to marry the daughter of another self-made Jewish millionaire who has retained his German name.

The principal drama of the story centres on George, who, with the world at his feet, rejects his English upbringing and prospects. He wants to revert to a German Jewish identity and to devote his life to becoming a great pianist. This brings the two branches of the family together, both equally horrified that so much that has been achieved should be thrown away and neither believing that he has the talent to fulfil his ambition. After much toing and froing the old lady brokers a deal whereby the parents agree to his studying in Munich for two years at the end of which he will submit himself to the judgement of a professional pianist. If the professional believes that he will in due course make the grade, he will be allowed to continue. If not, he will revert to the life of an English gentleman. He fails the test. The professional says he will never be first rate and he knows in his heart that this is true. His parents are devastated on his behalf and even willing to let him continue with his music, but he cannot live without the hope of his ambition being fulfilled and shoots himself.

The secondary drama concerns the unravelling of the Blands' integrationist dream and the extent to which, when gathered together, the two branches are so alike, with the old lady the ultimate authority whom none will defy. On the day of the test they all lunch with the famous Jewish woman pianist who is to conduct it. The narrator is the only Gentile present. 'All but old Lady Bland spoke perfect English,' he recounts, 'yet I could not help feeling that they did not speak like English people; I think they rounded their vowels more than we do, certainly spoke louder, and the words seemed not to fall, but to gush from their lips. I think if I had been in another room where I could hear the tone but not the words of their speech I should have thought it was in a foreign language they were conversing.'

This passage is part of a picture the first brush stroke of which had been Ferdy's profile. It is followed by Freddy bursting into tears when thwarted by his son, a spectacle that prompts the narrator to observe, 'he didn't behave very much like Sir Adolphus Bland, Bart., and the good old English gentleman he so much wanted to be, but like an emotional Adolph Bleikogel'. Finally, the narrator observes how 'her fleshy nose, the shape of her face and the back of her neck' revealed that the fair-haired, blue-eyed Muriel 'could not possibly be an Englishwoman'. In these and other references, as the story unfolds, attention is drawn to what the narrator regards as inherently Jewish features and characteristics and the enduring differences between alien and home-grown corn.

This was in accordance with the literary conventions of the time. References to stereotypical Jewish physical features and character traits are to be found in the works of almost all authors writing during the inter-war years. They reflected the way people thought and spoke. In some cases, the writer was anti-Semitic, but not necessarily, and the presumption should not be made on the basis of words attributed to fictional characters. Not until the end of the Second World War did the convention change.

In his book *Our Age*, an outstanding study of the generation born in the first two decades of the twentieth century, Noel Annan writes: 'The end of the war marked a change of manners concerning one topic. The revelation of the Holocaust in the concentration camps altered the way the educated classes spoke and felt about Jews. Anti-semitism never dies; like other forms of xenophobia it festers and erupts on strange issues. But at any rate after 1945 it became bad form and was regarded as disgusting to talk in a derogatory way about Jews, still less discriminate in public against them.'[7]

In the period after 1945 there was also a notable increase in the Jewish contribution to many aspects of British life through the work of those Jews who had fled to this country from the continent to escape the Holocaust. This is the subject of the following essay. But as I complete the writing of this book during the winter of 2018–19 against the background of the row over anti-Semitism in the Labour Party I have Annan's point about festering and erupting on strange issues ringing in my ears.

The Story of Art

by Ernst Gombrich (1950)

The Buildings of England

by Nikolaus Pevsner (1951–74)

Ernst Gombrich was born in Vienna in 1909, and Nikolaus Pevsner in Leipzig in 1902. They died in London in 2001 and 1982 respectively, loaded with honours awarded for their great contributions to British cultural life. Few individuals have exercised a more enduring influence on how people view and react to art and architecture than they. 'More people … have been introduced to the world of fine art in the last 45 years through Ernst Gombrich's *The Story of Art* than through any other single book,' wrote the Professor of Cultural History (and later Rector) at the Royal College of Art, Christopher Frayling, in 1995.* Reviewing a biography of Pevsner, the author and critic A. N. Wilson described him as 'one of our greatest cultural historians'.[8] They came to Britain in the 1930s and worked and wrote in English because they were Jews who had to flee from the Nazi persecution of the

* As quoted in the endorsements to the 16th edition of *The Story of Art*, Phaidon Press, 1995.

Jews that had begun in Germany and Austria and would culminate in the Holocaust.

They were part of an incredible transfer of talent to Britain from the countries that fell under Hitler's control. The actual numbers were small. Some estimates suggest around sixty thousand, but they were hard to count. Some, like Gombrich and Pevsner, arrived as adults with family members as a direct result of the Nazis' actions. Others, like the famous philosopher Ludwig Wittgenstein and my own father, both from Vienna, were working and established here before the Nazis came to power and decided to stay. Then there were those for whom Britain was a staging post en route to the United States, like the author Stefan Zweig. And there were unaccompanied children sent by parents who themselves could not escape, like my colleague in the House of Lords and former Labour opponent in two parliamentary elections, Alf Dubs. They were the lucky ones. As the Nazis tightened their grip it became increasingly hard for those without qualifications, connections or wealth to find a country that would take them in. By the end of 1940, when the Germans had overrun most of continental Europe, escape was almost impossible.

Their impact was out of all proportion to their numbers and benefited all branches of the arts, sciences, academia and business. In his standard work on the subject, *The Hitler Emigrés*, Daniel Snowman writes that by 1992 they or their children had won sixteen Nobel Prizes while seventy-four had become Fellows of the Royal Society.[9] There were many others who achieved great success in diverse fields. Three of the most notable were the artist Lucian Freud, who came with his family at the age of seven, Siegmund Warburg, the most innovative banker in the City of London for forty years after the Second World War, and George Weidenfeld, an equally innovative publisher for much longer. The economist Friedrich Hayek and the philosopher Karl Popper, who together provided Margaret Thatcher with much of her inspiration, were also refugees. The list is almost endless and so is the range of activities. It includes my father, Georg Tugendhat, who, together with a fellow émigré, Franz Kind, established a company that pioneered oil refining in the United Kingdom.

Many received British honours in recognition of their work as well as medals and prizes from other countries, including, after the war, those from which they had fled. Few garnered more than Ernst Gombrich, whose haul, as well as a knighthood and various academic distinctions, included the Order of Merit, one of the most exclusive British awards because there can be no more than twenty-four members at any one time. His output of books, articles and lectures was considerable, but the foundation on which the edifice of his fame and reputation was built is *The Story of Art*. Since it first appeared in 1950 it has never been out of print, has run into sixteen editions and been translated into more than thirty languages.

In 1995 Neil MacGregor, then Director of the National Gallery and later of the British Museum, wrote: 'Like every art historian, my way of thinking about pictures has been in large measure shaped by Ernst Gombrich. I was 15 when I read *The Story of Art* and like millions since, I felt I had been given a map of a great country, and with it the confidence to explore further without fear of being overwhelmed.'* This captures the essence of what Gombrich is about. He doesn't tell his readers what to think or like; he provides the means by which they can form their own judgements.

As it happens, when MacGregor read *The Story of Art* he was at the age that Gombrich was aiming at when he wrote it. As he explains in the book's preface: 'The readers I had first and foremost in mind were boys and girls in their teens who had just discovered the world of art for themselves.' To this end he was determined to 'avoid any

* As quoted in the endorsements to the 16th edition of *The Story of Art*, Phaidon Press, 1995.

trace of pretentious jargon or bogus sentiment', characteristics that all too often disfigure books on art, wine and other subjects in which connoisseurship is highly prized.

Reading *The Story of Art* is like being taken round a gallery by a curator who picks out the most important pictures, explains what makes them so, what to look for in them and how they relate to the other works around them. Great emphasis is placed on the importance of understanding what it was the artist was trying to achieve and the social, political and economic context within which he was working. A picture, Gombrich argued, should not be regarded as an object in isolation; it should be appreciated within the context in which it was created. It should be seen as an attempt by an artist, working in a particular time and place and governed by a set of beliefs to which he in some measure subscribes or rebels against, to convey an idea, story, concept or way of viewing the world around him.

The book is a phenomenal feat of memory. Because of the disruption caused by the war and post-war travel restrictions Gombrich would not have seen any of the pictures, sculptures and buildings outside this country about which he was writing for many years. He would have been able to look at photographs, but, like those in the original edition, they would almost all have been in black and white from which it is difficult to pick out details and finer features unless one knew them already and could remember where they were. In the 1950s his readers would have appreciated that. They wouldn't have been able to travel outside Britain either, except on active service during the war. The treasures he laid before them would have seemed out of reach in a way that is difficult to imagine today when foreign travel has become so easy.

Anyone now reading *The Story of Art* for the first time might be struck by the absence of any reference either to the destruction wrought by the war on Europe's architectural heritage or to the looting of works of art on a grand scale first by the Nazis and then by the Russians.

Many masterpieces had been lost and some have even now not been recovered. But this lacuna was symptomatic of the time when it was written. In the aftermath of the war people did not need to be reminded of its horrors. The memories were fresh and the scars in the form of bombsites were all around them in London and other British cities as well as on the Continent. In all countries people wished to blot out the worst of what had happened and to get on with rebuilding their lives and societies. Even in Israel in the 1950s, as Ari Shavit has written, 'The Holocaust was not to be mentioned and war was a heroic memory.'[10]

The structure of the book is chronological. Its twenty-seven chapters begin with pre-history and march steadily through the Egyptians, Greeks, Romans and each succeeding school and period of Western European art until tailing off in the twentieth century. Once the early periods are out of the way the emphasis is very much on pictures rather than sculpture or architecture. Gombrich was already in his lifetime criticized for not writing enough about women and for being too Eurocentric. On both he was representative of an era that still had many years to run. When, in 1969, Kenneth Clark presented his famous and ground-breaking thirteen-part BBC television series entitled *Civilisation*,* which is still the single most famous television production ever devoted to the arts, it dealt only with Western Europe and women barely featured.

Nikolaus Pevsner wanted to become an art historian from an early age. At sixteen he wrote in his diary of 'the dream I had been cherishing for some time: to see myself as a professor of art history, in a small house of my own, with the lady wife and a child, teaching, going about my business, maybe now and again writing – a German idyll'.[11] The German aspect of this ambition was denied him when, after being

* Shortly afterwards he received a peerage and took the title of Lord Clark of Saltwood. Both then and since, however, he has always been known as Lord Clark of Civilisation.

elected to power in 1933, the Nazis introduced race laws that prevented Jews from holding academic appointments as well as barring them from many other activities. But in Britain he was able to bring the art historical aspect to fruition.

While being interned for a short while as an 'enemy alien', like many other German and Austrian refugees (including an uncle of mine), he embarked on a book entitled *An Outline of European Architecture*, which was published after his release in 1942. Only a hundred and sixty pages long, it has since gone into seven editions and been translated into sixteen languages. It came out under the Penguin Books Pelican imprint and marked a turning point in his long and happy relationship with the firm's founder, Allen Lane.

As the war drew to an end Lane asked him for ideas. He came up with two. One was for a Pelican History of Art series and the other, which must at the time have sounded the more modest, was for a series of county-by-county guides to British architecture. The History of Art series, which aimed to encompass the whole world, was launched under Pevsner's editorial guidance in 1953. It achieved considerable success, but it is to the latter, entitled *The Buildings of England*, that Pevsner owes his enduring reputation. The guides have become so much of an institution that they – the originals, the revisions and the later ones written by his successors – are known and referred to as 'Pevsners'. For many they are the template against which other guides are judged.

The idea was not original. It was inspired by a handbook of German artists that dated back to 1900. There had also been county guidebooks before, notably those published by the Shell oil company to boost petrol sales. But these had been mostly written by amateur enthusiasts whereas Pevsner was a recognized scholar with his architectural book to his credit. The first volume on Cornwall appeared in 1951 to be quickly followed by two more. Timing was a key factor in the venture's early success. In 1950 petrol rationing had finally come to an end so that, for the first time since 1939, people could think about driving for pleasure instead of keeping their ration for work purposes and emergencies. It was in its way a liberation and Pevsner gave them a reason to take advantage of it by exploring their own country. As foreign travel was still very restricted because of the limits imposed on the amount of money individuals could take out of the country, there were many who wished to do so.

Pevsner's modus operandi became legendary and inspired many legends. Two German refugee ladies, later succeeded by graduate assistants, would gather all the material they could find on the target county. Pevsner, usually driven by his wife Lola until her death in 1963, would then visit all the places of interest that they had identified. The pace was frantic. One of those who drove him round Warwickshire recalled, 'Our record was nineteen parishes in a day, that is nineteen churches, say some forty other buildings and an assortment of other features of interest.' In the evening, 'the Professor went to his room and wrote up everything he had seen that day … so when we got back to London the book was finished and needed only an introduction'.* Pevsner and whoever was accompanying him always stayed in modest accommodation and, rather than interrupt his work schedule, he never accepted social invitations. In this way, between 1951 and 1974, he completed forty-six volumes of which he wrote thirty-two alone and the remainder with the help of an assistant. A truly Stakhanovite achievement.

Since Pevsner's retirement and death a succession of other authors has produced them. The originals have been revised and enlarged to take account of new material, new areas have been introduced and the series has been extended to include Scotland, Wales and Ireland. Whether readers agree with the views and judgements expressed in the Pevsner guides is immaterial. Their value lies in providing a yardstick against

---

* *Oxford Dictionary of National Biography*, entry by Brian Harrison.

which readers can form their own views and a means of ensuring that when they embark on an exploration of a town or region they see all there is to be seen.

Gombrich's and Pevsner's great contribution to this country – the country of their adoption – can be summed up in seven words: they opened the eyes of the British. Art and guidebooks galore had existed before they arrived here. But, though English was not their mother tongue, they found ways of conveying information and guidance in a clear and accessible way that enabled more people than ever before to appreciate and understand what they were looking at. This was perhaps because they had been brought up in German, which, until the Second World War, had always been the principal language of art history. When Clark began his career in the 1920s Bernard Berenson, the American who was at that time the most famous connoisseur in the world, advised him that if he wanted to write about art he would have to read the great art historians in their own language.[12]

I have written about Gombrich's and Pevsner's success. But, like all who came to Britain to rebuild their lives in exile, they experienced difficult adjustment periods. At one point after his internment Pevsner had to work as a labourer clearing rubble from bombed London streets. All had to adapt to a new language and environment and usually to having much less money than they had been used to. They had to put their former habits and ambitions behind them and set themselves new goals. Some could not do so. Gombrich and Pevsner, and the others whose names are mentioned in this essay, succeeded magnificently and Britain has gained accordingly. But they are the ones who stand out. There were many for whom migration resulted in blighted hopes and disappointing lives. And, whether successful or not, all had to contend with the knowledge of how the relatives and friends they left behind had suffered and died. 'I think of it every day,' I heard Claus Moser say at his 90th birthday celebration in 2012. He had arrived in this country in 1936 at the age of fourteen. After a long and successful career as a statistician, academic, adviser to governments, head of an Oxford college, chairman of the Royal Opera House, member of the House of Lords and much else, the memory continued to weigh heavily upon him, as it did on many others until the day they died.

The Lonely Londoners

by Sam Selvon (1956)

City Of Spades

by Colin MacInnes (1957)

Absolute Beginners

by Colin MacInnes (1959)

Of all the changes that have taken place in this country during my lifetime the most visible is in the composition of the population. Until the arrival of black American troops during the Second World War few Britons would ever have set eyes on a person of a different colour. The American army at that time was segregated into all-black and all-white formations and I can still remember, with some embarrassment, how my nanny and I stared at a large contingent of black troops camped in a park in rural Essex through which we were being driven to a children's party. When the war ended and life began to return to normal, some American military remained and a trickle of students from the colonies started to arrive, but the figures were very small. It is thought that the total number of people of non-European ethnic origin resident in this country was only about twenty thousand, although there are no reliable statistics to draw on.*

A sense of how rarely most people encountered members of this minority and how they were regarded is conveyed by a diary entry in the Mass Observation Project *Our Hidden Lives: The Everyday Diaries of Forgotten Britain, 1945–1948*, an invaluable record of how ordinary people felt and thought on issues of every kind in those years. On 12 December 1946 Maggie Joy Blount, a freelance writer and public relations agent, records an evening at the theatre in Windsor: 'The part of coloured servant played by a real Negro. When company took their call at the end they stood in line as usual, hand in hand, all except the Negro who stood separately a little behind them.'[13]

The turning point came in 1948. The British Nationality Act of that year conferred British citizenship and the right to enter and settle in the United Kingdom on all people living in the Commonwealth. On 22 June, while it was still being debated in Parliament, a ship called the *Empire Windrush* docked at Tilbury and some five hundred Jamaican immigrants, many of whom had served in the British forces during the war, disembarked. This is generally taken to be the moment when large-scale immigration from the Commonwealth began though few realized it at the time. The Colonial Secretary, Arthur Creech Jones, said he didn't expect the *Windrush* passengers to last more than one winter and many of them were in any case not intending to make their lives here.[14]

At first the flow of immigrants arriving each year increased slowly, but, as the 1950s progressed, the combination of full employment and an expanding economy stimulated a demand for cheap immigrant labour, especially in such state-run services as the NHS and London Transport. By comparison with conditions in the West Indies, parts of the Indian

---

* The 1991 UK census was the first to include a question about ethnicity.

subcontinent and Africa, prospects in Britain looked enticing and the number of new arrivals rose sharply – in the case of West Indians alone from two thousand in 1953 to twenty-seven thousand five hundred in 1955.[15] These three documentary novels, published in 1956, 1957 and 1959, are set in London during the period when the first arrivals were finding their feet and Londoners were coming to terms with what it meant to have strangers of another colour in their midst.

The barbed and uneasy relationship between the old and the new communities is encapsulated in two conversations. In Sam Selvon's *The Lonely Londoners* the Trinidadian Moses Aloetta, who has been in London some time, explains the realities of life to the recently arrived Galahad: 'It had a time when I was first here, when it only had a few West Indians in London, and things used to go good enough. These days spades all over the place, and every shipload is big news, and the English people don't like the boys coming to England to work and live.' Galahad asks if, 'Things as bad here as in America?' Moses replies that discrimination is less overt, but nonetheless real: 'In America you see a sign telling you to keep off, but over here you don't see any, but when you go in the hotel or the restaurant they will politely tell you to haul – or else give you the cold treatment.' In fact, as the immigrant population increased so did notices, especially at lodging houses, proclaiming 'No Blacks', 'No Coloureds' or, most notorious of all, 'No Blacks, No Irish, No Dogs'.

In *City of Spades* by Colin MacInnes, the white intellectual Theodora Pace declares her love for the Nigerian student dropout Johnny Fortune, after which they somewhat bizarrely embark on a discussion about the implications of immigration. 'We'd better change our immigration laws,' she says. 'Otherwise we'll soon have a half-caste population.' His response goes to the heart of the British dilemma: 'Always you preach in England against colour bars in other countries! Now you can practise what you preach at home.'

Sam Selvon and Colin MacInnes approached the subject from different and complementary standpoints. Selvon was among the first wave of West Indians to reach this country, arriving in 1950. MacInnes was an upper-class Englishman. Neither, however, was typical of his tribe. Selvon, who was of largely Indian ancestry with a dash of white, had been a successful journalist in Trinidad and his first novel, *A Brighter Sun*, which was set there, was published in London in 1952. MacInnes, who had been educated in Australia, was openly gay when homosexuality was still against the law. He was also one of the white 'slummers' of both sexes, who went in search of sex and excitement among the West Indian community. Darcus Howe, one of this country's foremost campaigners for black rights for many years before his death in 2017, was, as a young man, among those MacInnes propositioned, in this case unsuccessfully.[16] But, unlike most such 'slummers', MacInnes recognized a responsibility towards the black community as he showed when becoming one of the founders of the legal charity Defence, set up to help black people who had been arrested or harassed by the police.

Selvon sets out to chronicle what it was like to be a West Indian immigrant by fictionalizing the experiences of a group of young men among whom he lived when he first came to London. Initially he tried to write in standard English. When he found that wouldn't work he created a sort of fusion between the idiom of the people he was writing about and the way English is written, an effective device that has since been followed in varying degrees by other writers. Nearly all the action takes place in the area where the West Indians first congregated, bounded in the west by 'the Gate' (Notting Hill), in the east by the 'Arch' (Marble) and in the north by 'the Water' (Bayswater).

That practically all the characters are young men reflects the fact that, whenever large numbers of people start to move from one part of the world to another, it is young men who lead the way. Women and families follow and not many had done so at the time about which

Selvon is writing. Only one family features in *The Lonely Londoners* though Moses feels a sense of failure when he sees other men, who have been in London for less time than he, saving up enough money to bring their families over.

He is sometimes asked by people in Trinidad to meet new arrivals. They get off the boat train at Waterloo station in summer suits, clutching cardboard suitcases and thinking they know what to expect because Britain, the mother country of the empire, has loomed so large in their education and in the lives of the colonies from which they come. In fact, they are completely unprepared for the cold, the fogs, which are brilliantly evoked, the food and the mix of metropolitan glamour on the one hand and squalor on the other that characterized London at that time. They have to learn that a sum of money that would represent wealth at home buys little in London, so that the high wages they thought they were coming to earn are actually quite modest, and that in any case jobs are harder to find and pay less for black men than for white.

At the employment office, Moses explains to Galahad: 'Suppose a vacancy come and they want to send a fellar, first they find out if they want coloured fellars before they send you. That save a lot of time and bother, you see. In the beginning it cause a lot of trouble when fellars went and said they came from the labour office and the people send them away saying it ain't have no vacancy. They don't tell you outright that they don't want coloured fellars, they just say sorry the vacancy get filled.' When another veteran finds a job for a recently arrived relative, he explains, 'the work is a hard work and mostly is spades they have working in the factory, paying lower wages than they would have to pay white fellars'.

Selvon describes how the immigrants cope with this strange and hostile environment – crowding together for company to talk about home, to eke out scarce resources and to eat rice and peas; how they learn to navigate the city, to find jobs, to adjust to prejudice and where to buy 'weed'. There is nothing self-pitying or sentimental about his account. Some prosper as hustlers or in more or less legitimate businesses, others rub along on whatever wages they can pick up. One resourceful character, living in a top-floor room in what is today the exclusive Dawson Place, in Notting Hill, finds a way to save money on food by trapping and cooking seagulls. Like many working-class people in those days before the lottery, the immigrants do the weekly football pools and dream of winning the top prize of £75,000 (almost £2 million in today's money).*

They dream of, and often succeed in, dating English girls – a 'skin' or 'a sharp piece of skin', a 'frauline' (sic), a 'cat', a 'number', a 'chick' or 'white pussy'. On his way to his first date with a white girl, 'a nice piece of skin waiting under the big clock at Piccadilly Tube Station', Galahad rhapsodizes: 'This is London, this is life oh lord, to walk like a king with money in your pocket, not a worry in the world.' But mostly the contacts are less romantically tinged as white women seek out black men for experience and excitement and black men take advantage of the opportunities at illicit drinking clubs known as shebeens or private parties. As Darcus Howe later remembered it: 'The girls were Australian, Swedish, whatever – it was black men and white girls – mine was Italian. That's how it was.'[17] In his books Colin MacInnes describes other parties of a more louche variety that take place in white people's homes.

Then there was the Bayswater Road, in those days famous for the large number of prostitutes who solicited openly from the 'Arch' to the 'Gate'.[18] The women often took their clients into the park, in the quieter parts of which others too engaged in sexual activities and assignations of various sorts.

The most striking passage in *The Lonely Londoners*, extending over ten pages without a full stop, is Moses Aloetta's stream-of-consciousness

---

* A complex form of betting through a pool on the results of the following Saturday's football matches.

reminiscence of his own and others' experiences in the park during the warm summer months. From buying sex from prostitutes for a pound, to white women looking for black men to have sex with there or to take home, to voyeurs offering to pay him to have sex with their wives while they watch, to 'white fellars who feel is a big thrill to hit a black number and the girls does make them pay big money' – 'people wouldn't believe you when you tell the things that happen'. Significantly, this is not a happy memory. As the reminiscence ends, 'Moses sigh a long sigh like a man who live life and see nothing at all in it and who frighten as the years go by wondering what it is all about.' In this and numerous other passages, Selvon conveys the pain and perplexity felt by so many immigrants who had come to London to seek their fortune only to end up trapped in lonely and aimless lives.

There is no violence in *The Lonely Londoners*. That came later when, in the late summer of 1958, the resentment Moses had referred to in his conversation with Galahad reached boiling point in the form of the so-called Notting Hill race riots. In *Absolute Beginners*, which is mainly about what, in the 1960s, came to be called 'swinging London' rather than the black community, MacInnes captures the atmosphere of sinister foreboding that preceded the riots and how they escalated from individual acts of violence by white on black to ambushes and pitched battles.

The book's white narrator is attacked for being a 'Darkie-luvver' when he is found talking to a group of black men. Among other violent incidents that are described, a particularly arresting image is that of a black youth fleeing from a white mob down Bramley Road and seeking refuge in a greengrocer's shop whose elderly white female proprietor then confronts his pursuers as they shout, 'Bring him out' and 'Lynch him'. In *Having It So Good*, about the 1950s, the contemporary historian Peter Hennessy records being told by a West Indian, who had served in the RAF during the war and returned to live in Notting Hill, of white gangs rampaging down Portobello Road and Colville Road chanting,

'Kill the niggers!'[19] The diarist and future Labour Cabinet minister Tony Benn, who lived nearby, was appalled by the gangs' use of petrol bombs, iron bars and razors during the riots.[20]

The impact of the riots on public opinion was profound and among the factors that, in the 1960s, led to political action on two fronts: the imposition of restrictions on immigration and the introduction of laws against racial discrimination. Both were progressively tightened over the following decades. Also during those decades, as Britain became more prosperous, parts of the area in which the immigrants had settled were 'gentrified' and gradually transformed into the fashionable area that the name Notting Hill conjures up today. The immigrants moved to other parts of London. Today only the annual August Bank Holiday Carnival remains as a reminder of its West Indian past.

City of Spades is a play on words, the description given by one of the book's white characters to 'a world where you've never set foot before' – the 'spade city' being created by West Indians, Africans and American GIs in the heart of London. MacInnes describes it with all the relish of a man who enjoys the milieu and wants both to convey that enjoyment and to shock his readers. It is a world of loosely disguised and, for those familiar with the scene, instantly recognizable clubs, pubs, restaurants and dance halls where black people gathered and black and white mixed. But the black characters are by no means representative. There are no ordinary individuals in boring jobs and struggling to look after the families, which, by the late 1950s, were beginning to arrive. They are colourful rogues engaged in petty thievery, drug trafficking and prostitution with always a hint of violence just below the surface. MacInnes clearly got a kick out of consorting with them and deals amusingly with the fumbling ineptitude of his white characters as they try to find their way around.

The result is a book damaging to race relations in two respects. The nature of its characters and the activities they are engaged in confirmed the prejudices held by whites about the alleged fecklessness, lawlessness and unreliability of black people. And, for that reason, it diminished the impact of his accounts of how the police abused their powers when dealing with black people, a problem that was to blight race relations for many years afterwards.

City of Spades represents a landmark as the first novel by an established white writer set mainly among black people. Moreover, it is the black rather than the white characters who, for the most part, set the terms of engagement between them. Individual black and ethnic minority characters were beginning to appear in plays and novels in the late 1950s. Shelagh Delaney's play *A Taste of Honey*, first shown in 1958, and Alan Sillitoe's *Saturday Night and Sunday Morning*, published in the same year,* are two examples, but *City of Spades* is of an altogether different order. That it should have been a voyeur's guide to the seamier side of life in itself speaks volumes about how white people regarded black and the disadvantages the newcomers were up against.

---

* See essay on *Love on the Dole* and *Saturday Night and Sunday Morning*.

Diverse Perspectives

The Doctor's Dilemma, 1906, to which is linked the *Preface on Doctors*, 1911, by George Bernard Shaw, and *The Citadel* by A. J. Cronin, 1937.

The Green Hat by Michael Arlen, 1924, and *The Vortex* by Noël Coward, 1924.

The Old School edited by Graham Greene, 1934.

Scoop by Evelyn Waugh, 1938, and *Brideshead Revisited* by Evelyn Waugh, 1945.

Strangers and Brothers by C. P. Snow, 1940–70, and *The Two Cultures and the Scientific Revolution* by C. P. Snow, 1959.

A Book of Mediterranean Food by Elizabeth David, 1950.

The Doctor's Dilemma (1906) and the *Preface on Doctors* (1911)

by George Bernard Shaw

The Citadel

by A. J. Cronin (1937)

Few books have so comprehensively captured the mood of the moment when they were published as A. J. Cronin's *The Citadel* in 1937. Within four months this novel excoriating the medical ethics and practices of its day had sold over one hundred and fifty thousand hardback copies. In the following year, a Gallup poll reported that it 'impressed' more people than any other book except the Bible.[1] It traces the career of Andrew Manson, a young Scottish doctor, from being an assistant general practitioner, or GP, in South Wales to a rich London practice and draws heavily on the experiences of its author, a Scottish doctor who had himself started in South Wales in the early 1920s and later practised in London before retiring to write novels. *The Citadel* was his fifth and most successful.

George Bernard Shaw was already established as a leading playwright when *The Doctor's Dilemma* was first performed in 1906, since when it has been frequently revived. It is a satire on both the ethics of the medical profession and on the artistic temperament as personified by the brilliant and corrupt Louis Dubedat, an artist dying of tuberculosis. It also deals with the issue of trying to weigh the value of one individual's life against another's, the dilemma that gives the play its title, and with the blindness of romantic love. Depending on the production, the medical ethics issues can become somewhat overshadowed by other aspects of the play. Shaw, however, attached such importance to them that in 1911, when the play was published in book form, he added a *Preface on Doctors* of nearly a hundred pages. In this he sets out his criticisms of the medical profession's methods and ethics as well as expounding some theories of his own.

He approached these matters as a sceptic about how much doctors could achieve or indeed really understood about what they were doing, an attitude attributed by some to his having caught smallpox as a young man after having been vaccinated against it.[2] His circle of friends, however, included the celebrated bacteriologist Sir Almroth Wright and the play was inspired, at least in part, by a visit he paid to Sir Almroth's laboratories at St Mary's Hospital in London and the discussions he had with those working there. The character of Sir Colenso Ridgeon in the play draws on that of Sir Almroth, who, it is believed, helped Shaw a good deal with its technical medical details.

Shaw's central concern in the *Preface* is with the conflicts of interest inherent in the provision of medical services in return for money. He deals first with the relationship between rich patients and their doctors where, he argues, it will always be in the doctor's interest to prescribe the most expensive form of treatment. He rejects as hypocritical the profession's claim to be impartial in making this choice. By that he doesn't mean doctors deliberately putting their own financial interest ahead of the welfare of their patients or recommending harmful courses of treatment in order to earn more money, although, of course, there must always be the risk of that. He has in mind something more nuanced.

He believed that, 'As to the honor [sic] and conscience of doctors, they have as much as any other class of men, no more and no less.' They are therefore, he argues, as likely as other men (they are all men in both the *Preface* and the play) to believe that a particular course of action is objectively the best if it also happens to coincide with their own pecuniary interest. The extent to which their judgement may be swayed by this consideration will vary from one individual to another, but it must always, he believed, play some part, consciously or subconsciously, in a doctor's diagnosis and prescription. As there is so often more than one valid course of action in treating a condition, it will always be possible to make the case, and genuinely to believe, that the most expensive treatment is the most appropriate.

The temptation to err on the side of profit is enhanced by the propensity of consumers of all forms of goods and services to equate price and fame with quality. This is especially true of medicine about which most people know very little. The more fearful a person is, Shaw argues, either on their own behalf, or that of a loved one, the more likely they are to demand 'the best' regardless of cost in the hope of avoiding suffering and death. When they are advised that the newest treatment, or the most expensive, or the most fashionable, which are often one and the same, is the most suitable for their condition, it is often what they want to hear. If, nonetheless, the loved one dies, a large bill can reassure the survivor that no effort or expense was spared.

An incident in *The Citadel* illustrates this point. Andrew Manson refers a patient to a fashionable and expensive but incompetent surgeon with whom he has a financial relationship. The patient dies during the operation and Manson is overcome by remorse. But when he tries to apologize to the patient's widow for referring her husband to such an incompetent, she will have none of it. She is proud that her husband had been in the hands of a famous surgeon, she has boasted about it to her friends and she is happy in the belief that everything money could buy was done on his behalf.

Shaw argues that there will always be those among the rich and privileged who, when sick or caring for someone who is, will seek out the most famous doctor in the relevant field and invest a blind faith in his powers, as Mrs Dubedat does in the play when she pleads with Sir Colenso to save the life of her husband. That she is not, in fact, rich is incidental. She comes from the social class of people who are and is confident that Sir Colenso will attach as much worth to her husband's talent and future fame as he would to money.

This credulity, Shaw suggests, is often misplaced. Among the characters in the play, Sir Colenso has earned respect for his new treatment for tuberculosis. But Sir Ralph Bloomfield Bonnington, who takes on Dubedat's case when Sir Colenso says his hands are full, is casual to the point of negligence in his methods while the dandified surgeon Mr Cutler Walpole is a fraud. Shaw created these characters for dramatic effect, but their banter about misdiagnoses and operations that have gone wrong or served no useful purpose give substance to a serious accusation he makes against the medical profession in the *Preface*; namely that its members will always support each other when a mistake occurs: 'The only evidence that can decide a case of malpractice is expert evidence: that is, the evidence of other doctors; and every doctor will allow a colleague to decimate a whole countryside sooner than violate the bond of professional etiquette by giving him away.'

This was a fair point. Not only in medicine but in other professions too professional solidarity took priority over the public interest in Shaw's day. Today codes of behaviour, reporting procedures and regulatory structures are much stronger, but professional solidarity still exercises a powerful influence and abuses can still occur. Constant vigilance is required and whistle-blowers have a vital role to play.

If the practice of medicine was distorted by too much money among the rich, the opposite, Shaw argues in the *Preface*, was the case among the poor. When a poor man can't afford to pay more than a pittance, 'it is kinder to give him a bottle of something almost as cheap as water and tell him to come again with another eighteenpence if it does not cure him' than to suggest remedies that are beyond his means. In the play Dr Schutzmacher, who had begun his career working among the poor, boasts of how he had always prescribed the same medicine regardless of a patient's condition: 'Parrish's Chemical Food: phosphates, you know. One tablespoonful to a twelve-ounce bottle of water: nothing better, no matter what the case is.'

Whereas the rich were desperate to use their wealth to try new remedies, the poor, Shaw believed, were in thrall to ideas handed down from the past and suspicious of new ideas. 'The doctor,' he warns, 'learns that if he gets ahead of the superstitions of his patients he is a ruined man; and the result is that he instinctively takes care not to get ahead of them.' So, among both rich and poor there was a conspiracy between doctors and patients – among the rich to prescribe what is newest and most expensive, among the poor to stick with familiar remedies and the time-honoured bottle of coloured fluid.

Manson learns these lessons when he arrives in South Wales straight from medical school as an assistant GP full of enthusiasm and new ideas. He is shocked to find the surgeries, including that of the doctor for whom he works, dispensing medicines that are little more than coloured water. He is disappointed by his patients' reluctance to try unfamiliar remedies, sometimes with tragic results. When he advises a miner whose arm had been badly scalded by boiling water on how to treat it his prescription runs counter to the traditional remedy proposed by the District Nurse, a respected figure in the community. When he perseveres, he is told he is no longer wanted, with the result that the man is left with a permanently disabled arm and Manson loses a patient.

Another problem is the unwillingness of the local District Medical Officer of Health to stand up to the local council if that involves incurring expenditure, which leads to one of the most celebrated incidents in *The Citadel*. When Manson and another doctor identify contaminated water from a particular sewer as the cause of an outbreak of typhoid the Medical Officer fails to press the council to replace it. The two doctors thereupon take matters into their own hands by blowing up the sewer and successfully blaming the explosion on its own inert gases, thereby forcing the construction of a new one.

Over time, through sheer hard work and following a few spectacular successes, Manson wins the confidence of the local people, initially in one small town and then in another nearby. On one occasion he revives a baby the midwife had given up as stillborn. On another he saves a man from being certified as insane when he identifies and treats the illness that has given rise to the mental disorder. On a third he goes underground to amputate a miner's arm that that has been trapped under fallen rubble thereby freeing the man himself to be brought to the surface.

Yet his career cannot progress. In his first post the doctor for whom he works as an assistant has been incapacitated by a stroke and will never be able to resume his duties. Because there is no mechanism to remove him Manson does all the work while the doctor's wife* pockets the proceeds out of which she pays him a small salary. He moves to a neighbouring town to work for one of the medical aid societies set up by the miners' trade union. There he runs into more problems. His refusal to sign sick notes for malingerers and the methods by which he pursues his private research into the causes of lung disease among miners make him powerful enemies and he feels obliged to leave. His research enables him to secure a post in London with an official body

* This character in *The Citadel* so closely resembled the wife of the doctor for whom Cronin had worked as an assistant in South Wales that she successfully sued for libel. Cronin settled out of court and in subsequent editions wife was changed to sister.

concerned with the health of miners. He believes this will be his great opportunity, but soon discovers that it is controlled by the mine owners and he is sidelined as a troublemaker.

Manson at last achieves professional recognition when he buys a small general practice in a modest part of London with the intention of serving the local community. Here he comes into his own in a community that respects his talents. His reputation spreads and increasing numbers of prosperous people from other parts of London flock to consult him. At this point his moral compass deserts him.

He becomes infatuated by money and involved with a clique of self-serving physicians and surgeons who pass patients from one to the other, pander to hypochondriacs, promote pseudo-scientific remedies on behalf of their manufacturers and prescribe the most expensive treatments and operations. Only when one of his seriously ill patients dies while being operated on by an incompetent member of the clique in the incident referred to above are Manson's eyes opened. Appalled and remorseful, he decides to leave London and, with two old friends, to set up a new practice in the Midlands based on the most modern ideas.

Before he can do so disaster strikes and the novel reaches its crescendo. Manson had had under his care a young woman, the daughter of a dear friend, suffering from tuberculosis. Believing that the treatment she was receiving at a leading London hospital was doing her no good he had removed her to one run by an American pioneer of a new form of treatment. Together they had performed a procedure on her that had been entirely successful. But the American was not a formally qualified and registered doctor. His former associates, out to get him, report him to the General Medical Council for a breach of medical ethics and he is put on trial for his professional life. Friends and foes alike expect him to be struck off, but in a dramatic denouement he convinces his judges that he was acting in the best interests of his patient and is allowed to continue with his career. Thus, the book ends on a hopeful note with the medical establishment showing itself, on this occasion at least, willing to defy professional solidarity in favour of the outsider.

Cronin and Shaw can both reasonably be accused of unfairness and lack of balance in their portrayal of contemporary British healthcare. But they were not aiming at objectivity. They were polemicists inveighing against long-standing and deep-seated abuses and drawing attention to issues that needed to be tackled. They largely agreed on their diagnoses but differed on the remedy.

In the *Preface* Shaw argues that 'Until the medical profession becomes a body of men trained and paid by the country to keep the country in health it will remain what it is at present: a conspiracy to exploit popular credulity and human suffering.' He therefore welcomed the introduction of the National Health Service in 1948, two years before his death at the age of ninety-four. In *The Citadel*, when Manson reflects on the inadequacies of the hospital system he asks himself whether a state system might be the answer but rejects it: 'No damn it, that's hopeless – bureaucracy chokes individual effort – it would suffocate me.' The nearest he comes to setting out a reform programme is in his impassioned speech at the GMC in which he argues, 'We ought to be arranged in scientific units. There ought to be a great attempt to bring science into the front line, to do away with the old bottle-of-medicine idea, give every practitioner a chance to study, to co-operate in research.' He insists that commercialism must be taken out of medicine but does not suggest how that should be done.

Despite this, *The Citadel* helped to create the climate of opinion that, after the Second World War, led to the creation of the NHS. It also achieved fame and influence of a less welcome sort. In Germany during the war it was used with Cronin's other novels to discredit Britain. In April 1944 the Jewish diarist Victor Klemperer, who, despite dreadful privations and persecution, was still living in Dresden, wrote in his diary: 'Propaganda: English novels are banned of course;

but there are books by A. J. Cronin in every shop window: he's Scottish and exposes shortcomings of social and public services in England.'[3] Ironically Cronin himself was at that time propagandizing on behalf of the British war effort while working for the Ministry of Information in Washington.

The Green Hat

by Michael Arlen (1924)

The Vortex

by Noël Coward (1924)

In the mid-1920s Michael Arlen and Noël Coward, the one destined for obscurity, the other for immortality, were on a roll together. Arlen's novel *The Green Hat* was the literary sensation of 1924 while Coward's play *The Vortex* was its counterpart on the London stage. There was no doubt as to who was the bigger star. Coward had been unable to find a leading London theatre management to back his play and was only able to put it on at a small Hampstead theatre thanks to a loan from Arlen of £250 (£15,000 in today's money).[4] It was an immediate success, soon transferred to the West End and became his breakthrough into the big time. But when, in the following year, it opened in New York in the same week as a dramatized version of *The Green Hat* the *New Yorker* magazine reported, 'The Green Hat was consuming most of the attention with the opening attracting "every bigwig of Broadway", including Irving Berlin.'[5] In 1928 a film adaptation entitled *A Woman of Affairs* was produced, starring Greta Garbo.

It was not only in terms of sales and celebrity status that Arlen was highly regarded. In his memoir, *A Moveable Feast*, about his time in Europe in the 1920s, Ernest Hemingway records driving from Lyons to Paris with Scott Fitzgerald. 'Scott was very cheerful and happy and healthy and told me the plots of each and every one of Michael Arlen's books. Michael Arlen, he said was the man you had to watch and he and I could learn much from him.'[6] Sometime after this trip Hemingway sent Fitzgerald the draft of his first novel, *The Sun Also Rises*. Fitzgerald replied, 'You've done a lot of writing that honestly reminded me of Michael Arlen', which led Hemingway to cut out its first fifteen pages.[7] Even so his character Brett Ashley was considered by many American critics at the time to be derived from Iris Storm, the principal character in *The Green Hat*, although in fact she probably owed more to Lady Duff Twysden with whom Hemingway had been travelling in Spain.

Anthony Powell was another who fell under Arlen's spell. He recalls in his memoirs that when he arrived in London from Oxford in 1926 he decided not to live in the areas chosen by most of his friends and contemporaries. 'I had my own ideas, though I might not have admitted to everyone that the Shepherd Market seduction scene which opens Michael Arlen's novel, *The Green Hat* (1924) chiefly caused me to set my sights on that small enclave (also described in Disraeli's *Tancred*) so unexpectedly concealed among the grand residences of Mayfair.'[8] In *A Question of Upbringing*, the first novel in his own famous A Dance to the Music of Time sequence, which is set in the 1920s, Powell has two Oxford undergraduates discuss *The Green Hat* with one borrowing it from the other in the belief that it will unlock the secrets of what goes on in fashionable London society.[9]

The Green Hat is the story of Iris Storm, twice widowed and famously promiscuous. It was the first novel about the Bright Young Things of the 1920s – their parties, extravagances, fast cars, nightclubs and frivolity – to become a bestseller. Evelyn Waugh's *Vile Bodies*, published in 1930, has long since become the most famous example of the genre and a symbol of the decade. But in the decade itself it was *The Green Hat* which held that position. In the words of Waugh's novelist brother Alec, Michael Arlen was both 'the spokesman of a new type of woman who was demanding a man's right to live her life in the way she chose' and 'the spokesman of a disenchanted generation'.[10]

In the opening scene Iris Storm, wearing her signature green hat, arrives in Shepherd Market in her yellow Hispano-Suiza, one of the most glamorous cars of the period, to visit her alcoholic brother. The narrator, who lives in the flat below, shows her the way and, when they find him in a drunken stupor, is rewarded by spending the night with her. As the novel unfolds her history emerges. On her wedding night, when she was only nineteen, her husband fell to his death from their bedroom window. Her explanation, that he did so 'for purity', is widely taken to mean that he had committed suicide after finding that she wasn't a virgin. She bears out this interpretation by embarking on a string of affairs. Her second marriage, to an army officer with a Victoria Cross, is quickly cut short when he deliberately courts death in a shootout against Sinn Fein rebels in Ireland, thereby giving rise to more rumours and insinuations. Finally, after various other adventures, she has a miscarriage after sleeping with Napier Harpenden, an up-and-coming young diplomat she has known since childhood. They decide to elope, which, given the conventions of the time, means the destruction of his career and the hopes his father had for him as well as the end of his marriage.

The moral of the book lies in the last chapter, in which she and Napier's father confront each other. She reproaches him for having forced Napier to give her up when they were in love as eighteen-year-olds because he believed that with her as his wife Napier would be unable to fulfil the paternal ambitions he had for him. This had changed the course of her life. Though she had slept with many men since, 'I have only told one that I loved him', and that was Napier. She had married her first husband simply because she needed sex. The reason for his suicide was that he had syphilis and hadn't wanted to infect her. Her second went to his death because he had heard her declare her love for Napier in her sleep.

She denounces the father's values and the ambitions he held for his son. 'I despise your England,' she tells him and denies the right of old men like him to impose their ideas on the young since it was those ideas that 'have sent all Europe to the devil'. She rejoices in breaking Napier's diplomatic career because it was inherent in the nature of the diplomacy of the time that the world had been plunged into war. When they were young the father had been able to impose his will. But, instead of submitting as tradition demanded, Iris had rebelled. She had defied convention by her way of life and now at the age of thirty she is reclaiming the man she had always loved.

However, in a metaphor for the period, it is the old conventions that triumph in the same pyrrhic fashion as the Allied victory in the recent war. The unexpected arrival of Napier and his wife, who has acquiesced in the elopement, destroys her resolve. Iris flees back to her car, drives away at high speed and crashes into a tree beneath which she and Napier used to play as children. The narrator finds her green hat lying near the wreckage. Everybody has lost.

Today the way Arlen links the tragedy of Iris and Napier with the causes of the recent war and the great moral issues of the period seem absurdly over-dramatized and over-written. In 1924, coupled with Iris' scandalous behaviour, that link helped to propel the book up the bestseller lists while Arlen himself inspired the admiration of one of the greatest American writers of his generation.

The Vortex too is about intergenerational conflict, with cocaine as well as sex deployed to shock the audience. The chief protagonists are an ageing socialite mother with a much younger lover, the latest in a long line, and her drug-addict son, Nicky, the part Coward wrote for himself.

It begins as a light-hearted comedy of manners titillating the audience as a take-off of high society decadence and develops into a deeply serious confrontation between the mother and son as the son forces her to face up to the consequences of her selfish and immoral behaviour on those around her and above all on him. She is forced to accept her share of responsibility for him having become a drug addict and the play ends with both promising to try to overcome their addictions.

Both *The Green Hat* and *The Vortex* were entertainments, not political or social tracts, yet their popularity was a manifestation of the widespread post-war ambivalence about traditional values coupled with unease about their decline. The connection drawn between Napier's father's ambitions for his family and the attitudes that led to the horrors of the First World War struck a chord with Arlen's readers. When Coward presented high society as shallow and corrupt, his audiences both laughed and fretted that the country was losing its bearings.

The play transformed Coward into an icon of the age. Men everywhere wanted to ape the manners and appearance of Nicky, an image as far removed from the correct and upright ideal of the pre-war years as it is possible to imagine. As the famous photographer and arbiter of fashion Cecil Beaton puts it in his book *The Glass of Fashion*: 'All sorts of men suddenly wanted to look like Noël Coward – sleek and satiny, clipped and well groomed, with a cigarette, a telephone, or a cocktail at hand ... Coward's influence spread even to the outposts of Rickmansworth and Poona';[11] in other words to the outer London suburbs and to the best-known hill station of the British Raj in India. So ubiquitous was the image that it became one of the hallmarks of the decade.

The Vortex, in the words of his biographer Sheridan Morley, 'gave Coward as actor and as playwright his name, his reputation and his future'.[12] Arlen recognized the play's quality. 'If I had written that,' he said when he went backstage after the first night, 'I should have been so very proud.'[13] When their two plays were running together in New

York, rumours began to circulate that jealousy had come between them. To show that this was not so, they decided to dine together once a week at a nightclub.

Thereafter their careers diverged. With each succeeding decade Coward was able, with only a few mishaps, to capture the public mood on both sides of the Atlantic as one success followed another. His total output was enormous. At his death in 1973 it was estimated to include some forty plays and musicals, ten films and television scripts, fifteen musical reviews and cabarets plus books, short stories and memoirs. His 1942 film *In Which We Serve*, about a Royal Navy destroyer and its commander, based on the Duke of Edinburgh's uncle Lord Louis Mountbatten, and his ship, HMS *Kelly*, is one of the great classics of British wartime cinema. In 1964, forty years after his initial triumph, he was invited to direct his 1925 play *Hay Fever* at the National Theatre, the first living dramatist to be produced there.

Arlen was never able to repeat the success of *The Green Hat*, but he continued to write books and short stories that were highly popular both in Britain and the United States. Some were turned into films and he made a great deal of money. He also achieved indirect success when the lyricist and song writer Eric Maschwitz 'stole' and slightly adapted the title of one of his short stories to 'When the Nightingale Sang in Berkeley Square', which became one of the romantic classics of the 1940s on both sides of the Atlantic. Arlen, Maschwitz records, 'was genuinely delighted and insisted that the printed version of it should be dedicated to him'.[14] During the 1930s, Arlen enjoyed the fruits of his success, living with his family in some style near Cannes where Somerset Maugham, H. G. Wells, P. G. Wodehouse, Aldous Huxley and other famous writers had houses.

When war broke out in 1939, he and his family immediately returned to Britain. His wife joined the Red Cross and he was appointed Civil Defence Public Relations Officer for the East Midlands. However, when Bulgaria entered the war on the German side, questions were raised in the House of Commons about his loyalty, for Arlen had been born in that country of Armenian parents and his original name was Dikran Kouyoumdjian. In 1901, six years after his birth, his parents had moved to England and given him a public school education at Malvern College, after which he had acquired British nationality and changed his name. There had never been any secret about this. He himself had often[15] drawn attention to his foreign origins, in words calculated to raise a smile and disarm criticism, by describing himself 'as every other inch a gentleman'.* But faced with such questions he and his wife decided to leave the country. They settled in New York where, in the 1950s, Alec Waugh found him holding court every day at lunchtime in the King Cole Room of the St Regis Hotel. He died in 1956, while Noël Coward went on from one success to another.

* *Oxford Dictionary of National Biography*, entry by M. R. Bellasis, revised by Rebecca Mills.

The Old School

edited by Graham Greene (1934)

'Just as the heart of England is the middle class, so the heart of the middle class is the public school system,' wrote E. M. Forster in *Notes on the English Character* in 1920.[16] That is still true as I write nearly a hundred years later, which would have surprised many in the 1930s and 1940s. I remember the author and scientist C. P. Snow telling the Cambridge Union during a debate in the late 1950s that when the war ended he had been sure that, whatever else might happen in the coming years, the public schools would disappear and how surprised he was that they hadn't. In the early 1930s, Graham Greene, then at the outset of his literary career and himself the son of a headmaster,* was sure that they would. In his preface to *The Old School*, published in 1934, he writes, 'there can be no small doubt that the system which this book represents is doomed. Too few people can afford the fees of a public school.' He also believed that the class distinctions in society on which the public schools were based 'will not remain unaltered'.

Greene intended this collection of essays by various writers recalling their own school days to be the system's memorial, 'like a family photograph album'. For the purposes of comparison, it includes

* Of Berkhamsted School.

a few recollections by men who went to other sorts of school and by women who went to girls' schools, but the classical boys' public schools to which Forster referred form its core. The essays describe what it was like to be a public school boy – there were no girls – and what the schools were trying to achieve during the first quarter of the twentieth century.

The poet W. H. Auden, who was very happy at Gresham's School, Holt, in the early 1920s, describes their purpose as being 'the mass-production of gentlemen'. Another contributor, J. N. Richards, who went to Winchester, quotes with approval a suggestion that 'the public school system might be likened to a sausage machine – all kinds of meats were put into it, but only a monotony of sausages came out at the other end'. The diplomatic historian and diarist Harold Nicolson, who went to Wellington College in 1900, describes their aim in more hyperbolic terms as being 'to provide a large number of standardized young men fitted for the conquest, administration and retention of a vast Oriental Empire'.

Parents sent their sons to public schools so that, whatever their own background, their boys should emerge as gentlemen. That is to say as men instantly recognizable by their accent and manner as entitled to give orders, to employ others and to be treated with deference and respect by those who did not possess the same attributes. For some that was a sufficient basis on which to make a life. Richards, about whom I have been able to discover nothing, concludes his essay with an expression of gratitude to Winchester for an education that 'has admirably suited me to the life of leisure which I find most congenial to my temper'. For others it provided the foundation for building a successful career, whether, as Nicholson suggests, in running the empire, or in the arts, sciences, the professions, business or government.

There were men who had not been to public school at the apex of all these activities, more indeed than is often supposed. But they were always the exceptions who had had to overcome considerable difficulties to reach the top whereas public school old boys had been on an inside track. Whether or not a man's parents were well-established members of the middle and upper classes or new money, if he had been to a public school that fact in itself established him as a gentleman with all its consequential advantages. Some schools were, of course, more prestigious than others. To have been to Eton or Winchester provided access to better networks and more opportunities than Gresham's or Berkhamsted. Those who had been to the former would have looked down on those who had been at the latter. Nonetheless, for a man the crucial distinction between being a member of the upper or the lower orders – the leaders and the led – was whether or not he had been to a public school.

This privilege came at a price and not just in parental money. By the standards of today life at the public schools, though better than in Victorian times, was in some respects very harsh. Two features stand out: fagging and beating. Fagging was a system whereby junior boys acted as servants to their seniors. It took different forms at different schools, but often included such chores as cleaning the senior boy's study, lighting its coal fire and toasting crumpets for his tea. Sometimes they were more esoteric as the children's writer Roald Dahl recalls in his autobiography. At Repton in 1929 the lavatories were in an unheated outhouse where he was obliged each morning to sit on a seat to warm it before a senior boy used it.[17]

In some schools the juniors were at the permanent beck and call of their seniors so that if, for instance, a senior boy wanted a letter posted or a message delivered to some distant part of the school, he could stand in a corridor and shout 'Fag' at the top of his voice. The small boys would then have to interrupt whatever they were doing, including studying, and come running, with the last to arrive being assigned the task. When Anthony Powell, famous now for his great sequence of novels A Dance to the Music of Time, was at Eton, he found responding to summonses of this sort while trying to study 'very irksome', but this was more than made up for by the enjoyment of exercising power when he became a senior. 'Who again,' he writes in his essay, 'will be in a position to summon by a shout fifteen servants who know that physical agony will be the price of disobedience?'

By physical agony he meant a beating. Corporal punishment was commonplace in all public schools. It could be administered both by masters and by those senior boys who, as prefects or monitors, assisted the masters in maintaining discipline. The regime varied from one school to another, but in most it was often meted out for the most trivial offences, such as failing to respond to a senior boy's call, breaching a dress code or being late for an engagement. L. P. Hartley, now best remembered for his novel *The Go-Between*, records that, while at Harrow from 1910 to 1915, he was 'whopped for being late for House singing'. Later he became Head of House in which capacity he 'did not mind whopping delinquents' and would take 'practice shots against the curtain of my bed to get my hand in'.

Modern readers, who did not experience corporal punishment at school, will be surprised by the matter-of-fact tone in which the contributors to *The Old School* refer to beatings and the reasons why they were administered. They were regarded as part of daily life and none of them claims to have suffered any lasting ill effects because of them. This accords with my own experience between 1950 and 1955 at Ampleforth where, like many others, I was subjected both to beatings on my behind with a cane and on my hands with a leather strap, depending on the nature of the offence. Much as we disliked it, we did not, as I recall, consider it to be any big deal. In accordance with the psychological theories then becoming fashionable, the literary editor of the *Spectator* in the 1930s, Derek Verschoyle, who was at Malvern in the mid-1920s, provides an explanation for the prevalence of corporal punishment. He suggests, 'The tradition of corporal punishment grew up side by side with the tradition of unmarried masters', and that it provided a form 'of acute sexual release'. He also notes that 'with the increasing number of married masters, there has been a decline in the amount of corporal punishment inflicted'.

Another theme that runs through most of the contributions is sport. Auden gives thanks for the fact that at his school 'athletics were treated as they ought to be treated, as something to be enjoyed not made a fetish of'. This was by no means common. At many other schools, sport played a central, not to say dominant, role in the lives of the boys. It was the principle yardstick by which success was judged and prestige earned. Around it was constructed a culture of *esprit de corps* and loyalty to the school and the houses into which it was divided that was supposed to be a template for the emotions they would later be expected to feel towards their country and whatever institutions they became part of.

At Rugby during the First World War, the novelist, poet and critic William Plomer gained the impression 'that the ritual of the cricket field was more elaborate and just a trifle more sincerely performed than that of the chapel'. This is obviously somewhat tongue in cheek, but there is real resentment in Harold Nicolson's recollection that at Wellington his scholastic promise counted for nothing beside his inability to succeed at any sort of sport. He felt that it 'retarded the growth of any self-confidence or "will" or even "character for seven shrouded years"'. Others must similarly have suffered.

Other themes recur with varying degrees of frankness. Vice, by which was meant homosexual acts between boys, and the measures taken to combat it, such as the absence of doors on the lavatories at Malvern or the removal of their locks at Berkhamsted, receive only passing references. It was such a well-known feature of public school life during this period that it could not have been completely ignored, although most of the references are somewhat oblique. An exception is Verschoyle when he states: 'The fact of homosexuality is a natural and transitory condition of adolescence, and that the very conditions of school life designed to suppress it are the ones most likely to produce homosexual fixation, is naturally not recognized nor taken into consideration' by the school authorities. To express such an opinion showed how much times had changed since 1917 when Alec Waugh had brought a storm of obloquy down on his head as a result of the very circumspect references in *The Loom of Youth*[18] to homosexual relationships between boys at Sherborne, where he had been at school.

Most public schools had imposing chapels. Religious education and the formal practice of the Anglican religion were conspicuous features of their culture. It was not uncommon for headmasters to be clergymen and to go on to become bishops. The Headmaster of Rugby in Plomer's day, Albert David, later became Bishop of Liverpool. As late as after the Second World War Michael Ramsey followed Geoffrey Fisher as Archbishop of Canterbury, having earlier succeeded him as Headmaster of Repton. Even so, Auden captures a general sense that comes through in other contributions when he writes that 'a Christian world view has broken down among schoolmasters'. Religion had become a formality.

Catholics were forbidden by their own bishops from going to Protestant schools unless they received a special dispensation. Instead they went to exclusively Catholic establishments run on the same lines by the religious orders of which the Benedictine Ampleforth and Downside and the Jesuit Stonyhurst and Beaumont were the best-known. Some, though not all, other schools accepted Jews. The nature of the tensions this could cause can be detected from a revealing passage in Powell's essay. When he arrived at Eton in 1919, he found that his house had a poor reputation. This was in part due to lack of sporting success. But, 'Worse still there had been a period in the immediate past, happily drawing to a close at the time of my arrival, when the non-Aryan proportion in its membership seemed to many unnecessarily high.'

As most of the contributors were at school during or soon after the First World War, it is not surprising that the Officers' Training Corps, generally known as Corps, features in several of the memoirs. Designed to provide boys with a rudimentary understanding of military matters and weaponry, it involved parading in khaki at set times each week for drill and martial exercises of various kinds plus field days when mock battles were fought, and a summer camp with an army unit. It loomed equally large in the lives of those of us who were at school during the Second World War and the Cold War.

I believe that at some schools it was possible to get out of Corps on grounds of conscience. At Catholic schools that was not the case as the monks who ran them regarded themselves as experts on such matters. At Ampleforth, when we paraded on Monday and Friday afternoons and at other Corps occasions, Father Peter, the Housemaster of the Junior House, metamorphosed into Lieutenant Colonel Utley with other monks as his subordinate officers in military uniforms with badges of rank. As, unlike most men of their age, they had not fought in the war because of being in Holy Orders, this was somewhat ironic. The real work was done by a former regular army sergeant major.

Several contributors pay tribute to a particular master who inspired them. Auden, Powell and the writer and critic Arthur Calder-Marshall, who was at St Paul's in the early 1920s, all commend in varying degrees the quality of the teaching they received. Nicolson, on the other hand, has 'no affection for, nor gratitude towards, my own old school' though when he revisits it in the 1930s he finds it somewhat improved. Exams, which now mean so much to the schools, parents and pupils – as they did to us in the 1950s – are never mentioned. Nor is there any reference as to whether they weighed on the minds of the contributors during their school days or what passing or failing ever meant to them. It was the fact of having been at a public school that above all determined the opportunities a man would have in life, not the exams he took while there.

However, nearly all the contributors express views on the curricula their schools followed, believing them to be out of date and with too much emphasis on the Classics. They also express regret at the class-consciousness with which they had been so thoroughly imbued. In this context the contribution by the poet Stephen Spender, about University College School in London, where he was a day boy, stands out. Most unusually 25 per cent of the boys there had won scholarships from state schools and some came from very poor backgrounds. As a result, he felt he had a better idea than those who went to conventional public schools of how privileged his family was and of how most of the country lived. For his part Graham Greene looks forward to a more radical reform of the system than extending the UCS model. In his conclusion, he holds up Norway with its almost universal system of state education in the hands of non-political civil servants as the example Britain should follow.

Scoop

by Evelyn Waugh (1938)

Brideshead Revisited

by Evelyn Waugh (1945)

Evelyn Waugh was one of the best writers in the English language anywhere in the world during the twentieth century. His novels are a joy to read, his characters memorable, his satire coruscating and his scorn venomous. But it is for the beauty and clarity of his prose that he earns his place in the pantheon of greats. In the words of the Australian essayist and critic Simon Leys, 'the way in which Waugh manipulates language is akin to the poetic mode of literary creation: his is first of all an art of words'.[19]

His output was considerable. Besides the novels for which he is most famous, it includes travel books and biographies, some of which cast a penetrating light on the times in which he lived. As I have already described in an earlier chapter, he displayed the most remarkable foresight, when in his 1931 travel book, *Remote People*, he raised the question of whether the European colonization of Africa would survive for more than another twenty-five years. In these two books, *Scoop*, published in 1938, and *Brideshead Revisited*, published in 1945, he tackles two quite different subjects.

Scoop, as its title indicates, is about newspapers. It exposed their methods and satirized their morals and mores, the people who worked for them and the tycoons who owned them. As such it is unique. No other British author has mounted so powerful an attack on the press on such a wide front. Some have attacked the proprietors, others have mocked journalists. Waugh went for both simultaneously and he did so at a time when the press was at the height of its power. With radio still quite a new phenomenon in the 1930s, newspapers were the nation's principal source of news, the prism through which people saw and learned about the world and the catalyst for their political opinions and judgements.

Their proprietors were larger-than-life characters, who used their newspapers to wield political influence and who themselves sometimes became directly involved in politics. During the First World War Lord Rothermere of the *Daily Mail* and Lord Beaverbrook of the *Daily* and *Sunday Express* had both served in Lloyd George's government while Beaverbrook would do so again in Churchill's during the Second World War. The press and its proprietors could turn their fire on whoever they chose but were themselves to a great extent immune. As authors depended on newspapers for reviews, coverage and commissions, it took unusual courage or recklessness for a writer to make them and their owners objects of ridicule.

That is what Waugh did. His portrait of Lord Copper, the proprietor of the *Daily Beast*, is both mocking and patronizing. Within his own empire Copper is an omnipotent dictator whose employees quail before him. 'Up to a point, Lord Copper', the words his foreign editor uses to indicate dissent when his proprietor says something blatantly wrong, has entered the language as the epitome of obsequiousness. Yet Lord Copper is largely unaware of anything beyond his own interests, in awe of society hostesses and putty in their hands. He cares nothing for either the moral issues at stake in the news his papers carry or for the veracity of their reports. When a war breaks out abroad he is concerned only with whether it will be a 'promising' source of copy. What he wants is for his journalists to scoop the opposition in order to generate the excitement that will boost circulation and profits.

Contemporaries would have immediately recognized the *Daily Beast*'s office as being based on the Express Group's black-glass palace in Fleet Street. Lord Copper is a more composite figure embodying aspects of, among others, both Beaverbrook, who threatened to sue when he saw the original dust jacket of *Scoop**, and Rothermere. The *Daily Beast* and its great rival the *Daily Brute* are obviously modelled on the *Daily Express* and the *Daily Mail*.

The novel is built on a misunderstanding. To please the society hostess Mrs Stitch, Lord Copper agrees to send her protégé, the fashionable young novelist John Boot, to cover an African civil war. When the foreign editor receives the instruction, he thinks his proprietor must be referring to William Boot, the young man who writes the paper's weekly nature notes. William is accordingly dispatched to the war zone with an unlimited expense account and a mountain of expensive equipment that provides Waugh with a running joke. A comic farce then unfolds. The hapless William Boot, with no idea of what he is supposed to be doing and outmanoeuvred at every turn by the ruthless professionals of rival papers, stumbles from one absurd misadventure to the next. Finally, however, through a mix of good luck and good nature, he secures the story about a British financier outwitting foreign competitors to obtain a vital minerals concession that is the scoop that gives the book its title. As a result, he returns home a celebrity.

Like all true satire, *Scoop* is not pure invention. The central features of the story are loosely based on facts, which Waugh embroiders and exaggerates to render ridiculous. The African civil war is drawn from his experience covering the 1935 Italian invasion of Abyssinia (as Ethiopia

---

* The book's original dust jacket, a clear pastiche of the *Daily Express* masthead, was quickly withdrawn and replaced by another. Very few of the originals survive.

was then known). He had done this for the *Daily Mail*, an assignment he had secured thanks to Lady Diana Cooper, the society beauty on whom Mrs Stitch is based, intervening on his behalf with Lord Rothermere. William Boot is, to a great extent, based on the young and totally inexperienced Bill Deedes, who went out to Abyssinia for the *Morning Post* without achieving Boot's success. Waugh's descriptions of how the journalists competed with each other by spoiling each other's stories, stealing each other's cables and filing eyewitness accounts of events before they had taken place were derived partly from his experiences covering the Italian invasion and partly from his earlier assignment in Abyssinia reporting on its Emperor's coronation.*

Almost seventy years after the publication of *Scoop*, Deedes, who by then had achieved the unique distinction of having been both the editor of a national newspaper and a Cabinet minister, wrote a memoir[20] describing the incidents and characters that provided Waugh with his raw material. This includes how, like Boot, he had been taken to a London store to acquire a mountain of equipment, in his case weighing six hundred pounds, that required two taxis to take away. He also provides details of the incident that inspired Boot's scoop. In real life it was obtained by one of the professional journalists Waugh mocks in the novel, with Waugh himself completely out of touch with what was happening.

Deedes doesn't dwell on how the journalists in the novel were able to make so much money from their expenses but I can provide supporting evidence for that. The culture of treating expenses as a tax-free supplement to salary was still going strong on some papers in the early 1960s when I was offered a job on the *Daily Express*' 'William Hickey' gossip column. 'You can double your money on expenses,' its editor told me, adding, 'and girls will do anything for you'. Despite these inducements, I declined and remained on the *Financial Times*.

---

* This led to his novel *Black Mischief*, published by Chapman & Hall in 1932.

Scoop is about a world Waugh despised. By contrast *Brideshead Revisited* is a lament for a lost world of great country houses, privilege, luxury and ease that he adored. The great French statesman Talleyrand is reputed to have said in old age, 'He who did not live in the years before the Revolution cannot understand what the sweetness of living is.' In 1945 many members of the middle class and aristocracy – the book-buying classes – felt the same when they looked back to their pre-war world. They rejoiced in Britain's victory, but mourned the loss of their comforts and privileges that the war had brought about. Their servants had disappeared, their taxes had risen steeply and they suffered the same privations as everyone else from food, clothes, petrol and coal rationing. As Waugh himself later put it, 'the book is infused with a kind of gluttony, for food and wine, for the splendours of the recent past'.* When they read of the way of life he describes and, above all, of the meals the book's characters consume, his British readers were transported back to happier days. It cast their pre-war world in a golden haze of romanticism and they flocked to buy it.

Not only those readers; its appeal went and continues to go much wider. It was published in the United States a few months after the United Kingdom and was an immediate success there too, selling over half a million copies as a Book of the Month choice and thereby transforming Waugh's finances. It has remained one of his most widely read novels ever since, above all because it is a brilliant exercise in nostalgia that conveys the excitement he himself felt when breaking into fashionable society during the inter-war period. The evocative 1981 Granada Television series and the less good 2008 feature film based on it have generated further sales, but these were inspired by the book's enduring popularity, they did not create it.

---

* Preface written in 1959 for the new Penguin edition of *Brideshead Revisited.*

When he wrote *Brideshead* in 1944 Waugh was a captain in the army on six months' unpaid (at his request) leave. It opens with the narrator, Captain Charles Ryder, arriving at an unknown destination where his battalion is to be billeted. With a shock of recognition he realizes it is Brideshead Castle, which before the war he had known well when it was the home of the aristocratic Flyte family. Memories come flooding back, beginning with a blissful holiday he spent there in 1923 with his lover, the beautiful and eccentric Lord Sebastian Flyte, and their time together as Oxford undergraduates. This is the most important relationship in the book; everything else flows from it.

Throughout, the parallels with Waugh's own life are close. At Oxford he had an affair with a young man called Alastair Graham, who shared both Sebastian's beauty and his addiction to drink. After Oxford Ryder's connection with the Flyte family plus his burgeoning reputation as an artist enable him to climb from his Bayswater background into aristocratic circles. Waugh made a similar progression from the environs of Golders Green, where he was brought up, thanks to his burgeoning reputation as a novelist and his friendship with the aristocratic Lygon family among others. Apart from its chapel, the Lygons' stately home at Madresfield bears no resemblance to Waugh's description of Brideshead, but the head of their family, the Earl of Beauchamp, lived abroad because of an earlier scandal, as does Lord Marchmain, the head of the Flyte family. Both return home in order to die with Marchmain's death playing a crucial role in the novel's denouement.

The book is a mine of period detail and social nuance of the most varied kinds. For instance: if, after a drunken evening, of which Sebastian and Ryder have many, an undergraduate leaves vomit on the floor of his room for his College servant to clear up, he should tip the servant five shillings (about £15 in today's money). And: although Sebastian's sister, Julia, is the daughter of a Marquess and one of the most beautiful debutantes of her year, there were grand families who would not regard her as a suitable match for an eldest son because the Flytes are Catholic.* Partly for this reason she marries a worldly and ambitious Canadian, who, having amassed a fortune, is making his way in politics.

It is on their commitment to the austere and authoritarian form of Catholicism that held sway among English Catholics at that time, and to which Waugh himself was devoted, that the book turns. In the end, whatever they might have done to resist it, their religion determines the fate of each of the major characters in a way that Waugh later described as 'the operation of divine grace'.† When, after years as an alcoholic bumming around the Mediterranean and having lost his male lover, Sebastian can no longer cope with life, he persuades a monastery in Tunisia to take him in. When Lord Marchmain, having deserted his wife and his faith many years before, returns, accompanied by his mistress, to die at Brideshead, he accepts a priest's absolution and the last rites of the Church on his deathbed.

The drama and symbolism of this event have a profound effect on Julia. By then divorced and having left the Church, she is having an affair with Ryder and planning to marry him. The circumstances of her father's death force her back to her original beliefs and to throw Ryder over. 'I need God. I can't shut myself off from his mercy,' she explains. To go ahead with the marriage would, she feels, be 'to set up a rival good to God's' and she cannot do that. The non-Catholic and sceptical Ryder is left speechless and denied the shared inheritance of Brideshead that would have been his if the marriage had gone ahead. Yet in the final pages, when he is back at the Castle in uniform we learn that he too has become a Catholic.

---

* Though not precisely analogous, the disapproval of the Duke and Duchess of Devonshire when, during the war, their eldest son, the Marquess of Hartington, wanted to marry Kathleen Kennedy, the Catholic daughter of the immensely rich former United States Ambassador to Britain, Joe Kennedy, illustrates this point. The Kennedys disapproved even more strongly, but the wedding went ahead. Hartington was killed in action shortly afterwards and she died in an air crash in 1948. Her brother, Jack, became President of the United States in 1960.

† Preface for the 1959 Penguin edition.

When the book came out Waugh was abroad with the army. His friend, the writer Nancy Mitford, reported to him on what their mutual friends thought of it. Many, like her, admired it, but a common reaction was 'too much Catholic stuff'.[21] Waugh did not allow that to put him off. His subsequent and much-admired Sword of Honour trilogy about the Second World War also has a strong Catholic theme.* Catholicism, to which he had converted in 1930, was integral to his life and gave it a purpose and meaning that is reflected in the character of Guy Crouchback, the central figure in the trilogy. Readers in a post-religious age find this aspect of his novels hard to understand and tend either to ignore it, as the television and film directors did, or to feel uncomfortable with it. It has, I think, contributed to him being taken less seriously as a novelist than he deserves.

More damaging blows to Waugh's reputation have, however, been delivered by his views on other matters and by his own behaviour. His love of the aristocracy, with which he so much wanted to be identified and which permeated his life as well as his work, attracted mockery even when *Brideshead* was published. The patronizing contempt with which he writes about Africans in *Scoop* and *Black Mischief* was in tune with public attitudes when the books were published; now it is completely unacceptable. Throughout his life he consumed vast quantities of alcohol. These took their toll. In his later years he was deeply depressed and seemed determined to present himself to the general public in the most reactionary and misanthropic colours.[22] When his diaries[23] were published in 1976, eleven years after his death, they confirmed this impression of him. That, despite such handicaps, his novels continue to be so widely read and enjoyed throughout the English-speaking world is a tribute to his skill as a novelist and to the beauty and clarity of his prose.

---

* *Men at Arms* (1952), *Officers and Gentlemen* (1955) and *Unconditional Surrender* (1961). All published by Chapman & Hall.

Strangers and Brothers

by C. P. Snow (1940–70)

The Two Cultures and the Scientific Revolution

by C. P. Snow (1959)

C. P. Snow, as he was always known, introduced two phrases into the English language, 'the Corridors of Power' and 'the Two Cultures', that continue to be used long after their origins have been forgotten. The first is the title of one of the novels in his *Strangers and Brothers* sequence, the other an abbreviation of the title of a celebrated lecture, 'The Two Cultures and the Scientific Revolution', that he gave at Cambridge in 1959. In his heyday, in the twenty years after the Second World War, his novels were bestsellers in Britain, widely read abroad, particularly in the United States and the Soviet Union, and adapted for stage and television. His lecture on the gap that existed between scientists and, in his words, 'literary intellectuals' – the two cultures – and their mutual incomprehension and disdain for each other influenced opinion and aroused controversy across the world. In the United States the soon to be President Jack Kennedy described it as 'one of the most provocative discussions I have ever read of this intellectual dilemma, which at the same time is of profound consequence to public policy'.[24]

Snow himself was a polymath with a foot in both cultures. As a young academic scientist in the 1930s he worked at the Cavendish Laboratory in Cambridge during its golden age of research into nuclear fission. When war broke out in September 1939 he wrote a far-sighted article forecasting that, if an atomic bomb could be developed, it would most likely be in the United States while warning of the danger that Germany might get there first.[25] The government brought him into Whitehall to mobilize scientists to work on the British nuclear programme as well as radar and other high-priority technology projects. After the war, besides devoting himself to his writing, he took up a position with English Electric, then one of the country's largest industrial companies. When Labour won the general election in 1964 he became a government minister with a seat in the House of Lords. Few novelists have enjoyed such a varied career.

Strangers and Brothers is a sequence of eleven overlapping novels chronicling the life and times of their narrator, Lewis Eliot. They span the years from 1914 to 1968 with the emphasis on the 1930s, 1940s and 1950s and were published between 1940 and 1970. Like Snow, Eliot was born and brought up in a lower-middle-class family in a provincial city (in Snow's case Leicester). He breaks free as the result of receiving a small legacy and by qualifying as a barrister. Marital problems make it difficult for him to pursue this profession and he puts together an alternative, which involves dividing his time between a fellowship at a Cambridge college (based on Christ's where Snow was a fellow) and part-time work for a large company in London.

When war comes Eliot, like Snow and many others, is swept up into Whitehall where he achieves success as a civil servant involved with the bureaucratic aspects of the British nuclear programme. In the post-war years he attains an important but shadowy role at the interface between defence and science policy, but declines an offer of a ministerial post under the Labour government elected in 1964. By the time Snow came to describe that incident in *Last Things*, published in 1970, he had himself left office. Inevitably, this gives the impression that Eliot's decision reflected a feeling on his part that he had made a mistake in becoming a minister. His element, and Eliot's, was the bureaucracy, not politics.

Both Snow and Eliot enjoyed unusually successful and diverse careers, but there were many others of that generation whose lives were transformed for the better by the war. It gave British society a huge shake-up that broke down barriers between classes and occupations. For those lucky enough to have the right attributes, military or civilian, and to be in the right place at the right time, it opened up previously undreamed-of opportunities. Snow was very conscious of this and of his good fortune. What it meant to rise from obscurity to the heart of the British Establishment is a constantly recurring theme in the novels.

He and his alter ego remained firmly on the left in politics. They welcomed the social changes brought about by the war and the 1945 Labour government. But, far from rejoicing in the pain of those whose privileges were being stripped from them, as many on the left did, Snow admired their grace in making sacrifices in the national interest. In *The New Men*, set during the war, he has Eliot record his admiration for the way in which the aristocracy and well-to-do put the national interest before their own class interest. This is often now taken for granted, but it was a point that at the time impressed overseas observers of the British scene. One such was the Canadian diplomat Charles Ritchie, who, in April 1941, wrote in his diary: 'They are Englishmen before they are capitalists or landlords (unlike the same class in France) ... England's ruling class are committing suicide to save England from defeat.'[26]

The most famous of Snow's novels is *The Masters*, published in 1951. Although set in Eliot's Cambridge college, it has nothing to do with undergraduates. Nonetheless when I first read it in 1955, between leaving school and joining the army for my National Service, it made me frantic with worry that I might be prevented by another war from ever taking up my place there, or be inordinately delayed, as happened to so many in 1939. It revolves round the election of a new Master of the college in the late 1930s and deals in enthralling detail with the machinations, clash of personalities and points of contention involved. These have nothing to do with the great ideological issues of the period. It is a study of pure politics in the sense of how men (women were confined to separate colleges at that time) succeed and fail to get their way within a closed community. As such it is a classic of its kind. The same is true, except that it is less good, of *The Affair*, about how the college deals with a miscarriage of justice involving a piece of abstruse scientific research in the early 1950s.

The same theme is pursued in a completely different context in *The New Men*, published in 1954, which deals with the development of nuclear fission and the atomic bomb during and immediately after the war. The action is all behind the political scenes at the research establishment where the work is taking place and in Whitehall, Snow's home ground. Besides the rivalries and personality clashes of the college novels, the plot involves the conscience-stricken agonizing of the scientists as they confront the possible implications for the human race of what they are doing while being driven forward by their own determination to resolve technical problems and the overwhelming need to win the war. Everything comes to a head when two atomic bombs developed by their American colleagues are dropped on Japan, a Soviet spy is uncovered in their midst and the government decides to develop an independent British nuclear capability. *The Corridors of Power*, set in 1958 and 1959 and published in 1964, is on a related matter: the downfall of an ambitious young Conservative minister who wants Britain to relinquish the bomb.

The other books in the sequence relate to Lewis Eliot's previous life as he progresses from the provincial backstreets to Cambridge and London. The first, originally called *Strangers and Brothers* but renamed *George Passant* when that title was given to the whole oeuvre, is about the efforts of a charismatic but flawed solicitor's clerk in a provincial city to encourage the young people around him to make the most of their lives. *Time of Hope* and *Homecomings* are about Eliot's early career and his unhappy first marriage culminating in his wife's suicide, which is followed by an affair with a married woman that leads to a second marriage and middle-aged fatherhood.

The Light and the Dark explores the character and dilemmas of a brilliant but manic-depressive Cambridge scholar of oriental languages, who, when told that RAF Bomber Command is where a man is most likely to meet an early death, volunteers for it and is duly killed while on a mission over Germany. *The Conscience of the Rich* is a study of a rich Jewish family in the 1930s and the oppressive effect of their wealth on their eldest son, a barrister friend of Eliot's, who decides to give up his life of privilege to become a doctor in the East End of London.

When Snow was approaching the halfway mark in the *Strangers and Brothers* sequence the political columnist Henry Fairlie, writing in the *Spectator*,[27] coined the term 'The Establishment' to describe the informal network of influential individuals who, working through informal as well as formal channels, made the country tick. That was Snow's world.

His Cambridge and Whitehall novels provide a direct insight into how those individuals thought, acted, spoke, behaved towards each other, deployed arguments and took decisions during the period between the late 1930s and the early 1960s. Reading his dialogue is like listening into their conversations. He also provides a wealth of period detail, such as how, during the wartime winters, when there wasn't enough coal to heat Whitehall offices, officials wore their overcoats at work, how it was customary for even the closest of colleagues to address each other by their surnames and how, in some of the circles in which Eliot moved, men were expected to shake hands on meeting and in others not.

In his lifetime Snow's novels were often compared with those of Trollope, through the prism of which we enter the lives of mid-Victorian churchmen and politicians. The difference between them is that Trollope was not a player in the worlds about which he wrote whereas Snow was. Trollope, however, had a better understanding than Snow of the link between the public and the private sphere in men's lives. In the worlds in which both men operated women played no official part, but Trollope understood that they could wield considerable influence behind the scenes, as does Mrs Proudie in the Barchester novels and Lady Glencora (later Duchess of Omnium) in the political ones. Snow's novels demonstrate no such understanding. Nor, unlike Trollope, did he create memorable characters that live on in the minds of his readers like those two women and several others.

Trollope's reputation declined after his death and did not fully recover until he came into vogue during the Second World War, since when it has remained high. The beginning of the decline in Snow's literary reputation was a vitriolic attack launched on him in 1962 by F. R. Leavis,[28] the leading Cambridge academic and literary critic, who took exception to his lecture on the 'Two Cultures'. Leavis had many followers among the younger generation of academics and critics among whom it became fashionable to denigrate Snow's work. By the time of his death in 1980 to say that one liked his novels was to define oneself as a philistine.

A different and, I think, fairer view than that of Leavis and his acolytes was expressed by the novelist and author of *A Clockwork Orange*, Anthony Burgess, who in 1984 included *Strangers and Brothers* in his anthology *Ninety-Nine Novels: The Best in English Since 1939*. 'This sequence,' he wrote, 'is a very considerable achievement, despite the flatness of the writing ... it deserves to be reconsidered as a highly serious attempt to depict the British class system and the distribution of power. The work has authority: it is not the dream of a slippered recluse but of a man actively involved in the practical mechanics of high policy-making.'[29] A more recent accolade has come from another novelist, Zadie Smith. In 2017, in an obituary tribute to Bob Silvers, the legendary editor of the *New York Review of Books*, she wrote: 'Many of Bob's writers were Nobel Prize winners, true geniuses, all rounders of the C. P. Snow variety.'[30]

The Two Cultures and the Scientific Revolution itself lives on and continues to be cited in the United States[31] as well as Britain more than half a century after it was delivered. The mutual incomprehension of scientists and non-scientists, and the inability of political and business leaders educated in the arts and humanities to take scientific factors sufficiently into account in their decision-making, are as much a cause of concern in both countries today as they were then.

The terms in which the lecture is couched are redolent of the intellectual climate and assumptions of the 1950s. To read it now is to be transported back to the arguments it provoked in those days in newspaper leading articles, politics, university common rooms and among the chattering classes. It assumes that, if the West can't resolve the problems of poverty in Africa and Asia, 'the Communist countries will'. The permanence and continuing success of Soviet Communism is taken for granted. British performance is measured only against developments in the United States and the Soviet Union. There is barely mention of the economic transformation being wrought at that time in Western Europe and of the challenges and opportunities posed for Britain by the newly formed European Economic Community, as it was then called. In this Snow was typical of the British Establishment, which completely failed to appreciate the importance of what was happening on the Continent or to foresee that in the following decade the question of whether or not to join that Community would become a central issue in British politics.

In the early 1970s my wife and I lived a short distance away from Snow and his wife, the novelist Pamela Hansford Johnson, and we became friends. We kept in touch after I became a European Commissioner and our move to Brussels. When I acquired a first edition of the original *Strangers and Brothers* novel I telephoned to ask Snow to inscribe it for me on my next visit to London. When I arrived at his house to take him out to lunch I was told by Pamela that he had died a few hours earlier.

A Book of Mediterranean Food

by Elizabeth David (1950)

Traditionally in Britain the preparation, presentation and eating of food has not been regarded as a means of expressing creativity. In France and Italy, they have for long been an integral part of popular culture and even attained the status of an art form. What the British traditionally wanted was plain fare and plenty of it, with quantity rather than creativity denoting wealth and status. Our popular culture has for long been the tending and creation of gardens, which, in the right hands, can also be an art form.

In recent decades tradition has been turned on its head. While gardening and gardens remain a national obsession, there are now millions of people interested in how to cook, present and enjoy food. Programmes on every aspect of these subjects have become a staple of television and the shelves in bookshops groan under the weight of cookery books. The stars of the former and authors of the latter become celebrities and chefs can achieve the status, or nearly so, of leading sportsmen and women. Eating out is a popular pastime and the quality of food served in restaurants at all price levels is infinitely better than it used to be. Such a massive change in popular culture can only be the result of several factors. Rising living standards, the arrival here of people from other countries and foreign travel have all played a part. But if there is one person above all others who can be credited with kickstarting the process it is Elizabeth David with *A Book of Mediterranean Food*, published in 1950.

Her biographer, Artemis Cooper, claims that she 'was the best writer on food and drink this country ever produced'.* That is impossible to prove, but she is certainly among the most celebrated. In 2012 to mark the Queen's Diamond Jubilee she was chosen by BBC Radio 4 as one of the sixty Britons who had been most influential during the sixty years of the Queen's reign. In 2013 her portrait was on one of the first-class stamps honouring ten 'Great Britons'. A film has been made about her life† and she has been the subject of a novel.[32] Her fame spread to the United States where her papers are now housed in the Schlesinger Library at the Radcliffe Institute for Advanced Study at Harvard University.

Yet in the year of its publication, *A Book of Mediterranean Food* was not so much a cookery book as a book of dreams – hers and her readers'. It would in practice have been impossible to produce most of her recipes. With the system of food rationing introduced in 1940 still in full swing, such basic foods as meat, bacon, butter, cheese, sugar and tea could only be purchased in the small quantities that each person was permitted to buy. Olives, olive oil, garlic, cloves, aubergines, lemons and other staple ingredients of Mediterranean cooking, though not rationed, were virtually unobtainable except in very limited amounts from obscure shops in Soho. I still remember the conspiratorial way in which the head waiter at Manchester's Midland Hotel whispered to my father, a frequent and highly valued guest, as we took our seats in the dining room in September 1950, that some black olives had been specially saved for him.

---

* *Oxford Dictionary of National Biography*.

† *Elizabeth David: A Life in Recipes*, written by Amanda Coe, directed by Catherine McCormack and first screened by BBC2 on 3 January 2006.

As David herself wrote in a preface to the book's second and revised edition published in 1958, 'even if people could not very often make the dishes here described, it was stimulating to think about them; to escape from the deadly boredom of queueing and the frustration of buying the weekly rations; to read about real food cooked with wine and olive oil, eggs and butter and cream, and dishes richly flavoured with onions, garlic, herbs, and brightly coloured Southern vegetables'. Her readers could not produce the dishes she described, but they were transported into another world in the same way as when they read a novel set in an exotic location.

A Book of Mediterranean Cooking was a long time in the making and grew directly out of Elizabeth David's adventures during the war years. These began in the early months of 1939 when, despite the looming threat of war, she had set off in a small yacht with her lover, Charles Gibson Cowan, to sail to Greece, an extremely unconventional thing for a young (she was twenty-five), unmarried, upper-class woman to do at that time. When they reached Marseilles she fell under the spell of the then famous author and traveller Norman Douglas to whom the enjoyment of food was as integral a part of a civilized life as appreciation of the arts. He became her mentor. As Artemis Cooper puts it, 'Norman taught her that with a little care and attention, one could eat good food every day. He also taught her how to search out the best, insist on it, and reject all that was bogus and second rate.'[33]

In 1940, as the German army advanced into France, she and Gibson Cowan resumed their journey only to be stopped and briefly interned as enemy aliens by the Italians, who had just entered the war on Germany's side. Eventually, after their boat was impounded, they were put on a train to still neutral Greece where he found a job as an English teacher on the island of Syros. There, with very little money, she learned to cook using only the ingredients available on the island and drawn from the sea around it, the most practical possible course in

Mediterranean cooking and a complete contrast to the sophistication of the South of France.

It did not last long. After a few months, the Germans invaded Greece and they again had to flee, this time to Crete. From there they were evacuated by the British Army to Egypt, where she and her lover decided to separate.

As a former debutante with aristocratic connections in England and speaking good French and German, Elizabeth David was quickly able to find a job working for the vast British military establishment in Cairo. She also joined the glittering and cosmopolitan society that surrounded it, a world immortalized by Lawrence Durrell in those of his novels known as the Alexandria Quartet and by Olivia Manning in her Levant Trilogy. Both became friends. Now she had servants to cook for her. The supply of food was plentiful and varied and from them she learned a great deal. She also cooked herself and, unlike most British women in her position, scoured the bazaars for the ingredients she needed rather than relying on the servants to do her shopping for her. It was during this time that she married an army officer called Tony David and acquired the name by which she was to become famous. However, by the time she returned to Britain when the war ended they were, to all intents and purposes, already separated.

After the warmth of the Mediterranean and the glamour and plentiful food of her life in Cairo, she found the cold, the shortages and the sheer grimness of post-war London hard to bear. Writing her book was a form of therapy. For many years she had collected recipes and when she and a lover from her Egyptian days were trying to find some escape from the horrors of London in a hotel in Ross-on-Wye in November 1946, he suggested that she put them down on paper. The hotel was warm, but its food dreadful. Recalling the recipes she had once enjoyed helped her, David later wrote, 'to work out an agonized craving for the sun and a furious revolt against that terrible, cheerless heartless food by writing down descriptions of Mediterranean and Middle Eastern cooking. Even to write words like apricot, olives and butter, rice and lemons, oil and almonds produced assuagement';[34] the same feelings Evelyn Waugh records having experienced when he was writing *Brideshead Revisited* two years earlier.*

Several publishers turned the book down, with one suggesting that it needed a linking text. It was this that provided David with an inspiration. She decided that instead of writing the links herself, she would interweave what she had already written with apposite extracts drawn from the works of a wide range of authors. These included her friends Norman Douglas and Lawrence Durrell, some who were famous, like Henry James, Arnold Bennett and D. H. Lawrence, and others who were not. They injected a further element of romance into her lists of ingredients and instructions on how to use them while giving the book something of the character of a literary anthology. They also conjured up visions of travelling in the countries from which the recipes came and consorting with their inhabitants; in that respect giving it something of the same appeal to the imagination as Durrell's Alexandria novels which came out a few years later.

The publisher John Lehmann accepted David's amended manuscript and commissioned the artist John Minton to do the illustrations. This proved to be another inspiration and one that played a significant role in the book's success. His cover, depicting a table loaded with bottles of wine, a lobster, melon and other delicacies set against the background of a harbour on a bay encircled by mountains, evoked memories among those who had been to the Mediterranean before the war and dreams among those who yearned to see it.

The book's timing turned out to be ideal. Rationing had been popular during the war when it enabled the whole population and not

---

* See essay on *Scoop* and *Brideshead Revisited.*

just the well-to-do to enjoy a balanced and sufficient diet. By 1950, five years after the war had ended, people had become thoroughly fed up with it and with the austerity foods, such as dried eggs, dried milk and whale meat that went with it. They couldn't wait for it to end.

Within a year of the book's publication a new Conservative government committed to abolishing rationing and loosening the rules that severely restricted the amount of money that individuals could take out of the country was elected. More people began to go abroad and to envisage producing meals derived from ingredients they had tasted there. There was not a mass market for either. Far from it. Nobody, except the well-to-do, would have contemplated travelling abroad for a holiday or experimenting with unfamiliar recipes. But those who could needed help and there were sufficient of them to generate a large demand for David's book. Before the war, the people who bought it would have had cooks and other servants. In the post-war world they had to do their own cooking, housekeeping and shopping.

As the 1950s progressed and scarcity gradually gave way to plenty, there was a growing demand for advice among the more prosperous classes, especially the younger generation, on how to improve their cooking skills. Elizabeth David produced articles for magazines and periodicals and wrote further books, *French Country Cooking* and *Italian Food*, during the preparation of which she travelled extensively in both countries. She then turned her attention to books on various aspects of English cooking. Where she led, others followed and became well known in their own right. In the years after we married in 1967, my wife's favourites were Robert Carrier for his books and Fanny Cradock on television.

Over time cookery books were transformed from a niche into a mass market, television cookery programmes built up vast audiences and chefs and writers on food and drink became celebrities. But none matched the influence of Elizabeth David either on the way the genre developed or in their influence over other writers. And not just in this country. Alice Waters, sometimes described as the 'mother of modern American cooking', has described David as 'her greatest inspiration': 'When I go back and read her books now I feel I plagiarized them,' she was quoted as saying on David's death in May 1992.[35] Nor did other writers achieve a similar cult status of the sort illustrated by a 1999 Channel 4 television documentary. Entitled *In the Footsteps of Elizabeth David*,* it featured the former Cabinet minister and the last Governor of Hong Kong Chris Patten visiting the various places mentioned in her books as he recalled how, in the early days of their marriage, he and his wife had worked their way through her canon. There were many other less famous couples who did the same.

* Shown on Channel 4, 26 and 27 December 1999.

Conclusion

The Economic Consequences of the Peace by J. M. Keynes, 1919, and *The General Theory of Employment, Interest and Money* by J. M. Keynes, 1936.

Homage to Catalonia by George Orwell, 1938,
Animal Farm by George Orwell, 1945,
and *Nineteen Eighty-Four* by George Orwell, 1949.

The Economic Conequences of the Peace

by J. M. Keynes (1919)

The General Theory of Employment, Interest and Money

by J. M. Keynes (1936)

John Maynard Keynes – always Maynard to his friends – was the twentieth century's most famous economist as well as one of its most innovative and influential. His great work, *The General Theory of Employment, Interest and Money*, published in 1936, changed the terms in which economic theory and issues were discussed and policy implemented and continues to influence policy-makers all over the world. He is one of that select body of individuals whose ideas have had such a far-reaching impact that a belief system has been named after them – Keynesianism, like Marxism. Marx explained how capitalism must inevitably collapse under the weight of its contradictions and lead via revolution to socialism. During the Great Depression in the 1930s this outcome, with Soviet Russia as its model, began to appear increasingly likely and, to many, desirable, if not in itself at least as an alternative to the Fascism of Nazi Germany. Keynes provided a countervailing theory that has helped capitalism to adapt and to avoid a recurrence of that form of economic collapse.

The Economic Consequences of the Peace, published in 1919, was directed at the crucial issue of how to enable Europe to rebuild a viable and prosperous economy after the devastation wrought by the First World War. Had its warnings and analysis been heeded the conditions that led to the rise of Nazism in Germany and thus to the Second World War might have been avoided.

Robert Skidelsky subtitles the second volume of his magisterial three-volume biography of Keynes *The Economist as Saviour*.[1] That is what Keynes aspired to be. He regarded the management of the economy as providing the underpinning of a civilized society, just as plumbing does for life in the home. When it breaks down or ceases to function in the public interest the way is opened for violence and revolution. His huge output of books, treatises and articles culminating in *The General Theory* was aimed at resolving the economic problems that threatened peace and stability internationally as well as nationally. They were leavened by his experience working in the Treasury during the First World War (he returned during the Second) and at the Paris Peace Conference that followed it. They were reinforced by his ability to combine an active participation in public life with his teaching and other responsibilities at Cambridge.

The Economic Consequences of the Peace arose out of Keynes' experiences at the Paris Peace Conference, which led to the Treaty of Versailles that formally ended the First World War. He served there as the Chancellor of the Exchequer's deputy on the committee dealing with economic issues and was therefore both a participant and a ringside spectator. Nobody in such a position had ever before exposed the inner workings of international diplomacy to the public gaze. The book created a sensation. It immediately became an international bestseller and continues to provide the principal prism through which the treaty is studied and judged. It also created a precedent for politicians and officials to write about events in which they have participated and to argue their case in public as well as behind closed doors.

The book was very much a personal statement. Its style, in Skidelsky's words, is 'angry, scornful and, rarely for Keynes, passionate'.[2] This reflected his belief that the treaty was ill-conceived and would have disastrous consequences. Personal considerations were involved as well. He was a member of the Bloomsbury Group of intellectuals surrounding Virginia Woolf described in earlier chapters. Many of its members had been conscientious objectors during the war. His own views on the war had been complex and he had felt guilty about serving a government so determined on victory at any price that it would not countenance a negotiated compromise peace. His conscience and his yearning for the approbation of his friends both demanded that he should do all that he could to create the conditions in which such a war could never happen again and be seen to condemn those responsible if the attempt failed.

He evokes the atmosphere of the meetings and negotiations and portrays the principal characters – Lloyd George for Britain, Clemenceau for France and Woodrow Wilson for the United States – in vivid and unforgettable terms. His description of how the pre-war European economy, including Britain's, revolved round the pivot of Germany is a model of clarity and his recollection of the material benefits it yielded is a delicate combination of analysis and nostalgia. The subsequent chapters with their tables, statistics and technical arguments about the financial and economic arrangements on which the treaty is based are harder to read. But the way in which he marshals his material to make his case provides a masterclass in the art of advocacy.

The first plank of that case was that the treaty imposed such harsh conditions on Germany that it would not be able to resume its role as the pivot of the European economy. In setting out to punish Germany for starting the war, Britain and France were not only condemning the

Germans to deprivation and instability, they were denying their own citizens, and the rest of Europe, the means to rebuild the integrated European economy that was essential if their own national economies were to prosper. The United States was equally culpable, but protected from the full consequences of its actions by the scale and self-contained nature of its economy on the other side of the Atlantic.

The second plank was a powerful warning of how the Germans might react against these conditions: 'If we aim deliberately at the impoverishment of Central Europe, vengeance, I dare predict, will not limp. Nothing can then delay for very long that final civil war between the forces of Reaction and the despairing convulsions of Revolution, before which the horrors of the late German war will fade into nothing, and which will destroy, whoever is the victor, the civilization and the progress of our generation.'

Nothing is inevitable. If some of the initiatives taken and proposed by various statesmen during the 1920s had succeeded and, above all, had the Great Depression that began in the United States in 1929 been avoided, all might have been well. The European economy might have recovered its equilibrium and again provided the basis for Europeans to live in peace with each other. As it was, Germany's descent into inflationary chaos in the first part of the decade opened the way for extremists, which in due course led to the Nazis coming to power, Hitler's revanchism and the Second World War. To that extent Keynes' judgement was vindicated. The consequences were not, as it turned out, as catastrophic as he and many others had feared,* but they easily might have been.

A fundamental problem at the conference was that the political leaders attending it had not grasped the extent to which political and economic stability in each of their own countries was influenced by what happened in other countries. They did not understand the implications

---

* See essay on *Challenge to Death* edited by Storm Jameson and *Guilty Men* by 'Cato'.

of economic interdependence adumbrated by Norman Angell before the war in his book *The Great Illusion*, which I discussed in an earlier chapter. They were still for the most part living in an earlier era when national economies in Europe were much less interdependent than they had become in the early twentieth century. In their minds what mattered after a war was the distribution of territory and populations. In Keynes' words: 'The future life of Europe was not their concern; its means of livelihood was not their anxiety. Their preoccupations, good and bad alike, related to frontiers and nationalities, to the balance of power, to imperial aggrandisements, to the future enfeeblement of a strong and dangerous enemy, to revenge, and to the shifting by the victors of their unbearable financial burdens on to the shoulders of the defeated.' They thought in old-fashioned balance-of-power terms rather than those of economic interdependence.

They were also being driven by the demands of their electorates for revenge, in France more strongly than in Britain, a factor to which Keynes does not give sufficient weight. Both countries had suffered a terrible loss of life, but the war had not touched either the British or the German national territory. It had been fought on French soil causing severe damage to the manufacturing industry, coal mines and agriculture of eastern France. The French wanted compensation and to secure a competitive advantage against Germany when peacetime conditions were restored. For these reasons as well as their own inclinations the leaders could not see what was required through the same objective eyes as Keynes. When the Second World War ended there was a much better understanding of what was required. In the words of Alec Cairncross, Head of the Government Economic Service in the 1960s: 'Keynes's thinking in 1919 was remarkably similar to the thinking behind the Marshall Plan in 1947.'*

---

* *Oxford Dictionary of National Biography.*

The General Theory was conceived and born in very different circumstances from *The Economic Consequences of the Peace*. It was not an attack on a fait accompli. It was an attempt to solve the overriding economic problem of the day. And, like its predecessor, it was influenced by personal considerations. In the final chapter Keynes expresses the fear that unless the crisis of capitalism can be resolved people will turn away from democracy to 'authoritarian state systems', which would mean 'Dictators and others such, to whom war offers, in expectation at least, a pleasurable excitement'. That some of the brightest young men he knew at Cambridge* were already subscribing to Communist ideas and even becoming Communists appalled him and intensified his fears.

He was in no doubt about the importance of what he was doing. In 1935, he wrote to the playwright George Bernard Shaw: 'I believe myself to be writing a book on economic theory which will largely revolutionize – not, I suppose, at once but in the course of the next ten years – the way the world thinks about economic problems.'[3] To do that, he believed, he had first to convince his fellow economists. He states in the preface that he is addressing them rather than the general public and the book is correspondingly hard to read.

Yet its central – and at the time revolutionary idea – emerges very clearly. It is that governments both can and should act to prevent economic depressions, a concept now so much part of the conventional wisdom that it is hard to believe it was ever revolutionary. Until *The General Theory*, the prevailing economic orthodoxy was that governments were largely at the mercy of economic forces, as sailing ships had been at the mercy of the winds. Just as their captains could influence neither the force nor the direction of the winds but had to adjust their sails accordingly, so governments had to trim their policies to economic

* They included two men who later achieved notoriety as Soviet spies – Guy Burgess, who escaped to Moscow in 1951, and Anthony Blunt, who was 'outed' by Margaret Thatcher in 1979.

forces. Keynes introduced the idea of counter-cyclical policy. When the economy was sinking, he argued, governments did not have to wait until unemployment had risen and wages fallen to the point where the supply and demand for labour were again balanced. They could pump money into the economy by undertaking investment on their own account and, by cutting taxes, printing money and keeping interest rates low, encourage the private sector to do the same.

The idea challenged two core concepts of prevailing economic orthodoxy. These were that governments should always try to balance their budgets by maintaining an equilibrium between income and expenditure and that the supply of money should not outstrip the reserves of gold available to back it. These rules had been broken by governments in time of war when the integrity and what were thought to be the vital interests of their state were threatened, leading to an increase in their national debt and a reduction in the value of their currency. But that was regarded as a matter of necessity the consequences of which should be corrected as soon as possible.

Keynes' suggestion, that as a deliberate act of policy in peacetime a government should increase its debt and, if necessary, reduce the value of its currency in order to create demand and so reduce the level of unemployment, was as shocking to the economic establishment as Luther's assault on the doctrines and practices of the Catholic Church had been to Catholics in the sixteenth century. Such a policy, it was argued, would not achieve its objective, would saddle the country that adopted it with debt and would lead to inflation. Besides which, it would result in an increase in the power of the state at the expense of the individual as in a dictatorship. Keynes countered this last criticism by claiming that only by some 'enlargement of the functions of government' could 'existing economic forms in their entirety and as the condition of the successful functioning of individual initiative' be maintained. The same thought is expressed more concisely by a character in Giuseppe

Tomasi di Lampedusa's novel *The Leopard*, in the famous line, 'If we want things to stay as they are, things will have to change.'[4]

The younger generation of economists was for the most part as excited by Keynes' proposition as the Establishment was shocked precisely because they thought he had found the means by which prosperity could be achieved without recourse to revolution and dictatorship. In the words of the American economics Nobel Prize-winner Paul Samuelson, it 'caught most economists under the age of thirty-five with the unexpected virulence of a disease … Economists beyond fifty turned out to be quite immune to the ailment.'[5] One of Keynes' own postgraduate students spoke for many of the younger generation when he wrote, 'what Keynes supplied was hope: hope that prosperity could be restored and maintained without the support of prison camps, executions and bestial interrogations'.[6] At a time when it was widely feared that the future might lie between Nazi Germany and Soviet Russia – between Hitler and Stalin – hope was something the younger generation badly needed.

It was the outbreak of the Second World War rather than the policy prescriptions in *The General Theory* that brought the Great Depression to an end. But because measures of a Keynesian nature, introduced on an ad hoc basis rather than as part of a coherent theory, mitigated its worst effects they helped to validate his theory. President Roosevelt's New Deal, launched in the United States in 1933, was the most important. Rearmament in the United Kingdom during the build-up to war was another. When people saw how effective these were at reducing unemployment, it made them more receptive to the idea that similar government expenditure on other public works could achieve the same result.

The golden age of Keynesianism came after 1945. Those who had been young in the 1930s had by then risen to positions of authority, while during the war the British and American governments had shown how effective they could be at mobilizing the total resources of the state in pursuit of victory. Throughout the Western world Keynesianism exercised a great influence on governments and nowhere more so than in Britain where it provided the framework for policy-making and was credited with the sustained economic growth that characterized the post-war years.

This lasted until the late 1960s when, under the pressure of events, the criticisms originally levied against Keynesianism began to gather renewed strength. Inflation was becoming more of a worry than unemployment as trade unions used the power that full employment gave them to drive up wages with a knock-on effect on prices to a degree Keynes had not foreseen. Limits were also reached on the extent to which governments could run annual deficits. Over time the control of inflation and the reduction of deficits once again became the dominant considerations and the policy prescriptions associated with Keynes no longer attracted the support they once had. But his central idea that, when faced with the threat of a depression, the government must do all in its power to prevent it remains embedded in the national consciousness, as shown by the way in which the government responded to the financial crash of 2008 by comparison with its predecessor's reaction to the Great Depression in 1929 and will be again in the face of future crises.

Keynes died in 1946 at the age of sixty-two, worn out by his efforts in two important sets of negotiations. One, held in 1944 at Bretton Woods in the United States, successfully laid the foundations for post-war international economic relations, in sharp contrast to what had happened after the First World War. The other secured loans from the United States that kept Britain afloat immediately after the war. He was honoured with a memorial service in the National Cathedral in Washington as well as one in Westminster Abbey where his parents led the mourners, a sad and unusual distinction. Had he, like them, lived on into his nineties, he would have come up with new and, most likely, unexpected ideas about how to tackle the economic and social problems that bedevilled the country in the decades after the war. As it is, he remains a prophet in his own country as well as being revered across the world.

Homage to Catalonia

by George Orwell (1938)

Animal Farm

by George Orwell (1945)

Nineteen Eighty-Four

by George Orwell (1949)

George Orwell, whose real name was Eric Blair,* is one of the giants of the twentieth century, famous throughout the world for *Animal Farm*, published in 1945, and *Nineteen Eighty-Four*, which appeared four years later. Both were instant bestsellers in Britain and the United States and have since been translated into more than sixty languages and sold many millions of copies. They are universally recognized as being among the most powerful works of literature in defence of freedom and against totalitarianism, which is why they were banned in the Soviet bloc countries of Eastern Europe until after the fall of Communism

* His biographer Bernard Crick writes in the *Oxford Dictionary of National Biography* that he adopted the pseudonym when he started writing to avoid embarrassing his parents and as a hedge against failure. He also disliked the name Eric.

in 1989. The word 'Orwellian' has become a synonym for attempts by governments to subvert democratic institutions and to distort facts and news. The extent of its continuing grip on people's imagination was shown in the United States when President Trump was inaugurated in 2017. A new edition of *Nineteen Eighty-Four* was rushed out in response to the fears of liberal-minded Americans. They bought it in such numbers that it went straight to the top of the Amazon bestseller list.

Homage to Catalonia, published in 1938, is in a different category. It is about his time fighting in the Spanish Civil War in 1936 and 1937, which Orwell later described as the defining experience of his life. 'Thereafter I knew where I stood,' he wrote in 1946 in his essay 'Why I Write'. 'Every line of serious work I have written since 1936 has been written, directly or indirectly, against totalitarianism and for democratic socialism.'* The book is one of the best eyewitness accounts of a war that sparked immense controversy and division in Britain. The reasons why left-wing circles in London rejected it and ostracized him for expressing the views it contains tell us much about British political attitudes in the late 1930s.

I cannot think of another author whose sales and reputation are so much higher in death than in life. For most of his career Orwell's books sold in small numbers, including *Homage to Catalonia* and *The Road to Wigan Pier*, about poverty in the North of England, which has since become a classic of its kind. He lived a hand-to-mouth existence from journalism and writing, was helped by friends and worked at various times as a school teacher and in a second-hand bookshop. In the late 1930s his essays put him on the literary map in a minor way. When war broke out in 1939 he was, despite his best efforts to join up, rejected by the army on health grounds. Thereafter he became known to a wider

---

* First published in the summer 1946 issue of the magazine *Gangrel* and subsequently widely republished. In the collection of his essays entitled *England Your England*, published by Secker & Warburg in 1953, the original date is given as 1947.

public through his articles in the left-wing weekly *Tribune*, the literary journal *Horizon*, the *Observer* and the *Partisan Review* in New York. He also broadcast on the BBC. But he was still, in the words of his biographer D. J. Taylor, 'a faintly marginal figure'[7] when in 1945 *Animal Farm* catapulted him into the limelight.

He had little chance to enjoy it. His wife had died* shortly before its publication, leaving him with the task of caring for a newly adopted son while the tubercular problems from which had been suffering for some years were getting worse. He felt he had to get away from London to concentrate on his writing and retreated with his son and his sister, to look after the child, to a primitive cottage on the island of Jura off the west coast of Scotland. The production of *Nineteen Eighty-Four* was literally a life-and-death struggle, which he won in the sense that his death at the age of forty-six in January 1950 occurred just a year after finishing the manuscript and seven months after its publication.

It was not only in literary terms that Orwell was a marginal figure before *Animal Farm*. It was true politically as well because of his unremitting hostility to Stalin's Soviet Union, whose iniquities and cruelties he grasped long before most others on the left and never ceased to denounce. To many on the left in the 1930s this was tantamount to blasphemy. The tone was set by people like Sidney and Beatrice Webb, who had helped to set up the London School of Economics, the Fabian Society and the *New Statesman* periodical. After visiting the Soviet Union, they published a book in 1935 hailing it as a new civilization, a view that was widely welcomed in left-wing circles. The left also looked to the Soviet Union as a bastion against Hitler and the evils of Fascism. Even as hard-headed a man as Denis Healey, who in the 1960s and 1970s became a notably tough-minded Labour Minister of Defence and Chancellor of the Exchequer, was sufficiently carried

* While in University College Hospital, London, he married Sonia Brownell in October 1949, three months before his death.

away by these attitudes to become a member of the Communist Party. *Homage to Catalonia* brought Orwell into direct conflict with them.

As with most civil wars the politics that lay behind the war in Spain were extremely complicated, with numerous groups reflecting different interests and opinions struggling against each other in what was then a very backward society. But in Britain and other democracies it was seen among the intelligentsia and in left-wing circles as a definitive struggle between good and evil – a war, in the words of the historian of ideas Noel Annan, in which 'justice was solely on one side, perhaps the only such war known in history'.[8] The elected left-wing republican government represented good, the right-wing rebels seeking to overthrow it, led by General Franco and backed by Hitler and Mussolini, represented evil. To Orwell, when he and his wife arrived in Barcelona in December 1936, 'here at last, apparently, was democracy standing up to Fascism' after Hitler's accession to power in Germany, Japan's invasion of Manchuria and Italy's invasion of Abyssinia. He was one of thousands of volunteers from this country and across Europe and the United States who flocked to fight for the republic.

He was entranced by what he found. 'Everyone called everyone else Comrade' and 'waiters and shop-walkers looked you in the face and treated you as an equal'. Practically everyone wore rough working-class clothes and it looked as if the wealthy classes had either fled or turned themselves into proletarians. A revolution appeared to be in full swing and 'I did not realize that there were serious differences' between the plethora of political parties and trade unions 'with their tiresome names'. His credentials had been issued in London by the far-left Independent Labour Party so, as a matter of course, he joined the militia of the Spanish party to which it was affiliated, known by its initials as POUM.*

---

* Partido Obrero de Unificación Marxista.

His socialist idyll continued when he was sent to the front. 'Everyone from general to private drew the same pay, ate the same food, wore the same clothes and mingled on terms of complete equality.' The cold, the dirt, the lice and the shortage of cigarettes were hard to bear. But he enjoyed the comradeship and political discussions with men of different nationalities and backgrounds and felt he was experiencing what the first stages of a socialist society would be like. Fortunately, there was very little actual fighting and this unconventional form of military organization was not put to the test.

His problems began when he returned to Barcelona, where his wife had been waiting for him, to find that class distinctions had reappeared. From the start of the war the government of the republic had relied on the Soviet Union for arms. While Orwell was away at the front the Spanish Communist Party, manipulated by Soviet agents, had taken control. Its priority was winning the war rather than promoting revolution. In order to gain the support of the wealthier classes and those elements of the regular army that had not opted for Franco, it was clamping down on the more extreme parties and their militias. Foreign volunteers and men Orwell had served with at the front had been thrown into jail and he too was in danger of being arrested.

Although deeply disillusioned, he still felt nothing could be worse than a Fascist victory and that he must fight on. Accordingly, he returned to the front line where he was wounded and briefly hospitalized. On his release, with the Communist purge intensifying, he and his wife went on the run until, after various adventures, they reached France. His first action was 'to rush to the tobacco-kiosk and buy as many cigars and cigarettes as I could stuff into my pockets. Then we all went to the buffet and had a cup of tea', a suitably British ending to a foreign adventure. A short time later both Orwell and his wife were indicted in absentia under their real names of Eric and Eileen Blair at a court in Valencia for being Trotskyite rebels.

His reports were not well received when he returned to England. Most of the press favoured Franco. Those on the left were solidly behind the republican government and its Soviet backers. Far from being seen as the villains of the piece, the Communists were regarded by the left as essential to the government's success in the war while POUM and other dissident parties and their militias were seen as troublemakers.

Orwell's articles were rejected by the *New Statesman*, the flagship periodical of the left, and he had to settle for the lesser *New English Weekly*. His regular publisher, Victor Gollancz, turned down the manuscript of *Homage to Catalonia* sight unseen because he had been a member of POUM. Fredric Warburg, who had recently established Secker & Warburg, took it on, but their high hopes for it were disappointed when it sold only seven hundred copies. By contrast a Penguin Special taking a straightforward pro-government line by the colourful Duchess of Atholl sold one hundred thousand copies in a week.

The publication of *Animal Farm* turned out to be even more fraught. Orwell wrote it between November 1943 and February 1944, before the Allied invasion of France and at a time when the Soviet army was at last pushing back the German invader. The mood of the nation was epitomized when, as Orwell was starting to write, Churchill presented Stalin with a bejewelled sword inscribed by King George VI, as a token of homage from the British people to the heroic Soviet defenders of Stalingrad during the siege of that city a few months earlier. There could not have been a worse moment to embark on a bitter satire of the Russian revolution in general and of Stalin in particular.

Gollancz again rejected the manuscript, as did Faber and Collins. Jonathan Cape decided to take it, but were persuaded to change their minds by an official from the Ministry of Information, the body charged with wartime propaganda, who later turned out to be a Soviet spy. For a while Orwell toyed with the idea of publishing it himself as a pamphlet with money borrowed from the proprietor of the *Observer*,

David Astor. Finally, Warburg again came to the rescue and the book was published in August 1945. The war in Europe had ended in May and attitudes towards the Soviet Union were no longer the same as eighteen months before. Not just commercially, but critically too, the book was an immediate success, with established authors as diverse as E. M. Forster and Evelyn Waugh writing congratulatory letters.[9]

Animal Farm is only ninety-three pages long and subtitled *A Fairy Story* in British editions, although not in the American and most others. It tells the story of how a farm is taken over by the animals, who expel the farmer and his workers and run it themselves, led by the pigs. They are inspired by a dream recounted by an old boar shortly before his death of how the farm could be run for the benefit of the animals rather than the humans. The terms in which he does so could perhaps have been inspired by the chapter entitled 'The Great Money Trick' in Robert Tressall's *The Ragged-Trousered Philanthropists*, which I cover in an earlier essay.

At first all goes well in an atmosphere that recalls Orwell's early days in Spain. But over time the pigs tighten their grip and the farm becomes a dictatorship led by a brutal tyrant in the shape of a boar called Napoleon. The other animals end up worse off than they were before the revolution though persuaded by his regime's lies and false statistics that their lives are much better. The pigs, meanwhile, have taken over all the privileges previously enjoyed by the farmer and, after teaching themselves to walk on two legs, become indistinguishable from humans. At the end of the book they invite the neighbouring farmers to a party in the farmhouse where they carouse together while the other animals peer through the windows unable to distinguish pigs from humans.*

The story of *Animal Farm* tracks that of the Russian revolution up to 1945. Another boar represents Trotsky, the rival Stalin had driven

* Ironically, in the Soviet Union in the 1930s Stalin had prosperous farmers portrayed as pigs on propaganda posters when preparing the way for them to be expropriated and persecuted.

into exile. There are purges and show trials as Napoleon establishes his power like those Stalin held in the 1930s. Many who were previously heroes are discarded, history is rewritten and the ideals of the revolution are trampled on. The 1939 alliance between Stalin and Hitler, known as the Ribbentrop–Molotov pact, is reproduced in a deal between Napoleon and a neighbouring farmer. It is followed by that farmer's double-cross and an attack on Animal Farm that recalls Hitler's subsequent invasion of Russia.

All would have been instantly recognizable to contemporary readers as would Napoleon's resemblance to Stalin. Orwell intended the book to be read as an attack on Stalin both personally and for the way in which he had betrayed the principles of the revolution that had brought the Communists to power in 1917. It was the revenge of a democratic socialist against the abuse of power in the name of socialist principles. He also intended it to be seen as a satire on all revolutions based on principle that end up as simply a change from one set of power-hungry masters to another. The satire is bitter, but the language throughout is couched in a gentle and ironic tone appropriate to a fairy story about animals.

Nineteen Eighty-Four is altogether different. In a report to his staff, Frederic Warburg described it as 'amongst the most terrifying books I have ever read'. He thought it was a 'great book, but I pray I may be spared from reading another like it for years to come'.[10] Later he told friends that some of the booksellers who had received advance copies had been so frightened that they were unable to sleep.[11] It remains a terrifying book to this day, but its impact would have been much greater in 1949 than in more recent decades. It is in many ways a compendium of the nightmares of that period to the point where some might almost have wondered whether they were reading faction rather than fiction.

Set in 1984, the story is about Winston Smith, who works at the Ministry of Truth in London, the capital of a province of Oceania, a state basically comprising the English-speaking countries and one of the three great powers into which the world is divided. They are in a permanent state of low-level war as a result of which rocket bombs periodically fall on residential areas, the necessities of life are rationed and constant propaganda exhorts the citizens to hate the enemy – siege conditions that the ruling party wishes to prolong as they help it to maintain its iron grip on society. Presided over by Big Brother, the Party's sole purpose is power for its own sake, which requires the total subordination of the human spirit and the obliteration of independent thought or action among its members.

Among its most useful instruments are two-way television screens installed in every room of every building that can both broadcast propaganda and enable the Thought Police to keep whoever they wish under surveillance at any time. Party members, like Smith, know that they can never know when they are being watched. Another is the constant rewriting of the past, both short and long term, to ensure that it complies with current orthodoxy. Smith's job at the Ministry is devoted to falsifying back numbers of *The Times* and air-brushing from history those who have fallen out of favour with the party.

Because of his work he knows that, contrary to what the Party claims, it has not always been in charge and that reality, history and facts are all subject to change and revision whenever the Party deems that to be necessary. Unfortunately for him, he is also still able to think for himself and to act independently. He begins to ask old people about the past, to recall his own childhood in the days before the Party was in full control and to look out for old objects no longer in use. He then commits the heinous crime of falling in love and having enjoyable sex with a woman, two activities forbidden because they create a world of their own outside the Party's control, sex being permitted only for the purposes of joyless reproduction. They are arrested and subjected to interrogation and torture. Smith betrays the woman and has the will to think for himself beaten out of him. The Party demands that regardless of any evidence to the contrary its members must believe – not passively accept but believe – whatever they are told to believe.

In 1949 much of this would have reflected the lives and fears of contemporary readers. Post-war London was still shabby and unkempt with rows of bombed-out houses, as described in Orwell's text. Food, clothing and fuel were still tightly rationed. Mysterious shortages of everyday items, such as the razor blades that Smith hoards, were a common occurrence. The disgusting meals in the Ministry canteen are only a few degrees more unpleasant than the institutional food of the late 1940s. Rocket bombs raining death and destruction from the skies were a recent memory and the unremitting wartime propaganda described in the book is a greatly exaggerated version of what they would have become used to during the war.

To the generation who had lived through the two world wars and was becoming accustomed to a Cold War that might at any time become hot, the idea of a perpetual war would not have seemed incredible. Nor would the concept of a world divided between three superpowers. If Britain had been defeated in 1940 and Germany had gone on to defeat the Soviet Union, Eurasia and Africa would in practice have been divided between German and Japanese spheres of influence with the United States left in control of the two American continents. That, of course, didn't happen, but when Churchill, Roosevelt and Stalin met in Tehran in 1943 Orwell felt that they were parcelling up the world into spheres of influence that would lead to all kinds of future trouble.

The Party's subordination of the human spirit and insistence on pain of death on absolute conformity to its wishes was not so very far removed from what had been the case in Nazi Germany and continued to be so in Communist Russia. If Germany had occupied Britain people believed that a regime backed up by executions and torture would have been imposed and they feared that the same would apply if the Cold

War should turn hot and the West be defeated. It was not as surprising as it might now seem that nervous booksellers should have been kept awake at night after reading *Nineteen Eighty-Four*.

Because of that title it is often supposed that Orwell was endeavouring to forecast the future. This was not his intention. The book is a satire on totalitarian and authoritarian forms of government and a warning of the horrors they could lead to. As with *Animal Farm* its model is Stalin's Soviet Union and the description of Big Brother's moustache in his ubiquitous portraits drives home the point. In the United States right-wing circles, ignoring his statement of belief in 'Why I Write', mistakenly believed Orwell to be anti-socialist as well as anti-Communist, which led some socialists to brand him a traitor. Later, in the 1950s, after Stalin's crimes had been fully exposed, he was posthumously attacked by some ex-Communists for being 'prematurely correct',* an accusation that might well have given him sardonic pleasure.

The irony is that while Orwell was writing *Nineteen Eighty-Four* democratic socialism was enjoying an apotheosis in Britain. At home, while post-war conditions remained hard and the cities scarred by bomb damage, the Labour government, elected to power in 1945, was introducing the National Health Service and the welfare state that over time would transform the lives of the great mass of the people. Abroad, in conjunction with the United States, it led the opposition to the Soviet Union and the spread of Communism while beginning the dismantlement of the empire that Orwell had always wanted.

* Crick, *Oxford Dictionary of National Biography*.

Acknowledgements

I have been helped and encouraged in many ways by good friends during the years it has taken me to write this book. In particular I thank Chas Foulds for putting the idea into my head in the first place and Kenneth Baker, John Eidinow, Peter Hennessy, Giles Radice and Robert Skidelsky for help in enabling me to overcome self-doubt as I pursued my project and in other ways as well. I am also grateful to John Bond, George Edgeller, Richard Collins and all at whitefox for bringing it to fruition and to Ruth Killick for her work in publicising it.

My two sons, James and Gus, have provided invaluable technical assistance as well as encouragement. Above all I thank my wife, Julia. We met and married while I was writing my first book in the 1960s. Since then she has been my constant support in everything I have ever done and my love and gratitude know no bounds.

Notes

Introduction

1 L. P. Hartley, *The Go-Between*, Hamish Hamilton, 1953, p. 9.

Debunking Victorianism

1 Introduction to the Penguin Classics edition of *The Way of All Flesh*, reprinted 1986, p. 7.

2 Leonard Woolf, *Sowing: An Autobiography of the Years 1880 to 1904*, Hogarth Press, 1960, p. 166.

3 Samuel Butler, *Samuel Butler: Victorian Against the Grain: A Critical Overview*, ed. James G. Paradis, University of Toronto Press, 2007, p. 363.

4 Samuel Butler, *The Way of All Flesh*. Essay by Brooke Allen, *Barnes & Noble Review*, 7 January 2008.

5 James Southall Wilson, 'Time and Virginia Woolf', *VQR*, Spring 1942, quoting an article from *The Nation and the Athenaeum*, December 1928.

6 BBC Home Service Talks for Schools, 15 June 1945. Reprinted in *The Complete Works of George Orwell*, Vol. 17, *I Belong to the Left: 1945*, ed. Peter Davison, Secker & Warburg, 1998, p. 186.

7 *The New Republic*, 21 September 1932.

8 Cyril Connolly, *Enemies of Promise*, George Routledge & Sons, 1938.

9 Michael Holroyd, *Lytton Strachey: A Critical Biography*, Vol. 2, *The Years of Achievement*, Heinemann, 1968, p. 264.

10 Ibid., p. 250.

11 The Romanes Lecture, June 1918, entitled 'Some Aspects of the Victorian Age'.

12 For an account of the event as well as a more objective portrait of Manning see Robert Gray, *Cardinal Manning: A Biography*, Weidenfeld & Nicolson, 1985.

War 1 – Warnings and Reality

1 Published for Queen Victoria's Diamond Jubilee, it first appeared in *The Times*, 17 July 1897.

2 Official Report, House of Commons, 18 February 1901: col 407.

3 Jim Ring, *Erskine Childers*, John Murray, 1996, p. 153.

4 Ibid., p. 289.

5 Lady Diana Cooper, *Darling Monster: The Letters of Lady Diana Cooper to Her Son John Julius Norwich, 1939–1952*, Chatto & Windus, 2013, p. 2.

6 Alan Judd and David Crane, *First World War Poets*, National Portrait Gallery Publications, 1997.

7 Ronald Blythe, *Akenfield: Portrait of an English Village*, Allen Lane The Penguin Press, 1969, p. 38.

8 John Bew, *Citizen Clem: A Biography of Attlee*, riverrun, 2017, p. 78.

War 2 – Warnings and Reality

1 Richard Overy, *The Morbid Age: Britain Between the Wars*, Allen Lane, 2009, p. 221.

2 Official Report, House of Commons, 10 November 1932.

3 Rodric Braithwaite, *Armageddon and Paranoia*, Profile Books, 2017, p. 43.

4 Roy Jenkins, *Churchill: A Biography*, Macmillan, 2001, p. 429.

5 William Manchester, *The Last Lion, Winston Spencer Churchill*, Vol. 1, Little, Brown & Co., 1983, p. 768.

6 John W. Wheeler Bennett, *King George VI: His Life and Reign*, Macmillan, 1958, p. 460.

7 Marie Vassiltchikov, *Berlin Diaries, 1940–1945*, Alfred A. Knopf, 1987.

8 Geoffrey Wansell, *Terence Rattigan: A Biography*, Fourth Estate, 1995, p. 126.

9 Ibid., p. 126.

Cold War

1 Peter Hennessy, *Having It So Good*, Allen Lane, 2006, p. 320.

2 Richard Luce, *Ringing the Changes*, Michael Russell, 2007, p. 26. In a remarkably varied and successful career he has also been a government minister and Vice-Chancellor of the University of Buckingham. We met at the Eaton Hall Officer Cadet School in 1956 while doing our National Service and have been friends ever since.

3 Elizabeth Jenkins, *The View from Downshire Hill*, Michael Russell, 2004, p. 96.

4 Luce, *Ringing the Changes*, p. 33.

5 For further information on this and other matters relating to conscription, see Richard Vinen, *National Service, Conscription in Britain, 1945–63*, Allen Lane, 2014.

Imperialist Complexities

1 Maya Jasanoff, *The Dawn Watch: Joseph Conrad in a Global World*, William Collins, 2017, p. 4.

2 Barack Obama, *Dreams from My Father*, Canongate, 2008, p. 103. In 2014, President Obama visited a Washington bookstore with his family to publicize his support for independent retailers. Among the books he purchased was *Heart of Darkness*, MailOnline, 30 November 2014.

3 Jan Karski, *Story of a Secret State*, Hodder & Stoughton, 1945, pp. 277–94.

4 David Gilmour, *The Ruling Caste: Imperial Lives in the Victorian Raj*, John Murray, 2005, p. xiii; Ian Kershaw, *Hitler 1936–45: Nemesis*, Allen Lane The Penguin Press, 2000, p. 401.

5 Leonard Woolf, *Growing: An Autobiography of the Years 1904–1911*, Hogarth Press, 1961, p. 174.
6 George Orwell, *Burmese Days*, Victor Gollancz, 1935, p. 19.
7 Selina Hastings, *The Secret Lives of Somerset Maugham*, John Murray, 2009, p. 280.
8 Ibid., p. 276.
9 *The Diary of Virginia Woolf*, Vol. IV, *1931–1935*, Hogarth Press, 1982, p. 210.
10 Elizabeth Bowen, *Bowen's Court & Seven Winters*, with an introduction by Hermione Lee, Vintage, 1999, p. 459.
11 *The Macmillan Diaries: Prime Minister and After, 1957–66*, ed. and with an introduction by Peter Catterall, Macmillan, 2011, p. 356.

Provincial Life

1 *Guardian*, 3 February 2011.
2 '9 novels that changed the world' by Rosamond Hutt, World Economic Forum, 3 March 2016. The others are: *Uncle Tom's Cabin* by Harriet Beecher Stowe, *The Jungle* by Upton Sinclair, *All Quiet on the Western Front* by Erich Maria Remarque, *Things Fall Apart* by Chinua Achebe, *The Grapes of Wrath* by John Steinbeck, *Nineteen Eighty-Four* by George Orwell, *To Kill a Mockingbird* by Harper Lee and *Beloved* by Toni Morrison.

Early Feminism

1 Introduction to the single-volume edition of *A Room of One's Own* and *Three Guineas*, Vintage, 2001, p. VII.
2 Hermione Lee, *Virginia Woolf*, Chatto & Windus, 1996, p. 148.
3 Diana Athill, *Stet: An Editor's Life*, Granta Books, 2000, p. 57.
4 *The Diary of Virginia Woolf*, Vol. IV, *1931–1935*, ed. Anne Olivier Bell, Hogarth Press, 1982, p. 147.
5 Anthony Burgess, *Ninety-Nine Novels: The Best in English Since 1939 – A Personal Choice*, Allison & Busby, 1984, p. 86.
6 Motoko Rich and Sarah Lyall, 'Nobel to Lessing, Incisive Voice of Women's Fate', *New York Times*, 12 October 2007.
7 Michiko Kakutani, 'President Obama on What Books Mean to Him', *New York Times*, 16 January 2017.
8 Preface to the 1972 edition of *The Golden Notebook*, published by Fourth Estate, p. 7.
9 Ibid., p. 10.
10 Doris Lessing, *Walking in the Shade: Volume Two of My Autobiography, 1949–1962*, HarperCollins, 1997, p. 305.
11 Ibid., p. 308.
12 1972 preface to *The Golden Notebook*, p. 8.
13 Ibid., p. 9.

14 Lessing, *Walking in the Shade*, p. 309.
15 'Doris Lessing's Golden Notebook, 50 years on', *Guardian*, 6 April 2012.

Sex and Relationships

1 June Rose, *Marie Stopes and the Sexual Revolution*, Faber & Faber, 1992, p. 116.
2 Denis Healey, *The Time of My Life*, Michael Joseph, 1989, p. 6.
3 Richard Ellman, *Oscar Wilde*, Hamish Hamilton, 1987, p. 435.
4 Ibid.
5 Jago Morrison and Susan Watkin, *Scandalous Fictions: The Twentieth-Century Novel in the Public Sphere*, Palgrave Macmillan, 2007, p. 63.
6 Report of the Committee on Homosexual Offences and Prostitution chaired by Sir John Wolfenden, Cmnd 247, Her Majesty's Stationery Office, 1957. The offences are listed under three headings: Buggery, Indecent Assault and Gross Indecency, of which the last two covered a range of activities.
7 Michael Howard, *Captain Professor*, Continuum, 2006, p. 128.
8 Introduction by David Leavitt to the Penguin Classics 2005 edition of *Maurice*.
9 Diana Souhami, *The Trials of Radclyffe Hall*, Weidenfeld & Nicolson, 1998, p. 151.
10 Ibid., p. 167.
11 *Sunday Express*, 19 August 1928.

Race and Immigration

1 Geoffrey Field, *The Evangelist of Race: The Germanic Vision of Houston Stewart Chamberlain*, Columbia University Press, 1981.
2 John C. G. Rohl, *The Kaiser and his Court*, Cambridge University Press, 1994, p. 205.
3 *Fabian News*, June 1911.
4 *Spectator*, 25 February 1911.
5 Shlomo Avineri, *Herzl*, Weidenfeld & Nicolson, 2013.
6 Anthony Julius, *Trials of the Diaspora*, Oxford University Press, 2010, p. 237.
7 Noel Annan, *Our Age: Portrait of a Generation*, Weidenfeld & Nicolson, 1990, pp. 207, 208.
8 Review of Susie Harris, *Nikolaus Pevsner: The Life*, *Financial Times*, 10 August 2011.
9 Daniel Snowman, *The Hitler Emigres*, Pimlico, 2003, p. 104.
10 Ari Shavit, *My Promised Land*, Scribe, 2014, p. 347.
11 Susie Harris, *Nikolaus Pevsner: The Life*, Chatto & Windus, 2011, p. 40.
12 James Stourton, *Kenneth Clark: Life, Art and Civilisation*, William Collins, 2016, p. 47.
13 *Our Hidden Lives: The Everyday Diaries of a Forgotten Britain*, ed. Simon Garfield, Ebury Press, 2004, p. 323.
14 Richard Cavendish, 'Arrival of SS *Empire Windrush*', *History Today*, Vol. 48, 6 June 1998.

15 Peter Hennessy, *Having It So Good*, Penguin Books, 2007, p. 223.

16 Robin Bruce and Paul Field, *Darcus Howe: A Political Biography*, Bloomsbury, 2014, p. 95.

17 Ibid., p. 96.

18 Soliciting in the street became illegal as a result of the Street Offences Act, 1959. Details of the kind of thing that went on in Hyde Park may be found in Julia Laite, *Common Prostitutes and Ordinary Citizens*, Palgrave Macmillan, 2012, chapter 10, p. 171.

19 Hennessy, *Having It So Good*, p. 498.

20 Tony Benn, *Years of Hope: Diaries, Letters and Papers 1940–62*, ed. Ruth Winstone, Hutchinson, 1996, p. 286.

Diverse Perspectives

1 Ross McKibbin, 'Politics and the Medical hero: A. J. Cronin's *The Citadel*', *English Historical Review*, Vol. 123, No. 502, June 2008.

2 Sally Peters, 'Bernard Shaw's dilemma: marked by mortality', *International Journal of Epidemiology*, Vol. 32, Issue 6, 1 December 2003.

3 *To the Bitter End: The Diaries of Victor Klemperer, 1942–45*, abridged and translated by Martin Chalmers, Weidenfeld & Nicolson, 1999, p. 294.

4 Sheridan Morley, *A Talent to Amuse*, Heinemann, 1969, p. 78.

5 'The Talk of the Town', *New Yorker*, 26 September 1925.

6 Ernest Hemingway, *A Moveable Feast*, Jonathan Cape, 1964, p. 158.

7 Carlos Baker, 'The Sun Rose Differently', *New York Times*, 18 March 1979.

8 Anthony Powell, *Messengers of Day*, Heinemann, 1978, p. 2.

9 Anthony Powell, *A Question of Upbringing*, Heinemann, 1951, p. 203.

10 Alec Waugh, *My Brother Evelyn and Other Profiles*, Cassell & Co., 1967, pp. 257, 258.

11 Cecil Beaton, *The Glass of Fashion*, Weidenfeld & Nicolson, 1954, p. 153.

12 Morley, *A Talent to Amuse*, p. 77.

13 Ibid., p. 81.

14 Eric Maschwitz, *No Chip on My Shoulder*, Herbert Jenkins, 1957, p. 36.

15 Alec Waugh, *My Brother Evelyn and Other Profiles*, pp. 255, 256.

16 E. M. Forster, *Abinger Harvest*, Edward Arnold, 1936, p. 3.

17 Roald Dahl, *Boy: Tales of Childhood*, Puffin Books, 2008 edition, p. 158.

18 Alec Waugh, *The Loom of Youth*, Grant Richards, 1917. It became a bestseller but resulted in his expulsion from the Old Shirburnian Society. He went on to become a successful novelist though overshadowed by his younger brother, Evelyn.

19 Simon Leys, *The Hall of Uselessness*, New York Review of Books, 2013, p. 192.

20 W. F. Deedes, *At War with Waugh*, Macmillan, 2003. Deedes was a Cabinet minister in the governments of Harold Macmillan and Sir Alec Douglas-Home in the early 1960s and editor of the *Daily Telegraph* from 1974 to 1985.

21 Selina Hastings, *Evelyn Waugh: A Biography*, Sinclair-Stevenson, 1994, p. 492.
22 For an account of Waugh's drinking and its effects on his character see Philip Eade, *Evelyn Waugh: A Life Revisited*, Weidenfeld & Nicolson, 2016.
23 *The Diaries of Evelyn Waugh*, ed. Michael Davie, Weidenfeld & Nicolson, 1976.
24 Philip Snow, *Stranger and Brother: A Portrait of C. P. Snow*, Macmillan, 1982, p. 117.
25 'A new means of destruction', editorial by C. P. Snow in *Discovery*, September 1939. Reproduced in C. P. Snow, *The Physicists*, Macmillan, 1981, pp. 176, 177.
26 Charles Ritchie, *The Siren Years: Undiplomatic Diaries*, Macmillan, 1974, p. 101.
27 *Spectator*, 22 September 1955.
28 'Two Cultures? The Significance of C. P. Snow by F. R. Leavis', Richmond Lecture, 1962. Published, with an essay on Sir Charles Snow's Rede Lecture, by Michael Yudkin, Chatto & Windus, 1962.
29 Anthony Burgess, *Ninety-Nine Novels: The Best in English Since 1939*, Allison & Busby, 1984, p. 31.
30 *New York Review of Books*, 11 May 2017.
31 See, for instance, Stephen Pinker, *Enlightenment Now: The Case for Reason, Science, Humanism and Progress*, Viking, 2018.
32 Roger Williams, *Lunch with Elizabeth David*, Abacus, 2000.
33 Artemis Cooper, *Writing at the Kitchen Table*, Michael Joseph, 1999, p. 67.
34 Ibid., p. 139.
35 *New York Times*, 28 May 1992.

Conclusion

1 Robert Skidelsky, *John Maynard Keynes*, Vol. 2, *The Economist as Saviour, 1920–1937*, Macmillan, 1992.
2 Robert Skidelsky, *John Maynard Keynes*, Vol. 1, *Hopes Betrayed, 1883–1920*, Macmillan, 1983, p. 384.
3 Skidelsky, *John Maynard Keynes*, Vol. 2, pp. 520, 521.
4 Giuseppe Tomasi di Lampedusa, *The Leopard*, translated from the Italian by Archibald Colquhoun, Collins Harvill, 1960.
5 Skidelsky, *John Maynard Keynes*, Vol. 2, p. 573.
6 Ibid.
7 D. J. Taylor, *Orwell*, Chatto & Windus, 2003, p. 328.
8 Noel Annan, *Our Age: Portrait of a Generation*, Weidenfeld & Nicolson, 1990.
9 Taylor, *Orwell*, p. 356.
10 Fredric Warburg's Report on *Nineteen Eighty-Four*, typewritten on 13 December 1948. Published in *The Annotated Edition of Nineteen Eighty-Four*, Penguin Books, 2013.
11 Taylor, *Orwell*, p. 402.

Index